Sexual Exploitation and Abuse by UN Peacekeepers

Sexual exploitation and abuse by United Nations (UN) peacekeepers is not an isolated or recent problem, but it has been present in almost every peacekeeping operation. A culture of sexual exploitation and abuse is contrary to the UN's zero-tolerance policy and has been the target of institutional reforms since 2005. Despite this, allegations of sexual abuse continue to emerge, and the reforms have not solved the problem. This book is a response to the continued lack of accountability of UN peacekeepers for sexual exploitation and abuse. Focusing on military contingent members, this book aims to analyse ways in which the UN can fill the accountability gap while taking a feminist perspective and emphasising the needs of victims, their communities, and the host state.

This book directly challenges the status quo of relying on troop-contributing countries (TCCs) to hold their peacekeepers to account. It proposes first, the establishment of a series of hybrid courts, and second, a mechanism for dealing with victim rehabilitation and reparation. It addresses these topics by considering international and human rights law and will be of interest to researchers, academics, policymakers, and students with an interest in international criminal law, United Nations peacekeeping, and peace studies.

Cassandra Mudgway is a lecturer in law at Auckland University of Technology Law School, New Zealand.

Routledge Research in Human Rights Law

Available titles in this series include:

Human Rights Education and the Politics of Knowledge
Joanne Coysh

Resolving Conflicts between Human Rights
The Judge's Dilemma
Stijn Smet

The ECHR and Human Rights Theory
Reconciling the Moral and the Political Conceptions
Alain Zysset

Developing the Right to Social Security – A Gender Perspective
Beth Goldblatt

Shifting Centres of Gravity in Human Rights Protection
Rethinking relations between ECHR, EU, and national legal orders
Edited by Oddný Mjöll Arnardóttir and Antoine Buyse

Socio-Economic Rights in Emerging Free Markets
Comparative Insights from India and China
Surya Deva

Comparative Executive Clemency
The Prerogative of Mercy in the Commonwealth
Andrew Novak

Social and Economic Rights in Theory and Practice
A Critical Assessment
Helena Alviar Garcia, Karl Klare & Lucy A. Williams

For more information about this series, please visit: www.routledge.com/Routledge-Research-in-Human-Rights-Law/book-series/HUMRIGHTSLAW

Sexual Exploitation and Abuse by UN Peacekeepers

Towards a Hybrid Solution

Cassandra Mudgway

Routledge
Taylor & Francis Group
LONDON AND NEW YORK

First published 2019
by Routledge
2 Park Square, Milton Park, Abingdon, Oxon OX14 4RN

and by Routledge
52 Vanderbilt Avenue, New York, NY 10017, USA

First issued in paperback 2020

Routledge is an imprint of the Taylor & Francis Group, an informa business

British Library Cataloguing in Publication Data
A catalogue record for this book is available from the British Library

Library of Congress Cataloging in Publication Data
Names: Mudgway, Cassandra, author.
Title: Sexual exploitation and abuse by UN peacekeepers : towards a hybrid solution / by Cassandra Mudgway.
Description: New York : Routledge, 2018. | Series: Routledge research in human rights law | Includes bibliographical references and index.
Identifiers: LCCN 2018015343| ISBN 9781138298989 (hbk) | ISBN 9781351579568
(web pdf) | ISBN 9781351579551 (epub) | ISBN 9781351579544 (mobipocket)
Subjects: LCSH: United Nations--Peacekeeping forces--Legal status, laws, etc. | Sex crimes--Prevention. | Peacekeeping forces--Sexual behavior. | United Nations--Officials and employees--Legal status, laws, etc. | United Nations--Privileges and immunities. | Criminal liability (International law) | Criminal jurisdiction
Classification: LCC KZ6376 .M83 2018 | DDC 345/.0253–dc23
LC record available at https://lccn.loc.gov/2018015343

ISBN 13: 978-0-367-58728-4 (pbk)
ISBN 13: 978-1-138-29898-9 (hbk)

Typeset in Galliard
by Taylor & Francis Books

Contents

Acknowledgements

The completion of this work would not have been possible without the support and encouragement of my family and friends. I am grateful to both of my PhD supervisors when this book was at the thesis stage, Professor Annick Masselot and Senior Lecturer Natalie Baird at the University of Canterbury; their guidance, ongoing comments, and emotional support were invaluable.

Thank you to my colleagues at the Auckland University of Technology Law School for encouragement and guidance throughout this process, from book proposal to manuscript: particularly, Warren, Rod, Leonid, and Lida.

Finally, my heartfelt thanks go to Rosa, for her support and enduring patience while I completed the conversion from PhD thesis to book. Aroha nui.

Introduction

Jane Hull Lute, Special UN Coordinator on Preventing Sexual Exploitation and Abuse: "It turns out that for the women of the world [sexual exploitation and abuse] is an ever-present danger. There is nowhere where women are safe. There's no family, no church, no school, no organisation or workplace"

Interviewer: "Shouldn't the UN, under UN responsibility, [be] that one place? If there was one place in the world?"

Lute: "There is no one place." [1]

In 2007, a 12-year-old girl, "Elizabeth", was walking home from school along a solitary road in Côte d'Ivoire.[2] She was alone when a United Nations (UN) truck pulled up alongside her, and she was raped by ten peacekeeping soldiers on the side of that road. A year later, when her story was reported by world media, she was psychologically traumatised and afraid to leave her home. None of her attackers were ever identified or punished.

In a Human Rights Watch report, sexual exploitation by African Union Peacekeepers was revealed as systemic in Somalia.[3] In one case, a 19-year-old Somali woman was brought to base camp for the purpose of sex.[4] Although she was afraid, she was displaced, poor, and hungry.[5] She was paid ten dollars each time she visited the base for sex.[6]

In April, 2015, a report leaked by a non-governmental organisation (NGO)[7] and reported by world media revealed that French peacekeepers in the Central African Republic (CAR) had forced local children, aged 9 to 13 years old, to

1 Transcript from "Haiti by Force" *Al Jazeera* (Video feature by Fault Lines, 22 March 2017) <www.aljazeera.com>. Timestamp 18.36–18.58.
2 The following story comes from M Pflanz "Six-Year-Olds Sexually Abused by UN Peacekeepers" *The Daily Telegraph* (26 May 2008) <www.telegraph.co.uk/news> ("Elizabeth" is a pseudonym).
3 Human Rights Watch *The Power These Men Have over Us: Sexual Exploitation and Abuse by African Union Forces in Somalia* (September 2014).
4 At 22.
5 At 22.
6 At 22.
7 AIDS-Free World.

perform oral sex in exchange for food.[8] France was perhaps encouraged by the leaked report,[9] but still took over a year to launch its investigations into the allegations. In fact, the UN promptly disciplined the initial whistleblower.[10] No charges were brought against the peacekeepers in question due to lack of evidence.[11] No one has yet been held accountable for these allegations.

Unfortunately, sexual exploitation and abuse committed by peacekeepers is neither a recent nor an isolated problem. UN peacekeeping operations have been plagued with sex-related misconduct on and off since the early 1990s. Allegations of sexual exploitation and abuse (including rape, sexual violence, exchange of sex for aid or food, and paedophilia) have been reported from almost every mission area in which the UN works (for example, Cambodia, Côte d'Ivoire, Democratic Republic of the Congo [DRC], Haiti, Liberia, Somalia, and South Sudan).[12] Recent allegations have involved peacekeepers in CAR, with a 100% increase of sexual exploitation and abuse allegations from 2015 to 2016.[13]

Although initially blaming the proverbial few bad apples and effectively suggesting that boys will be boys, since 2003 the UN's response has been one of zero tolerance.[14] Currently, any form of sexual exploitation and abuse is defined as "serious misconduct" under two UN codes of conduct[15] and the Secretary-General's 2003 Bulletin on Special Measures for Protection from Sexual Exploitation and Sexual Abuse (S-G Bulletin).[16] Peacekeeping personnel are forbidden from buying sex from prostitutes or engaging in sexual conduct with persons under the age of

8 The following story comes from K Willsher and S Laville "France Launches Criminal Inquiry into Alleged Sex Abuse by Peacekeepers" *The Guardian* (7 May 2015) <www.theguardian.com>.

9 Dr T Awori, Dr C Lutz and General PJ Thapa *Final Report: Expert Mission to Evaluate Risks to SEA Prevention Efforts in MINUSTAH, UNMIL, MONUSCO, and UNMISS* (2013).

10 The whistleblower was vindicated months later. See C Lynch "The UN Official Who Blew the Lid off Central African Republic Sex Scandal Vindicated" (17 December 2015) *Foreign Policy*<www.foreignpolicy.com>.

11 A Chrisafis and S Laville "No Charges Sought over Abuse Claims against French Troops in CAR" *The Guardian* (5 January 2017) <www.theguardian.com>.

12 See for example G Machel *Promotion and Protection of the Rights of Children: Impact of Armed Conflict on Children* GA, A/51/306 (1996) at [98]; Human Rights Watch, above n 3; Pflanz, above n 2; and UNHCR and Save the Children-UK *Sexual Violence and Exploitation: The Experience of Refugee Children in Guinea, Liberia and Sierra Leone* (February 2002).

13 J Whalan *Dealing with Disgrace: Addressing Sexual Exploitation and Abuse in UN Peacekeeping* (2017) <www.providingforpeacekeeping.org> at 5.

14 A Harrington "Victims of Peace: Current Abuse Allegations against UN Peacekeepers and the Role of the Law in Preventing Them in the Future" (2005) 12 *ILSA Journal of International & Comparative Law* 125 at 126.

15 UN Conduct and Discipline Unit *Ten Rules: Code of Personal Conduct for Blue Helmets* (1999) <http://cdu.unlb.org>; and UN Conduct and Discipline Unit *We Are United Nations Peacekeeping Personnel* <http://cdu.unlb.org>.

16 United Nations Secretary-General's Bulletin *Special Measures for Protection from Sexual Exploitation and Sexual Abuse* SG B, ST/SGB/2003/13 (2003): [S-G Bulletin (2003)].

18 years.[17] Furthermore, sexual relationships between peacekeepers and beneficiaries are "strongly discouraged".[18] The UN codes and the S-G Bulletin are not written with the intention of establishing criminal liability, although criminal behaviour may be included. They do not purport to obligate member states to criminalise the described conduct. Instead, the codes are standards of behaviour that stand alongside other staff regulations and policies and apply to all peacekeeping personnel.[19] In any case, disciplinary action is expected if personnel contravene these codes.

Despite such a strong position, the UN does not currently have the capacity to undertake criminal investigations or enforce prosecution. In the particular case of military contingent personnel, the troop-contributing countries (TCCs) have exclusive criminal jurisdiction. Troops are granted immunity from host state jurisdiction under two bilateral agreements: the Status-of-Forces Agreements (between the UN and the host state) and the Memorandum of Understanding (between the UN and TCC).[20] Due to the unpredictable and hostile environment in which peacekeepers operate, immunities offer essential protection from the host state.[21] Nevertheless, they are not intended to benefit the individual.[22] Under the UN Model Memorandum of Understanding (MOU), the TCC assures the UN that they will exercise their criminal jurisdiction in respect of offenders.[23]

Since the early 2000s, the UN has attempted to respond to the problem of sexual exploitation and abuse in a number of key areas – namely, prevention, remedial response, and accountability. However, the central framework remains unchanged. The S-G Bulletin continues to be the applicable standard, military contingent personnel are still protected from host state prosecution by legal immunities, and TCCs retain exclusive criminal jurisdiction. The interests of victims, their communities, and the host state appear last on the agenda. Moreover, sexual exploitation and abuse continues to be committed with impunity.

17 At [3.3(b)]-[3.3(c)].

18 At [3.3(d)].

19 Will apply to military contingents through their incorporation in the MOU. See generally Z Deen-Racsmany "The Amended UN Model Memorandum of Understanding: A New Incentive for States to Discipline and Prosecute Military Members of National Peacekeeping Contingents?" (2011) 16 *Journal of Conflict and Security Law* 321.

20 *Model Status of Forces Agreement between the United Nations and Host Countries* GA, A/45/594 (1990) [SOFA] at [47(a)]; *Manual on Policies and Procedures Concerning the Reimbursement and Control of Contingent-Owned Equipment of Troop/Police Contributors Participating in Peacekeeping Missions (COE Manual)* GA, A/c.5/69/18 (2014) Ch 9 Memorandum of Understanding [MOU 2007] art 7 *quinquiens.*

21 F Rawski "To Waive or Not to Waive: Immunity and Accountability in UN Peacekeeping Operations" (2002–2003) 18 Conn J Int'l L 103 at 104.

22 At 106.

23 MOU 2007, above n 20, art 7 *quinquiens.*

Overview of initiatives so far

The institutional response to sexual exploitation and abuse can be described as reactive, often following significant allegations of sexual abuse exposed by world media or international NGOs. The first substantial UN initiative followed media reports in 2004 highlighting sexual abuse of refugees by UN and humanitarian aid workers in the DRC.[24] Prince Zeid Ra'ad Zeid Al-Hussein, Personal Adviser to the UN Secretary-General at the time, issued the first comprehensive report on the extent of sexual exploitation and abuse in peacekeeping and made various recommendations.[25]

2005–2015

As a result of the Zeid Report, a number of reforms of a preventative nature were initiated post-2005. These included reforms that sought to regulate the behaviour of troops – for example, the instalment of recreation facilities within the mission site, out-of-bounds areas, and curfews.[26] Additionally, women are continually encouraged by the UN to take up peacekeeping roles.[27] The Zeid Report argues that this kind of gender mainstreaming could have a positive influence on the behaviour of male personnel in relation to discouraging sexual exploitation and abuse.[28] However, the percentage of women in peacekeeping remains low,[29] and peacekeeping remains overwhelmingly male.[30] Other reforms have focused on

24 The following text comes from the author's previously published work: C Mudgway "Sexual Exploitation by UN Peacekeepers: The 'Survival Sex' Gap in International Human Rights Law" (2017) 21 *The International Journal of Human* Rights 1453 at 1434. See also, *Investigation by the Office of Internal Oversight Services into Allegations of Sexual Exploitation and Abuse in the United Nations Organisation Mission in the Democratic Republic of the Congo* GA, A/59/661 (2005).

25 Text from Mudgway, above n 24, at 1434; See Secretary-General *A Comprehensive Strategy to Eliminate Future Sexual Exploitation and Abuse in United Nations Peacekeeping Operations* A/59/710 (2005) prepared by Prince Zeid Ra'ad Zeid Al-Hussein [Zeid Report].

26 Deen-Racsmany, above n 19, at 333.

27 See for example *Security Council Resolution 1325* SC Res, S/Res/1325 (2000); *Report of the Secretary-General on Peacebuilding in the Immediate Aftermath of Conflict* GA, A/64/866-S/2010/386 (2010) at [32]-[32]; and *Report of the Secretary-General on Peacebuilding in the Immediate Aftermath of Conflict* GA, A/67/499-S/2012/746 (2012) at [24]-[33].

28 Zeid Report, above n 25, at 18–19.

29 In 2017, the number of female military contingent members fluctuated between 3.3% and 3.7% of total troops. See "Gender Statistics" (2017) *UN Peacekeeping Operations*<www.un.org>. See also S Karim and K Beardsley "Explaining Sexual Exploitation and Abuse in Peacekeeping Missions: The Role of Female Peacekeepers and Gender Equality in Contributing Countries" (2016) 53 *Journal of Peace Research* 100. There is no official data around the percentage of UN personnel who identify as transgender or otherwise gender-variant.

30 See generally O Simic "Does the Presence of Women Really Matter? Towards Combating Male Sexual Violence in Peacekeeping Operations" (2010) 17 *International Peacekeeping* 188.

improved education and training of peacekeeping personnel before they go on mission.[31]

Conduct and Discipline Teams were also set up in the field to raise local awareness of sexual exploitation and abuse and reporting mechanisms.[32] The UN rolled out pre-deployment training materials on the zero-tolerance policy, particularly focusing on national commanders.[33] However, it is the primary responsibility of TCCs to provide the pre-deployment training itself. Policymakers such as the Inter-Agency Standing Committee continued to look at ways to improve education and prevent sexual exploitation and abuse.[34] Nevertheless, a 2015 report by the Office of Internal Oversight Services (OIOS) indicated that there was little local awareness of the UN's zero-tolerance policy and that there was still confusion among personnel about what constitutes "sexual exploitation".[35]

The UN has been slow to implement an adequate remedial response to victims of sexual exploitation and abuse. Although an official strategy was adopted by the General Assembly in 2008, which would have seen victims receive emergency medical and psychosocial assistance, the strategy failed to be implemented at all due to lack of funding.[36] By 2015, only a few missions had referral systems in place to make sure victims received the necessary remedial support.[37] Where UN agencies such as UNICEF have intervened, they have been accused of being grossly incompetent.[38]

Since the Zeid Report, there have also been a number of reforms in relation to individual criminal accountability, although none challenge the exclusive criminal jurisdiction of TCCs provided for under the SOFA and MOU. However, the UN has attempted to increase cooperation between national investigation teams and

31 Secretary-General *Special Measures for Protection from Sexual Exploitation and Sexual Abuse* GA, A/65/742 (2011) at [20], [31] and [34].

32 M Odello "Tackling Criminal Acts in Peacekeeping Operations: The Accountability of Peacekeepers" (2010) 15 *Journal of Conflict & Security Law* 347 at 355.

33 For a list of training materials see the Protection from Sexual Exploitation and Abuse Task Force website: <www.pseataskforce.org>.

34 See for example Inter-Agency Standing Committee *Global Review of Protection from Sexual Exploitation and Abuse by UN, NGO and IFRC Personnel* (July 2010).

35 See Office of Internal Oversight Services *Evaluation Report: Evaluation of the Enforcement and Remedial Assistance Efforts for Sexual Exploitation and Abuse by the United Nations and Related Personnel in Peacekeeping Operations* (May 2015) at 22 and 24.

36 *United Nations Comprehensive Strategy on Assistance and Support to Victims of Sexual Exploitation and Abuse by United Nations Staff and Related Personnel* GA Res, A/RES/62/214 (2008); and Secretary-General *Special Measures for Protection from Sexual Exploitation and Sexual Abuse* GA, A/69/779 (2015) at [68].

37 In Liberia, Haiti, and DRC see Report of the Secretary-General *Overview of the Financing of the United Nations Peacekeeping Operations: Budget Performance for the Period from 1 July 2010 to 30 June 2011 and Budget for the Period 1 July 2012 to 30 June 2013* GA, A/66/679 (2010) at [129].

38 See for example M Deschamps, HB Jallow and Y Sooka *Taking Action on Sexual Exploitation and Abuse by Peacekeepers: Report of an Independent Review on Sexual Exploitation and Abuse by International Peacekeeping Forces in the Central African Republic* (December, 2015) at iv.

the OIOS, the investigative arm of the UN. Where a TCC fails to respond to a complaint of sexual exploitation and abuse within ten days, a preliminary fact-finding inquiry is undertaken by the OIOS.[39] A fact-finding inquiry is purely administrative and does not include, for example, collecting forensic evidence or interviewing witnesses.[40] The case needs to be transferred to the national government concerned for formal criminal investigation.[41] There are identifiable practical problems with investigation in peacekeeping areas; for example, due to the six-month rotation of troops, the individual peacekeeper concerned may have already left the host state when allegations arise. Although the Model MOU was amended in 2007 to incorporate the zero-tolerance policy, accountability of military contingents is still dependant on whether the TCC chooses to take appropriate action against the individual; by 2015 the situation could be best described as woeful.[42]

2015–present

Renewed calls to strengthen UN response to sexual exploitation and abuse followed mass allegations of the sexual abuse of children by peacekeepers in CAR, involving over 200 victims.[43] An Independent Review Panel report that followed exposed significant issues with the accountability process, labelling it as "bureaucratic", lacking in the necessary urgency and sensitivity, and, ultimately, flawed.[44] The framework, which had been continuously tweaked over the previous decade, had failed to protect local populations from exploitation, and perpetrators were seemingly still going unpunished.

Since 2016, a number of additional initiatives have been rolled out; these include further development of training and education materials about the zero-tolerance policy and gender sensitivity, the appointment of a Special Coordinator on the issue, and the establishment of a Trust Fund for Victims of sexual exploitation and abuse.[45] Furthermore, the Security Council, in an unprecedented move, passed Resolution 2272, which endorses the Secretary-General's decisions to remove entire contingents where a TCC fails to hold perpetrators accountable.[46]

In 2017, the freshly appointed Secretary-General, Antonio Guterres, released his first report on sexual exploitation and abuse, promising a new approach

39 Currently through the OIOS see MOU 2007, above n 20, art 7 *quarter* (2).
40 MOU 2007, above n 20, at Annex F [33].
41 At art 7 *quarter* (3) and (4).
42 At art 7 *quinquiens* (1).
43 For details see generally Deschamps et al, above n 38.
44 At i.
45 United Nations Field Support *Combating Sexual Exploitation and Abuse: Initiatives* (2016); "Secretary-General Appoints Jane Holl Lute of United States as Special Coordinator on Improving United Nations Response to Sexual Exploitation and Abuse" (8 February 2016) *United Nations Meetings Coverage and Press Releases*<www.un.org>; and Secretary-General *Special Measures for Protection from Sexual Exploitation and Sexual Abuse* GA, A/70/729 (2016) at [76].
46 *Security Council Resolution 2272* SC Res, S/Res/2272 (2016).

centred on victims.[47] Unfortunately, Guterres's proposal was not as new as it first appeared – the previous Secretary-General, Ban Ki-moon, had described the zero-tolerance policy as victim centred as well.[48] However, to his credit, Guterres's intended reforms, which were innovative, included establishing a Victims' Rights Advocate and proposing a meeting with victims and victim organisations to discuss the future of the zero-tolerance policy.[49] Nevertheless, none of the current or planned reforms challenge the primary role of TCCs to investigate and prosecute their nationals. In fact, the current UN Special Coordinator on Preventing Sexual Exploitation and Abuse has opined that there is nowhere in the world where women are safe from such conduct and has not indicated that the UN should be aiming to change this, not even within its own peacekeeping operations. This attitude seems at odds with other commitments the UN has made, such as the Security Council Resolution 1325. If this attitude continues, it is unlikely that justice will be done any time soon.

Overall, perpetrators are seemingly going uninvestigated and unpunished.[50] Notwithstanding two decades of sporadic UN reforms, there is a general lack of accountability, and sexual exploitation and abuse continues to be committed with impunity. If TCCs fail to investigate and prosecute their military contingent members, if the host state is precluded from doing so, and if the UN cannot enforce accountability, then there is an accountability gap.

Aim of the book and guiding principles

The aim of this book is to examine various ways the UN can improve individual criminal accountability for sexual exploitation and abuse committed by its peacekeepers, focusing on a particular category of personnel: military contingent members. There are three relevant international actors to consider when framing the problem of sexual exploitation and abuse: the UN, TCCs, and the host state. Illustrated by two decades of attempted reforms, the current framework remains anchored to the primary role of TCCs in responding to allegations, which has arguably resulted in the accountability gap itself. Although the UN has made various efforts to improve prevention of sexual exploitation and abuse and improve cooperation between itself and TCCs, the accountability gap still exists, and impunity remains the norm. The host state, and so victims of sexual exploitation and abuse, are left without justice and without access to justice.

This book contends that the primary role of TCCs must be directly challenged in order to improve the accountability gap. Thus, when examining the various possible avenues for improvement throughout this book, the interests of victims,

47 Secretary-General *Special Measures for Protection from Sexual Exploitation and Sexual Abuse* GA, A/71/818 (2017).
48 See for example, *Special Measures for Protection from Sexual Exploitation and Sexual Abuse* (2016), above n 45, at [78].
49 See *Measures for Protection from Sexual Exploitation and Sexual Abuse* (2017), above n 47, at [27]-[35].
50 Revealed in a number of recent reports including Awori et al, above n 9; *Evaluation Report*, above n 35; and Deschamps et al, above n 38.

their communities, and the host state will be centralised – a perspective currently absent from the UN framework. In doing so, analysis will be informed by a feminist lens as well as three guiding principles: first, justice being seen to be done; second, host state ownership; and third, UN leadership.

Feminist lens

UN peacekeeping is inherently a gendered enterprise. As already noted, personnel remain overwhelmingly male. Additionally, peacekeeping economies (the economies that inevitably spring up in the areas in which peacekeepers work) involve work primarily associated with women, such as food services and sex work.[51] Traditional gender roles tend to follow, along with any negative gendered stereotypes that previously existed within the host state and within the cultural and social backgrounds of foreign personnel.[52] The added presence of a hypermasculine community (especially those that favour harmful performance of masculinity, characterised by antagonism, heterosexual norms, and dominance over the feminine) within the military can compound discrimination against women.[53] Women are thus more likely to be dehumanised, hypersexualised, and the subject of male aggression.[54] A culture favouring harmful kinds of masculinity can also foster a "boys will be boys" attitude and a reluctance to report sexual misconduct or enforce standards.[55]

Local men and boys can also be subject to sexual violence associated with this kind of toxic masculinity. As a group, male victims of sexual violence are not often the subject of feminist critique, and there has been historic silence within the literature as to their existence.[56] However, patriarchy as a hierarchal structure oppresses those who are feminine, who do not conform to heteronormative and gendered stereotypes, or who are otherwise "othered" by the dominant group (of men). In the

51 K Jennings "Service, Sex, and Security: Gendered Peacekeeping Economies in Liberia and the Democratic Republic of the Congo" (2014) 45 *Security Dialogue* 313 at 315.

52 Awori et al, above n 9, at 6–7; N Puechguirbal "Peacekeeping" in L Shepherd (ed) *Gender Matters: A Feminist Introduction to International Relations* (Taylor and Francis, Hoboken, 2014) at 256.

53 J McGill "Survival Sex in Peacekeeping Economies: Re-reading the Zero Tolerance Approach to Sexual Exploitation and Sexual Abuse in United Nations Peace Support Operations" (2014) 18 *Journal of International Peacekeeping* 1 at 24; A Kronsell *Gender, Sex, and the Postnational Defense: Militarism and Peacekeeping* (Oxford University Press, Oxford, 2012) at 55.

54 Awori et al, above n 9, at 6–7; McGill, above n 53, at 24.

55 S Martin *Must Boys Be Boys?: Ending Sexual Exploitation and Abuse in UN Peacekeeping Missions* (Refugees International, October 2005) at 5; Awori et al, above n 9, at 7.

56 See for example DA Lewis "Unrecognized Victims: Sexual Violence against Men in Conflict Settings under International Law" (2009) *Wisconsin International Law Journal* 1; S Mouthaan "Sexual Violence against Men and International Law – Criminalising the Unmentionable" (2013) 13 *International Criminal Law Review* 665; S Sivakumaran "Male/Male Rape and the 'Taint' of Homosexuality" (2005) 27 *Human Rights Quarterly* 1274; and L Stemple "Male Rape and Human Rights" (2009) 60 *Hastings Law Journal* 605.

context of peacekeeping, personnel with regular income and legal immunities can view themselves as a privileged group or as saviours of the local population.[57] Moreover, as personnel are not encouraged to interact with local people, the disparity between the two groups can lead to the local population being "othered".[58] Where personnel perpetuate harmful masculinity, such male aggression can target men as well as women. Local men and boys can be, and have been, victims of sexual exploitation and abuse within this context.[59] Overall, social and cultural structures within peacekeeping groups and the host state can foster discrimination against women and support an environment of hyper-heteronormativity and toxic masculinity, which leads to male violence.[60] A feminist perspective is thus insightful.

This feminist lens is placed within the theories of anti-essentialism and intersectionality.[61] Anti-essentialism rejects the notion that there is one universal women's voice; instead, this theory recognises the variety of experiences among groups of women.[62] For example, law or policy that is based on the experiences of white, middle-class, heterosexual women will not necessarily be applicable to women of colour.[63] Ignoring historic social and cultural contexts and differences may support further discrimination against one group of women while another may significantly benefit.[64] My feminist lens also attempts to reflect the intersectional nature of oppression.[65] Intersectionality recognises that oppression may not only be based on gender, but also on class, race, and sexual orientation, and that these oppressions may be operating at the same time and be interrelated.[66]

57 A Essa "Do UN Peacekeepers Do More Harm Than Good? UN Peacekeepers Are Supposed to Help Vulnerable Communities but Can Their Presence Damage the Countries They Operate In?" (9 August 2017) *Al Jazeera*<www.aljazeera.com>.

58 Essa, above n 57.

59 See for instance, the most recent raft of allegation involving boys in CAR: Willsher and Laville, above n 8.

60 See generally B Kovatch "Sexual Exploitation and Abuse in UN Peacekeeping Missions: A Case Study of MONUC and MONUSCO" (2016) 7 *The Journal of the Middle East and Africa* 157.

61 For an overview of feminist legal theories, particularly how they have been applied in international law, see H Charlesworth and C Chinkin *The Boundaries of International Law: A Feminist Analysis* (Manchester University Press, Manchester, 2000) at 23–61.

62 Charlesworth and Chinkin, above n 61, at 44–46 and 52–56; see also discussion on essentialism and anti-essentialism by DL Brooks "A Commentary on the Essence of Anti-Essentialism in Feminist Legal Theory" (1994) 2 *Feminist Legal Studies* 115.

63 For a critique of essentialism's impact on women of colour see AP Harri "Race and Essentialism in Feminist Legal Theory" (1990) 42 *Stanford Law Review* 581.

64 Charlesworth and Chinkin, above n 61, at 44–46 and 52–56.

65 See further K Crenshaw "Demarginalizing the Intersection of Race and Sex: A Black Feminist Critique of Antidiscrimination Doctrine, Feminist Theory and Antiracist Politics" (1989) *The University of Chicago Legal Forum* 139; and K Crenshaw "Mapping the Margins: Intersectionality, Identity Politics, and Violence against Women of Color" (1991) 43 *Stanford Law Review* 1241.

66 See SN Hasse-Biber *Handbook of Feminist Research: Theory and Praxis* (2nd ed, SAGE, California, 2012) at 154ff; D Staunæ and DM Sondergaard "Intersectionality: A Theoretical Adjustment" in R Buikema, G Griffin and N Lykke *Theories and Methodologies in Postgraduate Feminist Research: Researching Differently* (Routledge,

Generally, anti-essentialism and intersectionality focus on the context in which gender discrimination exists. This feminist lens favours bottom-up approaches to accountability, centralising the interests of victims of violence and their communities. Therefore, in addition to the feminist lens, there are three core principles that emerge from the feminist lens and underlie analysis: firstly, the theory of open justice – that justice should be seen to be done; secondly, host state ownership; and thirdly, UN leadership. Ultimately, these principles are about legitimacy in responding to sexual exploitation and abuse, inclusivity of the host state and victims, and transparency to the international and local community.

Justice being seen to be done

The rhetoric of "justice being seen to be done" is a crucial element of the principle of open justice – the public administration of justice.[67] This principle has its roots in the common law courts of England.[68] As such, Commonwealth countries and the United States have embraced the principle as a central element of the common law justice system.[69] Open justice is tied to the notions of democracy and accountability.[70] Court proceedings, particularly criminal cases, should be visible and open to the public; the public should not only see justice being done, but also see how proceedings are delivered (a check and balance on the function and role of the judiciary) and participate in them (jury or judgement by peers).[71] Although primarily a common law principle, the theory of open justice is now reinforced in international law under article 14(1) of the *International Covenant on Civil and Political Rights* (and thus is part of international standards).[72] This book focuses on the "justice being seen to be done" element of the open justice principle. Under the status quo, TCCs have exclusive criminal jurisdiction, and prosecution, if any, is likely to occur in a country other than the host state. Although TCCs are required to report on outcomes of cases to the UN, such reports are inconsistent.[73] The UN is often in the dark in relation to cases, the host state rarely receives information,

London, 2011) 45; and Report of the Secretary-General *In-Depth Study of All Forms of Violence against Women* GA, A/61/122/Add.1 (2006) at 361.

67 See generally C Baylis "Justice Done and Justice Seen to Be Done – the Public Administration of Justice" (1991) 21 *Victoria University of Wellington Law Review* 177.

68 For historical overview of the principle of open justice see generally G Nettheim "The Principle of Open Justice" (1984) *University of Tasmania Law Review* 25.

69 Nettheim, above n 67, at 30–44.

70 Baylis, above n 66, at 184.

71 At 185–186 and 190–191; Hon JJ Spigelman CJ "Seen to Be Done: The Principle of Open Justice" (keynote address to the 31st Australian Legal Convention, Canberra, 9 October 1999) at 24–25 and 26–28.

72 *International Covenant on Civil and Political Rights* 999 UNTS 171 (opened for signature 16 December 1966, entered into force 23 March 1976).

73 MOU 2007, above n 20, art 7 *sexiens* (1); Report of the Secretary-General *Special Measures for the Protection from Sexual Exploitation and Abuse* GA, A/67/766 (2013) at [15].

and the victims and their communities are also left without closure. Therefore, from the point of view of the international community, justice is currently not being seen to be done. In order to centralise the interests of victims, their communities, and the host state, justice needs to be seen to be done.

It is important to note that the focus of this book is centred on individual criminal accountability and *criminal justice*. Some have argued that such an emphasis on criminal law and prosecution as justice and a solution to the harms being committed against (predominately) women neglects other concepts of justice that may exist.[74] Victims of sexual exploitation and abuse, for example, may not necessarily view the criminal prosecution of offenders as justice, but rather attach the word "justice" to receiving restorative measures or remedies. Therefore, while this book emphasises individual criminal accountability, it does not do so to exclude other measures that might be explored and utilised to deliver justice for victims of sexual exploitation and abuse.

Host state ownership

In addition to improving the public administration of justice, accountability mechanisms should also foster host state ownership. In recent years, the UN has placed value in host state ownership and active participation of the local population in peacekeeping and peacebuilding.[75] According to the UN, the eventual success of peacekeeping operations requires the cooperation, support, and general inclusivity of the local population to be prioritised.[76] It is not about outside contributors solving post-conflict situations, but about empowering local actors at all levels of society to exercise ownership towards sustainable peace.[77] Specifically, the active participation of women in peacekeeping and peacebuilding is an essential element for the success of modern missions.[78] Host state ownership is also part of

74 See generally, E Bernstein "Militarized Humanitarianism Meets Carceral Feminism" (2010) 36 *SIGNS* 45.

75 *Report of the Secretary-General The Future of the United Nations Peace Operations: Implementation of the Recommendation of the High-Level Independent Panel on Peace Operations* GA, A/70/375-S/2015/628 (2015) at [64]; *Report of the Secretary-General on Peacebuilding in the Immediate Aftermath of Conflict* GA, A/63/881-S/2009/304 (2009) at [7]-[14]; *Report of the Secretary-General on Peacebuilding in the Immediate Aftermath of Conflict* (2010), above n 27, at [26]-[31]; *Report of the Secretary-General on Peacebuilding in the Immediate Aftermath of Conflict* (2012), above n 27; and *Report of the Secretary-General on Peacebuilding in the Immediate Aftermath of Conflict* GA, A/69/399-S/2014/694 (2014) at [27]-[39].

76 *The Future of the United Nations Peace Operations,* above n 73, at [64]; *Report of the Secretary-General on Peacebuilding in the Immediate Aftermath of Conflict* (2010), above n 27, at [26].

77 *Report of the Secretary-General on Peacebuilding in the Immediate Aftermath of Conflict* (2010), above n 27, at [26]. See generally E Newman, O Richmond and R Paris *New Perspectives on Liberal Peacebuilding* (United Nations University Press, New York, 2009).

78 SCR 1325, above n 27; *Report of the Secretary-General on Peacebuilding in the Immediate Aftermath of Conflict* (2010), above n 27, at [32]-[32]; *Report of the*

the capacity-building element of peacekeeping and peacebuilding operations and brings legitimacy to international projects implemented within the host state.[79] There seems to be much debate about what national ownership means and what its scope is, which may differ between host states.[80]

Host state ownership as a concept is both crucial and broad. It has been argued that the broad conceptualisation of ownership is necessary for its practical application; each peacekeeping or peacebuilding mission is different, and a flexible understanding of "ownership" can realise the capacity of various local communities or stakeholders.[81] Such ownership, for example, can be understood as national ownership (government, including opposition parties) and local ownership (residents of communities).[82] Additionally, there are many different ways in which ownership may be realised – for example, by including local stakeholders in decision making, government consultation, outreach to communities, and information sharing.[83] In post-conflict settings not all of these methods of partnership may be practicable.[84] However, the concept of host state ownership, as implemented so far by the UN, has been criticised for prioritising liberal principles (such as human rights and democracy) over local, context-specific knowledge and experience.[85] Advancing a "one size fits all" approach can undermine the legitimacy hoped to be achieved through host state ownership.[86] Notwithstanding this criticism, host state ownership is a UN strategic principle and is crucial for sustaining peace after conflict.[87] Moreover, local ownership and participation can be essential for centralising the views of victims of sexual exploitation and abuse by peacekeepers in a legitimate way.

The UN's policy of host state ownership and the involvement and support of the local population should also be factors when assessing various ways to improve the accountability of UN peacekeepers. Host state ownership is yet another way to centralise the interests of victims and their communities; the focus is on the context in which the abuse occurs, rather than on where the perpetrator comes from. Sexual exploitation and abuse is committed against members of the local

Secretary-General on Peacebuilding in the Immediate Aftermath of Conflict (2012), above n 27, at [24]-[33].

79 R Machold and T Donais *From Rhetoric to Practice: Operationalising National Ownership in Post-Conflict Peacebuilding* (Workshop Report, 2011) at 3.

80 At 2.

81 Newman et al, above n 77, at 13–14.

82 UNPKO *United Nations Peacekeeping Operations: Principles and Guidelines* (2008) at 38–39.

83 A Hansen "Local Ownership in Peace Operations" in T Donais (ed) *Local Ownership and Security Sector Reform* (DCAF Yearly Books, 2008) at 43.

84 See S Chesterman "Ownership in Theory and in Practice: Transfer of Authority in UN Statebuilding Operations" (2007) 1 *Journal of Intervention and Statebuilding* 3.

85 See for example, OJ Sending "Why Peacebuilders Fail to Secure Ownership and Be Sensitive to Context" *Security in Practice* (NUPI Working Paper, 2009); SBK von Billerbeck "Local Ownership and UN Peacekeeping: Discourse versus Operationalization" (2015) 21 *Global Governance* 299.

86 Sending, above n 85, at 7.

87 *Principles and Guidelines*, above n 82, at 38–39.

population, breaching the trust the communities place in international personnel and abusing the unequal power dynamics that exist. To legitimise the UN's continued presence in the host state community after its peacekeepers have violated such trust, arguably there should be some form of national ownership over response mechanisms.

United Nations leadership

The UN plays the central role in any UN peacekeeping mission, and it follows that the organisation should take leadership in accountability mechanisms and directly challenge the primary role of TCCs. The UN needs to take leadership in accountability where its own standards have been breached to legitimise the zero-tolerance policy against sexual exploitation and abuse. Furthermore, the UN is a human rights promoter as specified by the UN Charter[88] and has an essential role in monitoring human rights through its particular organs. Being unable or unwilling to act when its peacekeepers have abused the people that the UN serve would be hypocritical at the very least.

Since the early 2000s, the UN has demonstrated leadership in responding to sexual exploitation and abuse allegations; for example, it has implemented preventative measures and reforms.[89] Such measures include a Security Council resolution endorsing the Secretary-General to remove and replace entire contingents where there is a pattern of sexual exploitation and abuse. The UN has further committed elsewhere to increase the "participation of women and incorporate gender perspectives in all [its] peace and security efforts" and to implement special measures to protect women and girls from conflict-related sexual violence.[90] Arguably, in order to fulfil these commitments, the UN is required to take into consideration the context in which sexual exploitation and abuse takes place and to respond accordingly.

Therefore, to maintain and support both the integrity of the UN as a human rights promoter as well as the legitimacy of its standards against sexual exploitation and abuse, the UN should take active steps in establishing or improving accountability mechanisms. Overall, the UN is best placed to fulfil its leadership role in the international community in improving accountability for sexual exploitation and abuse committed by its peacekeepers in a way that is legitimate, transparent, and inclusive. The organisation's leadership in enforcement would also express the depth of the international community's condemnation of this behaviour and recognise the gravity of harm caused to victims and their communities.

88 *Charter of the United Nations* 1 UNTS XVI (24 October 1945). See also the United Nations Human Rights Initiative, available online <www.un.org>.

89 Zeid Report, above n 25; *Special Measures for the Protection from Sexual Exploitation and Abuse* (2013), above n 73, at 16; Report of the Secretary-General *Special Measures for the Protection from Sexual Exploitation and Abuse* GA, A/68/756 (2014).

90 SCR 1325, above n 27.

Sexual exploitation and sexual abuse – concepts and critiques

Before examining ways to address the accountability gap, it is necessary to determine what "sexual exploitation and abuse" actually means. The underlying rationale behind the zero-tolerance policy is the purported power imbalance between UN peacekeepers and the local population. It has been argued by UN officials and academics alike[91] that peacekeepers hold a position of trust in the host state community. Often operating in post-conflict situations, UN peacekeepers are there to support the local population in various ways, such as offering humanitarian, legal, and similar assistance.[92] Not only can the local population be dependant on these services, but they can also be vulnerable to exploitation based on this dependency.[93] Therefore, it can be argued that it is the unequal power dynamics that can lead to sexual exploitation and abuse of local women and girls. Consequently, such deferential power is an important element of the S-G Bulletin's definitions, particularly of "sexual exploitation".

It appears that the accepted position for academics and policy-makers is to make reference to "sexual exploitation and abuse" or "SEA" as one complete and conjoined concept. However, for the purposes of this book, the acronym (SEA) will not be used. Not only does the acronym hide complex concepts, it also dilutes the gravity of the harm caused to victims. Sexual exploitation and abuse can encompass many different forms of sexual misconduct, and it is inappropriate and too simplistic to lump them into one phrase without first making certain distinctions. The S-G Bulletin makes an important distinction between "sexual exploitation" and "sexual abuse", giving them different definitions with different elements of conduct.[94] Moreover, existing literature can largely ignore the "exploitation" part of "sexual exploitation and abuse" altogether.[95] Ignoring sexual exploitation ignores a significant number of allegations.[96] For these reasons, sexual abuse and sexual exploitation will be (and should be) analysed separately.

91 For example *Investigation by the Office of Internal Oversight Services into Allegations of Sexual Exploitation and Abuse in the United Nations Organisation Mission in the Democratic Republic of the* Congo, above n 24, at [23]; Zeid Report, above n 25, at [6]; EF Defeis "UN Peacekeepers and Sexual Abuse and Exploitation: An End to Impunity" (2008) 7 *Washington University Global Studies Law Review* 186 at 189.

92 Zeid Report, above n 25, at [6].

93 At [6].

94 S-G Bulletin (2003), above n 16.

95 But see C Morris "Peacekeeping and the Sexual Exploitation of Women and Girls in Post-conflict Societies: A Serious Enigma" (2010) *Journal of International Peacekeeping* 184 at 190; Mudgway, above n 24.

96 For example, the OIOS received 35 allegations of sexual exploitation against military contingent members involving approximately 189 victims, see *Special Measures for the Protection from Sexual Exploitation and Abuse* (2017), above n 47, at [47]-[54].

Sexual abuse

According to the S-G Bulletin, sexual abuse means "the actual or threatened physical intrusion of a sexual nature, whether by force or under unequal or coercive conditions".[97] It can be argued that rape and other forms of sexual violence would fall under this definition from the words "physical intrusion of a sexual nature" and the reference to coercion and force. This is supported by similar definitions of rape used by the ad hoc international criminal tribunals (i.e., the International Criminal Tribunal for the former Yugoslavia [ICTY] and the International Criminal Tribunal for Rwanda [ICTR]).[98] Additionally, the term "sexual abuse" has been used to encapsulate rape and sexual violence in other international instruments, such as Security Council Resolution 1325 concerning the protection of women and children in armed conflict.[99]

"Sexual abuse" has also been referenced in some human rights treaties, particularly those concerning sexual activity with children. The Convention on the Rights of the Child (CRC)[100] proved to be particularly influential in the development of the Bulletin's definitions.[101] For instance, article 34(a) requires states parties to take measures to prevent the inducement or coercion of a child to engage in any unlawful sexual activity. Similar provisions are found in regional human rights treaties, including the Council of Europe Convention on the Protection of Children against Sexual Exploitation and Sexual Abuse and the African Charter on the Rights and Welfare of the Child.[102] The definition of "children" under the S-G Bulletin (and the CRC) includes those aged under 18 years.[103] This position does ignore the fact that the age of maturity will differ between states and that the host state may classify those under the age of 18 as adults for the purposes of local custom and law.[104] It also potentially erases the agency of young women to make decisions regarding their sexual relationships and their bodies. However, the context of unequal power dynamics and the purported

97 S-G Bulletin (2003), above n 16, at 1.

98 See *The Prosecutor v Jean-Paul Akayesu (Judgment)* ICTR Trial Chamber ICTR-96–4-T, 2 September 1998 at [688]; Leading definition of "sexual violence" for the purposes of international crimes can be found in *Prosecutor v Furundzijia (Judgment)* ICTY Trial Chamber IT-95–17/1-T, 10 December 1998 at [186].

99 SCR 1325, above n 27, at [10].

100 *Convention on the Rights of the Child* 1577 UNTS 3 (opened for signature 20 November 1989, entered into force 2 September 1990).

101 *Investigation into Sexual Exploitation of Refugees by Aid Workers in West Africa* GA A/57/465 (11 October 2002) at [9].

102 *Council of Europe Convention on the Protection of Children against Sexual Exploitation and Sexual Abuse* CETS No: 201 (opened for signature 25 October 2007, entered into force 1 July 2010) arts 18–23; *African Charter on the Rights and Welfare of the Child* OAU CAB/LEG/24.9/49 (entered into force 29 November 1999) art 27(1)-(c).

103 CRC, art 1.

104 M Kanetake "Whose Zero Tolerance Counts? Reassessing the Zero Tolerance Policy against Sexual Exploitation and Abuse by UN Peacekeepers" (2010) 17 *International Peacekeeping* 200 at 201.

vulnerability of the local population supports the inclusion of persons aged under 18 years as children within the definition of sexual abuse.[105]

Sexual exploitation

The S-G Bulletin defines sexual exploitation as "actual or attempted abuse of a position of vulnerability, deferential power or trust, for sexual purposes, including, but not limited to, profiting monetarily, socially or politically from the sexual exploitation of another."[106] "Sexual exploitation" is intended to address transactional sex, which includes both adult prostitution and survival sex. The definition itself was conceived in the early 2000s for investigations conducted by the OIOS of allegations against peacekeepers and humanitarian aid workers in West African refugee camps.[107] Of particular concern were instances of personnel exchanging sex for services, food, or money that was already owed by the UN to the local population.[108]

Although survival sex is arguably the target of the S-G Bulletin's definition of sexual exploitation, the definition is ambiguous enough to catch other types of relationships of a transactional nature, including those that fall in the grey area between exploitation and a mutually beneficial relationship between two consenting adults. This line is not easily drawn, and the question as to what constitutes an exploitative relationship and what does not has been left open by the Bulletin.

When looking for the term "sexual exploitation" (or similar) elsewhere in international law, it becomes apparent that it is more likely to be found in the context of anti-trafficking law (for the purposes of prostitution) or in relation to the exploitation of children. For example, the most recent use of "sexual exploitation" can be found in the Protocol to Prevent, Suppress and Punish Trafficking in Persons, Especially Women and Children, supplementing the UN Convention against Transnational Organised Crime (2000).[109] As noted above, sexual activity with children is captured by the Bulletin's definition of sexual abuse. Consequently, the Bulletin's use of "sexual exploitation" is unique to the zero-tolerance policy.

Transactional sex – prostitution

Prostitution can be described as an exchange of (often) money for sexual purposes. Peacekeeping missions tend to correspond with an increase in the sex trade

105 *Report of the Office of Internal Oversight Services on the Investigation into Sexual Exploitation and Abuse by Aid Workers in West Africa*, above n 101, at [9].
106 S-G Bulletin (2003), above n 16, at 1.
107 *Report of the Office of Internal Oversight Services on the Investigation into Sexual Exploitation and Abuse by Aid Workers in West Africa*, above n 101, Annex I at [8].
108 At [6].
109 *Protocol to Prevent, Suppress and Punish Trafficking in Persons, Especially Women and Children, Supplementing the UN Convention against Transnational Organised Crime* 2237 UNTS 319 (opened for signature 15 November 2000, entered into force 25 December 2003) art 3(a).

in mission areas.[110] The opportunity to pay for sex whilst temporarily deployed in a foreign country has, in some cases, formed part of the masculine culture of the military.[111] Hence, it is not uncommon to see an increase of brothels, cafes, clubs, and bars in and around areas in which there are long-term military deployments.[112] Associated risks can include trafficking in women and girls for the purposes of prostitution and organised crimes, including peacekeepers participating in trafficking itself.[113] Therefore, UN views all prostitution in the peacekeeping context as dehumanising, profoundly disturbing, and enabling of a life of dependency and exploitation.[114] However, it is difficult to find an example elsewhere in international law where prostitution is similarly treated.

According to sources of international human rights law, buying sex from prostitutes is not strictly speaking a breach of human rights. The Convention on the Elimination of All Forms of Discrimination against Women (CEDAW) details under article six that "states parties shall take all appropriate measures, including legislation, to suppress all forms of traffic in women and exploitation of prostitution of women." The Committee on the Elimination of All Forms of Discrimination against Women's General Recommendation 19 pointed out that prostitutes are often driven into such work due to economic hardship.[115] Consequentially, it is their marginalised status that makes them susceptible to violence. Essentially, article six is about providing prostitutes with protection from human rights violations, such as rape and other violent crimes, not necessarily from the engagement in prostitution itself. However, the act of trafficking young women and girls in order to exploit them for prostitution is recognised as a breach of human rights.[116] It should be acknowledged that prostitution does not solely involve women and

110 See SE Mendelson *Barracks and Brothels: Peacekeepers and Human Trafficking in the Balkans* (Centre for Strategic and International Studies, Wellington, 2005), at 11; see also KM Jennings and V Nikolic-Ristanovic *UN Peacekeeping Economies and Local Sex Industries: Connections and Implications* (MICROCON Research Working Paper 17, Brighton, 2009) at 3.

111 See generally Higate P "Peacekeepers, Masculinities, and Sexual Exploitation" (2007) 10 *Men and Masculinities* 99; Martin, above n 55.

112 Mendelson, above n 110, at 11.

113 See generally Amnesty International *"So Does That Mean I Have Rights?" Protecting the Human Rights of Women and Girls Trafficked for Forced Prostitution in Kosovo* (London, 2004) at 41ff. See generally Mendelson, above n 110; United Nations Department of Peacekeeping Operations *Human Trafficking and United Nations Peacekeeping* (Policy Paper, 2004) at [12]; and O Simic "Boys Will Be Boys: Human Trafficking and UN Peacekeeping in Bosnia and Kosovo" in L Holmes (ed) *Trafficking and Human Rights: European and Asia-Pacific Perspectives* (Edward Elgar, Cheltenham, 2010).

114 Zeid Report, above n 25, at [6].

115 Committee on the Elimination of Discrimination against Women *General Recommendation 19* (11th Session, 1992).

116 *Convention on the Elimination of All Forms of Discrimination against Women* 1249 UNTS 13 (opened for signatures 18 December 1979, entered into force 3 September 1981) art 6; see also the *Inter-American Convention on the Prevention, Punishment and Eradication of Violence against Women*, above n 63, art 2(b).

girls, but may also involve men, boys, and other genders. However, similarly, there is no international instrument that suggests buying sex from prostitutes who identify as genders other than female would be treated as a breach of human rights.

Transactional sex – survival sex

Arguably, the primary focus of sexual exploitation under the S-G Bulletin is to address the situation of survival sex, where sex is exchanged for assistance or aid already owed to the local population. Examples of typical items exchanged are small amounts of money, biscuits, water, and greater access to aid that is already due to the beneficiaries of assistance.[117] The goods or assistance exchanged are linked with basics necessary for survival. The Zeid Report described this conduct as creating a relationship of dependency.[118] Local women and children often do not have the power to negotiate and risk receiving nothing in exchange at all.[119] Moreover, Prince Zeid expressed concern that items may be given after the fact to "disguise rape as prostitution".[120]

Feminist critiques of "sexual exploitation"

The definition of "sexual exploitation" (and the zero-tolerance policy generally) has been the subject of much academic criticism, particularly from those with a feminist perspective. As the definition does not make a distinction between coerced or voluntary sex, feminist scholars have argued that the zero-tolerance policy wrongly denies women's agency in sexual relationships. In countries where peacekeepers are deployed, transactional sex (exchange of sex for money, gifts, or services) can be common or culturally condoned or acceptable.[121] Additionally, the presence of UN peacekeepers and international humanitarian aid workers often coincides with an increase in transactional sex in the areas in which they operate, developing peacekeeping economies.[122] In such settings, there may be many different reasons why local women enter into relationships with

117 See for example, *Report into Sexual Exploitation and Abuse by Aid Workers in West Africa*, above n 101, at 9–11.
118 Zeid Report, above n 25, at [6].
119 P Patel and P Tripodi "Peacekeepers, HIV and the Role of Masculinity in Military Behaviour" (2007) 14 *International Peacekeeping* 584 at 588.
120 Zeid Report, above n 25, at [6].
121 See for example AR Kolbe "'It's Not a Gift When It Comes with Price': A Qualitative Study of Transactional Sex between UN Peacekeepers and Haitian Citizens" (2015) 4 *Stability: International Journal of Security & Development* 1; B Beber, MJ Gilligan, J Guardado and S Karim "Peacekeeping, Compliance with International Norms, and Transactional Sex in Monrovia, Liberia" (2017) 71 *International Organization* 1; J Adjei and E Saewyc "Boys Are Exempt: Sexual Exploitation of Adolescents in Sub-Saharan Africa" (2017) 65 *Child Abuse & Neglect* 14. Text from Mudgway, above n 24, at 1456.
122 See for example, Jennings above n 51. Text from Mudgway, above n 24, at 1456.

peacekeepers that are not always about survival or exploitation, but could be about excitement, attraction, friendship, or marriage.[123] Moreover, feminist legal theorists such as Dianne Otto and Jena McGill argue that the zero-tolerance policy fails to consider the legitimacy of survival sex.[124] Often in post-conflict states there are few economic opportunities, especially for women.[125] As a result, male relatives will relocate for work or military purposes. Thus, family survival will often depend on the women finding work, collecting aid packages, and so on.[126] Accordingly, these women are not victims, but survivors, making calculated decisions based on their cultural or social role in the family or community and the surrounding situation of poverty.[127]

A related criticism of the definition of "sexual exploitation" is that the UN effectively marks sex as the problem, rather than the context in which abuse occurs.[128] Such context in peacekeeping operations would include poverty, the displacement of local people,[129] and the performance of toxic masculinity associated with militaries (both peacekeeping troops and troops of the host state).[130] For example, the OIOS 2002 investigation report observed that many reasons young women and girls in West African refugee camps entered into such relationships were connected with poverty and lack of real employment opportunities for women.[131] Additionally, two separate UN reports in 2015 underlined poverty as a significant factor for transactional sex (specifically noting DRC, Haiti, Liberia, and South Sudan) and highlighted that for some women sex work may be the only means of obtaining food or money.[132] However, the zero-tolerance policy itself takes no account of this context.

The context of peacekeeping is therefore unique, and arguments such as Otto's and McGill's can overestimate the level of agency local women can express where unequal power dynamics exist. It has been noted that some women do not have the power to negotiate when entering into survival sex–type relationships, or feel

123 O Simic *Regulation of Sexual Conduct in UN Peacekeeping Operations* (Springer Berlin, Heidelberg, 2012) at 111–113.

124 See D Otto "Making Sense of Zero-Tolerance Policies in Peacekeeping Sexual Economies" in VE Muno and CF Stuchin (eds) *Sexuality and the Law: Feminist Engagements* (Routledge-Cavendish, New York, 2007); McGill, above n 53; see also C Harrington *Politicisation of Sexual Violence: From Abolitionism to Peacekeeping* (Ashgate, Surrey, 2010); Jennings, above n 51. Text from Mudgway, above n 24, at 1456.

125 Patel and Tripodi, above n 119, at 588; McGill, above n 53, at 6.

126 McGill, above n 53, at 7.

127 Otto, above n 124, at 266; McGill, above n 53, at 30.

128 Otto, above n 124, at 260–66.

129 Patel and Tripodi, above n 119, at 588; McGill, above n 53, at 6. Text from Mudgway, above n 24, at 1456.

130 See Higate, above n 111; Martin, above n 55, at 5. Text from Mudgway, above n 24, at 1456.

131 *Report of the Office of Internal Oversight Services on the Investigation into Sexual Exploitation and Abuse by Aid Workers in West Africa*, above n 101, at [12].

132 Awori et al, above n 9, at 6; *Evaluation Report*, above n 35, at 22–23. Text from Mudgway, above n 24, at 1456.

they have no choice.[133] Furthermore, when considering the post-conflict context, it is difficult to argue that all women have legitimate freedom of choice. Arguably, where peacekeepers take advantage of this context of desperation for sexual purposes, by withholding assistance owed, for example, then it is rightly classified as exploitation.[134]

A study conducted in Haiti is an example of the complexity involved. In this study, over 200 Haitians who engaged in transactional sex with UN peacekeepers were interviewed about their relationships.[135] The study revealed a range of transactional interactions, including single exchanges, continuing relationships, and relationships described by some as "dating".[136] Interviewees who were deemed "very poor",[137] lived in rural areas, or both, cited money, food, medication, or other kinds of assistance that peacekeepers had access to as the most valued items exchanged for sex.[138] However, those who attended school or were from urban or suburban areas noted they received "gifts" in exchange for sex (such as payment of school fees, school books, and cell phones) and were more likely to describe these exchanges within the concept of dating (but distinguished from romantic relationships).[139] In both categories, the transactional sex was linked to tangible goods or services related to survival, but with differing levels of negotiating power and consent. Where some interviewees expressed desperation for money or assistance as a triggering driving force, others believed they could call the exchange off whenever they pleased.[140] Therefore, the assumption that *all women* are exercising agency in their "choice" to engage in survival sex oversimplifies the reality of such relationships.[141] Conversely, local women and girls should not be considered as inherently victimised, either.

Definitions

It is crucial that sexual abuse and sexual exploitation are clearly defined, as these definitions will underlie any policy or measure adopted to improve accountability. "Sexual abuse" is unambiguous and so this book will apply the S-G Bulletin

133 K Jennings "Unintended Consequences of Intimacy: Political Economies of Peacekeeping and Sex Tourism" (2010) 17 *International Peacekeeping* 229 at 234; Kolbe, above n 121, at 11. Text from Mudgway, above n 24, at 1456.

134 SW Spencer "Making Peace: Preventing and Responding to Sexual Exploitation by UN Peacekeepers" (2005) 16 *Journal of Public International Affairs* 167 at 171. Text from Mudgway, above n 24, at 1456.

135 Kolbe, above n 121, at 4, although the majority of individuals interviewed were women, some men and transgendered individuals were included in the study, see at 8.

136 Kolbe, above n 121, at 8.

137 An interviewee was deemed "very poor" under the study if their household generated an income of less than $800 (US), see Kolbe, above n 121, at 7.

138 Kolbe, above n 121, at 9–11.

139 At 9, 12 and 14.

140 At 9–11; similar findings were made in a study located in Liberia, see Beber et al, above n 121. See also Jennings (2014) above n 51, at 319.

141 Text from Mudgway, above n 24, at 1456–57.

definition. This will include conduct such as rape, sexual violence, and sexual activity with children. Taking note of the different feminist critiques of the term "sexual exploitation" discussed above and the associated uncertainty with the term as defined in the S-G Bulletin, this book will proceed with the following definition instead:

> Sexual exploitation means survival sex, where sex is exchanged for aid or assistance to which peacekeepers have access or which is already owed by the UN to the local population.

Feminist theories of anti-essentialism and intersectionality, through which this book's feminist lens is informed, challenge the dichotomy of "victims" versus "agency", because both terms ignore or do not adequately address women's experiences within patterns of systematic power and oppression.[142] As a starting point, women should have the ability to exercise their active agency in making decisions relating to their sexual relationships and their bodies. To support a blanket rule against all kinds of transactional sex and label all sex between peacekeepers and local women as inherently harmful may support further discrimination against women. This view places women in a passive role and enforces the continuation of negative gendered stereotypes. Nevertheless, differential power between peacekeepers and locals does exist and cannot be ignored. The unequal power dynamics stem from the context in which peacekeepers operate: typically in post-conflict zones, providing assistance, stability, and protection for civilians and aid for local people. They have access to money, food, and medicine needed for survival while the local population may not. The host state and locals place their trust in peacekeepers to do their job and supply such aid. Moreover, additional power dynamics swing in peacekeepers' favour since they have legal immunity from host state jurisdiction.[143]

For the purposes of this book, "sexual exploitation" will be defined and limited to survival sex. Although there is a spectrum of possible exchanges between peacekeepers and local people within the concept of survival sex, this book focuses on the most offensive form as the subject of discussion – where sex is exchanged for aid or assistance to which peacekeepers have access or which is already owed to the local population. This will include the scenario of a local woman waiting in line for aid and being forced by a peacekeeper to exchange sex for such aid.

However, this book excludes soliciting sex from prostitutes from the meaning of sexual exploitation. There is no internationally agreed position on the so-called exploitative nature of prostitution. Additionally, there are differing levels of legality across states: where in some prostitution is legal and regulated, such as New

142 MA Fineman and R Mykitick *The Public Nature of Private Violence: The Discovery of Domestic Violence* (Routlegde, New York, 1994) at 64; see generally, B Hooks *Feminist Theory: From Margin to Center* (2nd ed, Pluto Press, London, 2000); E Schneider "Feminism and the False Dichotomy of Victimization and Agency" (1993) 38 *New York Law School Review* 387.

143 See Simic (2012), above n 123, at 114.

Zealand,[144] it is illegal in others, such as Pakistan.[145] There is also a notable gap in research regarding the circumstances of prostitutes in peacekeeping economies.[146]

Outline

With the feminist lens and guiding principles as the foundation for discussion, this book is divided into seven chapters.

Chapters one and two explore and analyse the legal framework that (potentially) applies to sexual exploitation and abuse committed by UN peacekeepers. Chapter one examines the agreements between states and the UN that facilitate troop contribution to peacekeeping operations. These are the SOFAs and MOUs. This chapter argues that the MOU is a bilateral treaty, and as such, there may be far-reaching implications for states that fail to investigate and prosecute their nationals. Chapter two surveys international human rights law for obligations for states to positively respond to sexual exploitation and abuse, comparing those standards to the zero-tolerance policy.

Having detailed the legal framework, chapter three assesses the first option for the UN to improve accountability – that of directly sanctioning TCCs that fail to discharge their obligations as identified under the MOU and international human rights law. Both coercive and noncoercive measures are explored. Furthermore, Security Council Resolution 2272 is specifically discussed as a measure of such enforcement.

A second avenue for improving accountability is host state jurisdiction, which is the subject of chapter four. This chapter aims to summarise how jurisdiction is approached under the current system and then compares the different ways in which host state jurisdiction may be achieved. Chapter five explores the possible jurisdiction of the International Criminal Court (ICC) in circumstances where TCCs are unwilling or unable to investigate or prosecute their nationals. Both host state and ICC jurisdiction are argued as desirable yet unsatisfactory options.

The book's central proposal is two-fold and is covered in both chapters six and seven. Chapter six argues for the establishment of a series of hybrid courts, and chapter seven supports the development of victim participation and reparations. The hybrid model will be put forward as the best option, which serves the principles underlying the book and directly challenges the primary role of TCCs to respond to sexual exploitation and abuse. The interests of victims and their communities must be supported within a new system, so chapter seven will argue for restorative measures and transformative reparations. There is a number of potential hurdles that are also discussed, including the material jurisdiction and possible offences within sexual exploitation and abuse, the political will of states, and the need to secure adequate resources.

This book's main arguments are drawn together in the conclusion. Overall, this book argues that it is time for states to have uncomfortable conversations about

144 See Prostitution Reform Act 2003 (NZ).

145 See The Punjab Suppression of Prostitution Ordinance 1961 (PK); Pakistan Penal Code 1860 (PK), section 377.

146 But see Kolbe, above n 121; Beber et al, above n 121.

the primary role of TCCs. This requires consideration of alternative mechanisms, such as a series of hybrid courts and serious responses to victims of sexual exploitation and abuse that involve comprehensive support, assistance, and, where appropriate, transformative reparations.

References

A Adjei and E Saewyc "Boys Are Exempt: Sexual Exploitation of Adolescents in Sub-Saharan Africa" (2017) 65 *Child Abuse & Neglect* 14

African Charter on the Rights and Welfare of the Child OAU CAB/LEG/24.9/49 (entered into force 29 November 1999)

Amnesty International *"So Does That Mean I Have Rights?" Protecting the Human Rights of Women and Girls Trafficked for Forced Prostitution in Kosovo* (London, 2004)

T Awori, C Lutz and General PJ Thapa *Final Report: Expert Mission to Evaluate Risks to SEA Prevention Efforts in MINUSTAH, UNMIL, MONUSCO, and UNMISS* (2013)

C Baylis "Justice Done and Justice Seen to Be Done – the Public Administration of Justice" (1991) 21 *Victoria University of Wellington Law Review* 177

B Beber, MJ Gilligan, J Guardado and S Karim "Peacekeeping, Compliance with International Norms, and Transactional Sex in Monrovia, Liberia" (2017) 71 *International Organization* 1

E Bernstein "Militarized Humanitarianism Meets Carceral Feminism" (2010) 36 *SIGNS* 45

DL Brooks "A Commentary on the Essence of Anti-essentialism in Feminist Legal Theory" (1994) 2 *Feminist Legal Studies* 115

H Charlesworth and C Chinkin *The Boundaries of International Law: A Feminist Analysis* (Manchester University Press, Manchester, 2000)

Charter of the United Nations 1 UNTS XVI (24 October 1945)

S Chesterman "Ownership in Theory and in Practice: Transfer of Authority in UN Statebuilding Operations" (2007) 1 *Journal of Intervention and Statebuilding* 3

A Chrisafis and S Laville "No Charges Sought over Abuse Claims against French Troops in CAR" *The Guardian* (5 January 2017) <www.theguardian.com>

Committee on the Elimination of Discrimination against Women General Recommendation 19 (11th Session, 1992)

Convention on the Elimination of All Forms of Discrimination against Women 1249 UNTS 13 (opened for signatures 18 December 1979, entered into force 3 September 1981)

Convention on the Rights of the Child 1577 UNTS 3 (opened for signature 20 November 1989, entered into force 2 September 1990)

Council of Europe Convention on the Protection of Children against Sexual Exploitation and Sexual Abuse CETS No: 201 (opened for signature 25 October 2007, entered into force 1 July 2010)

K Crenshaw "Demarginalizing the Intersection of Race and Sex: A Black Feminist Critique of Antidiscrimination Doctrine, Feminist Theory and Antiracist Politics" (1989) *The University of Chicago Legal Forum* 139

K Crenshaw "Mapping the Margins: Intersectionality, Identity Politics, and Violence against Women of Color" (1991) 43 *Stanford Law Review* 1241

Z Deen-Racsmany "The Amended UN Model Memorandum of Understanding: A New Incentive for States to Discipline and Prosecute Military Members of National Peacekeeping Contingents?" (2011) 16 *Journal of Conflict and Security Law* 321

EF Defeis "UN Peacekeepers and Sexual Abuse and Exploitation: An End to Impunity" (2008) 7 *Washington University Global Studies Law Review* 186

M Deschamps, HB Jallow and Y Sooka *Taking Action on Sexual Exploitation and Abuse by Peacekeepers: Report of an Independent Review on Sexual Exploitation and Abuse by International Peacekeeping Forces in the Central African Republic* (December 2015)

A Essa "Do UN Peacekeepers Do More Harm Than Good? UN Peacekeepers Are Supposed to Help Vulnerable Communities but Can Their Presence Damage the Countries They Operate In?" (9 August 2017) *Al Jazeera* <www.aljazeera.com>

A Essa "Is the UN Doing Enough to Stop Peacekeeper Abuse?" *Al Jazeera* (6 August 2017) <www.aljazeera.com>

MA Fineman and R Mykitick *The Public Nature of Private Violence: The Discovery of Domestic Violence* (Routledge, New York, 1994)

"Haiti by Force" *Al Jazeera* (Video feature by Fault Lines, 22 March 2017) <www.aljazeera.com>

A Hansen "Local Ownership in Peace Operations" in T Donais (ed) *Local Ownership and Security Sector Reform* (DCAF Yearly Books, 2008)

AP Harri "Race and Essentialism in Feminist Legal Theory" (1990) 42 *Stanford Law Review* 581

A Harrington "Victims of Peace: Current Abuse Allegations against UN Peacekeepers and the Role of the Law in Preventing Them in the Future" (2005) 12 *ILSA Journal of International & Comparative Law* 125

C Harrington *Politicisation of Sexual Violence: From Abolitionism to Peacekeeping* (Ashgate, Surrey, 2010)

SN Hasse-Biber *Handbook of Feminist Research: Theory and Praxis* (2nd ed, SAGE, California, 2012)

P Higate "Peacekeepers, Masculinities, and Sexual Exploitation" (2007) 10 *Men and Masculinities* 99

B Hooks *Feminist Theory: From Margin to Center* (2nd ed, Pluto Press, London, 2000)

Human Rights Watch *The Power These Men Have over Us: Sexual Exploitation and Abuse by African Union Forces in Somalia* (September 2014)

Inter-Agency Standing Committee *Global Review of Protection from Sexual Exploitation and Abuse by UN, NGO and IFRC Personnel* (July 2010)

International Covenant on Civil and Political Rights 999 UNTS 171 (opened for signature 16 December 1966, entered into force 23 March 1976)

Investigation by the Office of Internal Oversight Services into Allegations of Sexual Exploitation and Abuse in the United Nations Organisation Mission in the Democratic Republic of the Congo GA, A/59/661 (2005)

Investigation into Sexual Exploitation of Refugees by Aid Workers in West Africa GA, A/57/465 (11 October 2002)

K Jennings and V Nikolic-Ristanovic *UN Peacekeeping Economies and Local Sex Industries: Connections and Implications* (MICROCON Research Working Paper 17, Brighton, 2009)

K Jennings "Service, Sex, and Security: Gendered Peacekeeping Economies in Liberia and the Democratic Republic of the Congo" (2014) 45 *Security Dialogue* 313

K Jennings "Unintended Consequences of Intimacy: Political Economies of Peacekeeping and Sex Tourism" (2010) 17 *International Peacekeeping* 229

M Kanetake "Whose Zero Tolerance Counts? Reassessing the Zero Tolerance Policy against Sexual Exploitation and Abuse by UN Peacekeepers" (2010) 17 *International Peacekeeping* 200

S Karim and K Beardsley "Explaining Sexual Exploitation and Abuse in Peacekeeping Missions: The Role of Female Peacekeepers and Gender Equality in Contributing Countries" (2016) 53 *Journal of Peace Research* 100

AR Kolbe "'It's Not a Gift When It Comes with Price': A Qualitative Study of Transactional Sex between UN Peacekeepers and Haitian Citizens" (2015) 4 *Stability: International Journal of Security & Development* 1

B Kovatch "Sexual Exploitation and Abuse in UN Peacekeeping Missions: A Case Study of MONUC and MONUSCO" (2016) 7 *The Journal of the Middle East and Africa* 157

A Kronsell *Gender, Sex, and the Postnational Defense: Militarism and Peacekeeping* (Oxford University Press, Oxford, 2012)

DA Lewis "Unrecognized Victims: Sexual Violence against Men in Conflict Settings under International Law" (2009) *Wisconsin International Law Journal* 1

C Lynch "The UN Official Who Blew the Lid off Central African Republic Sex Scandal Vindicated" (17 December 2015) *Foreign Policy* <www.foreignpolicy.com>

G Machel *Promotion and Protection of the Rights of Children: Impact of Armed Conflict on Children* GA, A/51/306 (1996)

R Machold and T Donais *From Rhetoric to Practice: Operationalising National Ownership in Post-conflict Peacebuilding* (Workshop Report, 2011)

Manual on Policies and Procedures Concerning the Reimbursement and Control of Contingent-Owned Equipment of Troop/Police Contributors Participating in Peacekeeping Missions (COE Manual) GA, A/c.5/69/18 (2014)

S Martin *Must Boys Be Boys?: Ending Sexual Exploitation and Abuse in UN Peacekeeping Missions* (Refugees International, October 2005)

J McGill "Survival Sex in Peacekeeping Economies: Re-reading the Zero Tolerance Approach to Sexual Exploitation and Sexual Abuse in United Nations Peace Support Operations" (2014) 18 *Journal of International Peacekeeping* 1

SE Mendelson *Barracks and Brothels: Peacekeepers and Human Trafficking in the Balkans* (Centre for Strategic and International Studies, Wellington, 2005)

Model Status of Forces Agreement between the United Nations and Host Countries GA, A/45/594 (1990)

C Morris "Peacekeeping and the Sexual Exploitation of Women and Girls in Post-conflict Societies: A Serious Enigma" (2010) *Journal of International Peacekeeping* 184

S Mouthaan "Sexual Violence against Men and International Law – Criminalising the Unmentionable" (2013) 13 *International Criminal Law Review* 665

C Mudgway "Sexual Exploitation by UN Peacekeepers: The 'Survival Sex' Gap in International Human Rights Law" (2017) 21 *The International Journal of Human Rights* 1453

G Nettheim "The Principle of Open Justice" (1984) *University of Tasmania Law Review* 25

E Newman, O Richmond and R Paris *New Perspectives on Liberal Peacebuilding* (United Nations University Press, New York, 2009).

M Odello "Tackling Criminal Acts in Peacekeeping Operations: The Accountability of Peacekeepers" (2010) 15 *Journal of Conflict & Security Law* 347

Office of Internal Oversight Services *Evaluation Report: Evaluation of the Enforcement and Remedial Assistance Efforts for Sexual Exploitation and Abuse by the United Nations and Related Personnel in Peacekeeping Operations* (May 2015)

D Otto "Making Sense of Zero-Tolerance Policies in Peacekeeping Sexual Economies" in VE Muno and CF Stuchin (eds) *Sexuality and the Law: Feminist Engagements* (Routledge-Cavendish, New York, 2007)

Pakistan Penal Code 1860 (PK)

P Patel and P Tripodi "Peacekeepers, HIV and the Role of Masculinity in Military Behaviour" (2007) 14 *International Peacekeeping* 584

M Pflanz "Six-Year-Olds Sexually Abused by UN Peacekeepers" *The Daily Telegraph* (26 May 2008) <www.telegraph.co.uk/news>

Prosecutor v Furundzijia (Judgment) ICTY Trial Chamber IT-95–17/1-T, 10 December 1998

Prostitution Reform Act 2003 (NZ)

Protocol to Prevent, Suppress and Punish Trafficking in Persons, Especially Women and Children, Supplementing the UN Convention against Transnational Organised Crime 2237 UNTS 319 (opened for signature 15 November 2000, entered into force 25 December 2003)N Puechguirbal "Peacekeeping" in L Shepherd (ed) *Gender Matters: A Feminist Introduction to International Relations* (Taylor and Francis, Hoboken, 2014)

F Rawski "To Waive or Not to Waive: Immunity and Accountability in UN Peacekeeping Operations" (2002–2003) 18 *Connecticut Journal of International Law* 103

Report of the Secretary-General In-Depth Study of All Forms of Violence against Women GA, A/61/122/Add.1 (2006)

Report of the Secretary-General The Future of the United Nations Peace Operations: Implementation of the Recommendation of the High-Level Independent Panel on Peace Operations GA, A/70/375-S/2015/628 (2015)

Report of the Secretary-General on Peacebuilding in the Immediate Aftermath of Conflict GA, A/63/881-S/2009/304 (2009)

Report of the Secretary-General on Peacebuilding in the Immediate Aftermath of Conflict GA, A/64/866-S/2010/386 (2010)

Report of the Secretary-General on Peacebuilding in the Immediate Aftermath of Conflict GA, A/67/499-S/2012/746 (2012)

Report of the Secretary-General Overview of the Financing of the United Nations Peacekeeping Operations: Budget Performance for the Period from 1 July 2010 to 30 June 2011 and Budget for the Period 1 July 2012 to 30 June 2013 GA, A/66/679 (2010)

E Schneider "Feminism and the False Dichotomy of Victimization and Agency" (1993) 38 *New York Law School Review* 387

Secretary-General *A Comprehensive Strategy to Eliminate Future Sexual Exploitation and Abuse in United Nations Peacekeeping Operations* A/59/710 (2005)

Secretary-General *Special Measures for Protection from Sexual Exploitation and Sexual Abuse* GA A/65/742 (2011)

SW Spencer "Making Peace: Preventing and Responding to Sexual Exploitation by UN Peacekeepers" (2005) 16 *Journal of Public International Affairs*

Hon JJ Spigelman CJ "Seen to Be Done: The Principle of Open Justice" (keynote address to the 31st Australian Legal Convention, Canberra, 9 October 1999)

Report of the Secretary-General *Special Measures for the Protection from Sexual Exploitation and Abuse* GA A/67/766 (2013)

Report of the Secretary-General *Special Measures for the Protection from Sexual Exploitation and Abuse* GA, A/68/756 (2014)

Secretary-General *Special Measures for Protection from Sexual Exploitation and Sexual Abuse* GA, A/69/779 (2015)

Secretary-General *Special Measures for Protection from Sexual Exploitation and Sexual Abuse* GA, A/70/729 (2016)

Secretary-General *Special Measures for Protection from Sexual Exploitation and Sexual Abuse* GA, A/71/818 (2017)

Security Council Resolution 1325 SC Res, S/Res/1325 (2000)
Security Council Resolution 2272 SC Res, S/Res/2272 (2016)
OJ Sending "Why Peacebuilders Fail to Secure Ownership and Be Sensitive to Context" *Security in Practice* (NUPI Working Paper, 2009)
O Simic "Boys Will Be Boys: Human Trafficking and UN Peacekeeping in Bosnia and Kosovo" in L Holmes (ed) *Trafficking and Human Rights: European and Asia-Pacific Perspectives* (Edward Elgar, Cheltenham, 2010)
O Simic "Does the Presence of Women Really Matter? Towards Combating Male Sexual Violence in Peacekeeping Operations" (2010) 17 *International Peacekeeping* 188
O Simic *Regulation of Sexual Conduct in UN Peacekeeping Operations* (Springer Berlin, Heidelberg, 2012)
S Sivakumaran "Male/Male Rape and the 'Taint' of Homosexuality" (2005) 27 *Human Rights Quarterly* 1274
D Staunæ and DM Sondergaard "Intersectionality: A Theoretical Adjustment" in R Buikema, G Griffin, and N Lykke *Theories and Methodologies in Postgraduate Feminist Research: Researching Differently*(Routledge, London, 2011)
L Stemple "Male Rape and Human Rights" (2009) 60 *Hastings Law Journal* 605
The Prosecutor v Jean-Paul Akayesu (Judgment) ICTR Trial Chamber ICTR-96–94-T, 2 September 1998
The Punjab Suppression of Prostitution Ordinance 1961 (PK)
UN Conduct and Discipline Unit *Ten Rules: Code of Personal Conduct for Blue Helmets* (1999) <http://cdu.unlb.org>
UN Conduct and Discipline Unit *We Are United Nations Peacekeeping Personnel*<http://cdu.unlb.org>
UNHCR and Save the Children-UK *Sexual Violence and Exploitation: The Experience of Refugee Children in Guinea, Liberia and Sierra Leone* (February 2002)
United Nations Comprehensive Strategy on Assistance and Support to Victims of Sexual Exploitation and Abuse by United Nations Staff and Related Personnel GA Res, A/RES/62/214 (2008)
United Nations Department of Peacekeeping Operations *Human Trafficking and United Nations Peacekeeping* (Policy Paper, 2004)
United Nations Field Support *Combating Sexual Exploitation and Abuse: Initiatives* (2016)
United Nations Meetings Coverage and Press Releases "Secretary-General Appoints Jane Holl Lute of United States as Special Coordinator on Improving United Nations Response to Sexual Exploitation and Abuse" (8 February 2016) <www.un.org>
UNPKO *United Nations Peacekeeping Operations: Principles and Guidelines* (2008)
United Nations Secretary-General's Bulletin *Special Measures for Protection from Sexual Exploitation and Sexual Abuse* SG B, ST/SGB/2003/13 (2003)
SBK von Billerbeck "Local Ownership and UN Peacekeeping: Discourse versus Operationalization" (2015) 21 *Global Governance* 299
J Whalan "Dealing with Disgrace: Addressing Sexual Exploitation and Abuse in UN Peacekeeping" (2017) <www.providingforpeacekeeping.org>
K Willsher and S Laville "France Launches Criminal Inquiry into Alleged Sex Abuse by Peacekeepers" *The Guardian* (7 May 2015) <www.theguardian.com>

1 Memorandum of Understanding

The overall objective of chapters one and two is to examine the international legal framework in relation to sexual exploitation and abuse as well as the extent to which there are positive obligations on troop-contributing countries (TCCs) to respond to allegations against their military contingent personnel. These chapters will expose the gaps that exist with respect to obligations to exercise criminal jurisdiction. Further, they will confirm the primary role of TCCs within the current legal framework, and that the interests of victims, their communities, and the host state remain largely absent.

There are two instruments that contribute to the legal framework of United Nations (UN) peacekeeping operations: The Status-of-Forces Agreements (between the UN and the host state) and the Memorandum of Understanding (between the UN and TCC).[1] They both govern the jurisdiction of states and the immunity of UN personnel. The current version of the UN Model Memorandum of Understanding (MOU) provides the most detailed provisions governing investigation and accountability requirements on behalf of TCCs and is therefore the most relevant and will be the focus of this chapter.

This chapter will begin with a brief overview of jurisdiction in UN peacekeeping operations generally, followed by an examination of the Status-of-Forces Agreements (SOFAs). This will provide the necessary background for a close analysis of the MOU. After providing a summary of the history of the use of MOUs in peacekeeping, the chapter will turn to their legal status. This section will argue that the MOU is a treaty. There are important implications if the MOU is accepted as a treaty; for example, TCCs may be in breach of treaty obligations rather than just policy if they fail to exercise their criminal jurisdiction over sexual exploitation and abuse. Consequentially, the MOU's provisions relating to accountability may carry more normative weight.

Secondly, this chapter will consider the provisions of the MOU itself. Standards related to sexual exploitation and abuse are annexed to the MOU, making it

1 *Model Status of Forces Agreement between the United Nations and Host Countries* GA, A/45/594 (1990) [SOFA]; *Manual on Policies and Procedures Concerning the Reimbursement and Control of Contingent-Owned Equipment of Troop/Police Contributors Participating in Peacekeeping Missions (COE Manual)* GA, A/c.5/69/18 (2014) Ch 9 Memorandum of Understanding [MOU 2007].

necessary to examine the extent to which these documents are incorporated into the MOU (to form part of the legally binding treaty). Articles 7 *quater*, 7 *quinquiens*, and 7 *sexiens* were added in 2007 to clarify obligations relating to criminal accountability of military contingent members. These provisions will be the main focus of analysis. Thirdly, this chapter will consider the possible consequences for breaching the MOU.

Jurisdiction

From the inception of the United Nations Emergency Force I (UNEF I)[2] in 1956 (established to help end the Suez Crisis), TCCs have received the benefit of exclusive criminal jurisdiction over members of their national military contingents.[3] The purpose of this policy was to encourage member states to contribute troops from their military forces without the fear of being subjected to foreign jurisdiction for crimes committed while on mission. Specifically, there was concern that TCCs' military personnel may be tried in a possibly defective legal system, perhaps without procedural safeguards in relation to evidence collection or relevant civil rights.[4] Immunity from host state jurisdiction provides important protection for foreign military forces so they can perform their official functions without interference.[5] Additionally, granting exclusive criminal jurisdiction to the TCC supports the practice of sovereign immunity.[6] The discipline or criminal punishment of members of military forces in particular is often considered a special matter of sovereignty for the sending state.[7]

Generally, customary international law dictates that states are not permitted to proscribe or exercise their jurisdiction unless it can be supported by certain

2 *General Assembly Resolution* GA Res, A/Res/998 (ES-I) (1956); *General Assembly Resolution* GA Res, A/Res/1000 (ES-I) (1956); *General Assembly Resolution* GA Res, A/Res/1001 (ES-I) (1956).

3 M Odello "Tackling Criminal Acts in Peacekeeping Operations: The Accountability of Peacekeepers" (2010) 15 *Journal of Conflict & Security Law* 347 at 366.

4 Such as the right to a lawyer or a fair trial, see Odello, above n 3, at 366; D Hammarskjold *Summary Study of the Experience Derived from the Establishment and Operation of the Force: Report of the Secretary-General* GA, A/3943 XIII (1958) at [136].

5 D Fleck "Introduction" in D Fleck (ed) *The Handbook of the Law of Visiting States* (Oxford University Press, Oxford, 2001) at 5.

6 See generally D Fleck "Securing Status and Protection of Peacekeepers" in R Arnold and GA Knoops (eds) *Practice and Policies of Modern Peace Support Operations under International Law* (Transnational Publishers, New York, 2006) 141. See also F Akada "The Enforcement of Military Justice and Discipline in External Military Operations: Exploring the Fault Lines" (2008) 47 *Military Law and the Law of War Review* 253 at 262; G Simm "International Law as a Regulatory Framework for Sexual Crimes Committed by Peacekeepers" (2012) 16 *Journal of Conflict & Security Law* 473 at 501; and Odello, above n 3, at 376.

7 Secretary-General *A Comprehensive Strategy to Eliminate Future Sexual Exploitation and Abuse in United Nations Peacekeeping Operations* A/59/710 (2005) prepared by Prince Zeid Ra'ad Zeid Al-Hussein [Zeid Report] at [80].

jurisdictional principles.[8] Jurisdiction over criminal conduct is primarily based on the territoriality principle, where a state establishes jurisdiction on the basis that the crime has been committed within the state's own territory.[9] In the peacekeeping context, this would mean that the host state would usually have jurisdiction over criminal offences committed by peacekeeping personnel based on the territoriality principle. However, under the Status-of-Forces Agreement (SOFA), the host state waives its jurisdiction in regard to military contingent members, confirming their immunity.

Status-of-Forces Agreements

SOFAs set out the privileges and immunities to be enjoyed by UN personnel when they enter the host state and execute their operational duties as mandated by the Security Council. The agreements also govern other concerns, such as liabilities for civil claims,[10] use of uniforms and arms,[11] transportation,[12] and the settlement of disputes.[13] The relevant provision in terms of criminal jurisdiction over military contingent members is article 47(b):

> Military members of the military component of the United Nations Peacekeeping Operation shall be subject to the exclusive jurisdiction of their respective participating states in respect of any criminal offences which may be committed by them in [host country].

This provision reinforces the doctrine of sovereign immunity; it also makes clear that the host state waives its criminal jurisdiction over such personnel. The host state is, however, relying heavily on the TCC to exercise its criminal jurisdiction.[14] Additionally, the footnote to article 48 states:[15]

> Upon conclusion of a specific agreement, the provision in question could instead be inserted in a memorandum of understanding where further clarifications on the terms of an agreement are usually provided.

TCCs retain exclusive criminal jurisdiction on the understanding they will indeed exercise it. The SOFA dictates that the Secretary-General is to ensure this by obtaining formal assurances from each TCC to this end – this is required (as opposed to being merely optional) by article 48. Further, the footnote of article

8 C Ryngaert *Jurisdiction in International Law* (Oxford University Press, Oxford, 2008) at 21.
9 G Simm *Sex in Peace Operations* (Cambridge University Press, Cambridge, 2013) at 56.
10 SOFA, art 49.
11 At art 37.
12 At arts 12–14.
13 See part VII.
14 At art 48.
15 At art 48 footnote h.

48 suggests that assurances could be inserted in the MOU as part of the usual terms of that agreement.

Since UNEF I, SOFAs have been concluded in one way or another.[16] The UN Model SOFA was drafted in 1991 to facilitate negotiation of such agreements based on past state practice.[17] Where a SOFA has not been concluded before the commencement of a particular mission, the Security Council has, on such occasions, stated that the Model SOFA will apply in the interim.[18] This continued state practice has brought about much scholarship on the legal status of the Model SOFA. Some academics[19] have debated the extent to which the Model SOFA now represents customary international law. If it were the case that the Model SOFA represents custom, then the requirement of a formal assurance is more cogent. As will be seen below, between 1997 and 2007 the Model MOU did not contain a provision on assurances, and there had also been a lack of state practice in providing them. The SOFA and its legal status have received a lot of scholarly attention; however, there is a gap in the literature on the MOU and its precise legal status, which is unexpected since it is the partner agreement to the SOFA.

Memorandum of Understanding

This section will provide an analysis of the MOU in regard to its legal status and the contents of its provisions. There is evidence to support the argument that the MOU is a treaty, rendering its provisions relating to sexual exploitation and abuse more than just UN standards or policy. Essentially this section will assert that there are obligations on states to exercise their criminal jurisdiction over sexual exploitation and abuse. However, this does not equate to an obligation to investigate or prosecute, rather to transfer cases to appropriate national authorities. Overall, the MOU supports the primary role of TCCs and defers to domestic prosecutorial discretion without enforcement mechanisms on behalf of the UN. Analysis will expose the MOU's central weakness concerning accountability: it does not promise that justice will be seen to be done, and it renders victims and the host state powerless to pursue justice at all.

History

Since UNEF I, agreements were concluded between the UN and TCCs governing financial administration and logistics of providing personnel and equipment to

16 See Z Deen-Racsmany "The Amended UN Model Memorandum of Understanding: A New Incentive for States to Discipline and Prosecute Military Members of National Peacekeeping Contingents?" (2011) 16 *Journal of Conflict and Security Law* 321 at 329.

17 For example, see *Security Council Resolution 1528* SC Res, S/Res/1528 (2004) at [9]; *Security Council Resolution 1542* SC Res, S/Res/1542 (2004) at [11].

18 Deen-Racsmany, above n 16, at 326.

19 For example, see D Fleck and M Saalfeld "Combining Efforts to Improve the Legal Status of UN Peacekeeping Forces and Their Effective Protection" (1994) *International Peacekeeping* 82.

peacekeeping operations.[20] The agreements also served to supplement the terms relating to immunity and privileges attributed to personnel under the SOFA.[21] In 1991, a Model Troop Contribution Agreement (TCA) was drafted, based upon previous state practice and exchanged letters, to serve as a basis of negotiation between TCCs and the UN.[22] This model agreement was subject to important amendments in 1997 and 2007. The 1997 amendment changed the TCA into a Memorandum of Understanding,[23] and its terms were stripped down to the most basic provisions. The Model MOU was again amended in 2007 to the current version.

The 2007 MOU is one of the most positive developments that came through the UN's many reforms post-2005. The amendments followed several recommendations made by official UN reports and academic commentary.[24] Both the Zeid Report and the first Report of the Group of Legal Experts identified the need for clear provisions governing accountability of personnel.[25] The second Group of Legal Experts Report focused particularly on the need to include the UN codes of conduct and the Secretary-General's 2003 *Bulletin on Special Measures for Protection from Sexual Exploitation and Sexual Abuse* (S-G Bulletin).[26] Before 2007, the UN codes were not standardised across all categories of UN personnel.[27] The 2007 amendments saw the introduction of several detailed

20 This was typically done through an exchange of letters, see for example *Exchange of Letters Constituting an Agreement concerning the Service with the United Nations Emergency Force of the National Contingent Provided by the Government of Finland* 271 UNTS 135 (1957).

21 Deen-Racsmany, above n 16, at 329; Odello above n 3, at 366.

22 *Model Agreement between the United Nations and Member States Contributing Personnel and Equipment to United Nations Peace-Keeping Operations* GA, A/46/1991 (1991) [1991 TCA].

23 *Reform of the Procedures for Determining Reimbursement to Member States for Contingent-Owned Equipment* GA, A/51/967 (1997) Annex [1997 MOU]. It has also been noted that the 1997 version was never adopted by the General Assembly, therefore the 1997 MOU was never technically a basis for negotiation, unlike the 1991 version and the subsequent 2007 MOU. See *Report of the Special Committee on Peacekeeping Operations and Its Working Group* GA, A/59/19/Rev. 1 (2005).

24 Zeid Report, above n 7, at [25]; *Report of the Special Committee on Peacekeeping Operations and Its Working Group* (2005), above n 23, at [39]; *Report of the Group of Legal Experts on Ensuring the Accountability of United Nations Staff and Experts on Mission with Respect to Criminal Acts Committed in Peacekeeping Operations* GA, A/60/980 (2006) [First Group of Legal Experts Report] at [64(c)].

25 Zeid Report, above n 7, at [38]-[46]; First Group of Legal Experts Report, above n 24.

26 United Nations Secretary-General's Bulletin *Special Measures for Protection from Sexual Exploitation and Sexual Abuse* SG B, ST/SGB/2003/13 (2003) [S-G Bulletin (2003)].

27 See generally *Report of the Group of Legal Experts on Making the Standards Contained in the Secretary-General's Bulletin Binding on Contingent Members and Standardising the Norms of Conduct so That They Are Applicable to All Categories of Peacekeeping Personnel* GA, A/61/645 (2006) [Second Group of Legal Experts Report].

provisions pertaining to the application of the UN standards of conduct,[28] discipline,[29] investigations,[30] exercise of jurisdiction, and accountability.[31]

Legal status

A common designation used among scholars to describe the Model MOU is an "international agreement" between the UN and TCCs.[32] However, the term "bilateral treaty" has seldom been used.[33] Although a treaty need not explicitly be designated as such, the absence of such designation does raise the issue of legal status. There has been some argument to suggest that the term "international agreement" is different from "treaty", even under the Vienna Conventions.[34] Michael Brandon argues that "international agreement" is more generic than "treaty".[35] The term "international agreement" includes treaties and other instruments that would not necessarily fall within the meaning of "treaty" in the relevant Vienna Conventions.[36] Thus, being designated as an "international agreement" by commentators does not necessarily mean that the said authors are suggesting that the MOU is (or is not) in fact a treaty.

Moreover, comments made by academics are conflicting on the issue of legal status. One academic has described the MOU as an instrument "adopted by the UN" and compared this with an international convention.[37] It is unclear whether the author has meant to instead compare the bilateral nature of the MOU with multilateral treaties. Another commentator has gone even further to suggest that neither the SOFA nor the MOU have been adopted in treaty form, referring to the UN model versions of these agreements.[38] Again it is unclear whether the author means to imply that concluded agreements based on the UN models are not adopted as treaties or that his comments are limited to the models alone. Furthermore, some other scholars do not list the MOU under "legal sources" or

28 2007 MOU, art 7 *bis*.
29 At art 7 *ter*.
30 At art 7 *quater*.
31 At arts 7 *quinquiens* and 7 *sexiens*.
32 See for example R Opie "Human Rights Violations by Peacekeepers: Finding a Framework for Attribution of Responsibility" (2006) *New Zealand Law Review* 1.
33 But see Simm "International Law as a Regulatory Framework", above n 6, at 501.
34 For example, see M Brandon "Analysis of the Terms 'Treaty' and 'International Agreement' for the Purposes of Registration under Article 102 of the United Nations Charter" (1953) *The American Journal of International Law* 49. Vienna Conventions include the *Vienna Convention on the Law of Treaties* 1155 UNTS 331 (opened for signature 1969, entered into force 1980) [1969 Vienna Convention] and the *Vienna Convention on the Law of Treaties between States and International Organisations or between International Organisations 1986* (opened for signature 21 March 1986, not yet in force) [1986 Vienna Convention].
35 Brandon, above n 34, at 51.
36 D Door and K Schmalenbach *Vienna Convention on the Law of Treaties* (Springer, Berlin, 2011) at 30.
37 Deen-Racsmany, above n 16, at 350–355.
38 Fleck "Securing Status and Protection of Peacekeepers", above n 6, at 150.

consider it within the legal framework of peacekeeping operations.[39] Nevertheless, as will be explored below, there is a case to be made for suggesting that the MOU is a treaty. Despite the evidence, there appears to be nothing in the literature that discusses the applicability of treaty law. This is a highly relevant area of law that needs more scholarly attention, particularly when considering the accountability issues for sexual exploitation and abuse.

The starting point when determining the status of an MOU is the presumption that it is a non-binding, informal agreement.[40] Nevertheless, there has been some extensive debate about the legal status of MOUs. Whereas Jan Klabbers[41] argues that all MOUs are in fact treaties, Anthony Aust[42] casts doubt on such a proposition. According to Aust, determining the status of MOUs requires looking for evidence of an intention to conclude a treaty.[43] Even after such evidence has been obtained, the MOU may still not in fact be a treaty.[44] For the purposes of the current context, it is helpful to compare the benefits of an MOU to a formalised treaty. This is an important consideration given the fact that the previous TCAs were deliberately renamed as "Memoranda of Understanding" in 1997.

There are many practical reasons why states or international organisations may choose to use an MOU as opposed to a formal treaty. MOUs are not typically subject to the same technical process of ratification.[45] Arguably, the form of an MOU suits the unpredictable nature of the peacekeeping operations. In missions where circumstances are likely to change rapidly or evolve unexpectedly, states must be able to change their agreement with the UN quickly and efficiently.[46] Agreeing to a formal treaty, even the bilateral kind, can be a lengthy and costly process, and amending one even more so.[47] Moreover, peacekeeping missions concern issues that are highly political.[48] Therefore, the practical benefits of a not-so-formalised instrument can have a positive impact on the efficient functioning of peacekeeping operations.

In fact, lack of formal ratification seems to be one of the principal reasons behind the formal change from "Troop Contribution Agreements" to

39 See for example, D Fleck *The Handbook of Visiting Forces* (Oxford University Press, Oxford, 2001) at 490–502.
40 A Aust *Modern Treaty Law and Practice* (2nd ed, Cambridge University Press, Cambridge, 2007) at 20.
41 J Klabbers *The Concept of Treaty in International Law* (Kluwer Law International, Boston, 1996).
42 See above n 40.
43 Aust, above n 40, at 33; Klabbers *The Concept of Treaty in International Law* also stresses the importance of determining an intention to conclude a treaty, above n 41, at 68.
44 Aust, above n 40, at 33.
45 C Lipson "Why Are Some International Agreements Informal?" (1991) 45 *International Organization* 495 at 514.
46 Fleck "Securing Status and Protection of Peacekeepers", above n 6, at 150.
47 Lipson, above n 45, at 514.
48 At 514.

"Memoranda of Understanding".[49] This implies that a TCA did require legislative changes at the domestic level and an MOU does not. Simply on this basis it could be argued that the MOU cannot be a treaty. However, despite the name change, and that the use of an MOU may avoid technicalities associated with formal ratification, it is still generally expected (from the point of view of the UN) that some legislative changes need to be made in order to incorporate the requirements of the MOU.[50] But this is not the case for all states. In some (monist) states, international agreements or treaties will directly apply as domestic law after ratification or accession, or approval of the legislature.[51] Few TCCs would classify as purely monist states, although France is an example. In other (dualist) states, international agreements may need legislative expression, thus needing extra steps taken by the legislature.[52] This is true for many top TCCs, such as India, Pakistan, and Bangladesh.[53] Therefore, there may be no practical difference between the processes of implementing a TCA as opposed to an MOU.

(i) Form of the MOU

The definition of "treaty" under the *Vienna Convention on the Law of Treaties between States and International Organisations or between International Organisations* (1986 Vienna Convention)[54] is confined to the following:[55]

a "treaty" means an international agreement governed by international law and concluded in written form:

  i between one or more states and one or more international organizations.

49 See 1997 MOU, note by the Secretary-General; see also *Report of the Advisory Committee on Administrative and Budgetary Questions* GA, A/61/646 (1996) at [7].

50 See *Report of the Special Committee on Peacekeeping Operations and Its Working Group* (2005), above n 23, at [40(b)], and was one of the tasks set for the Second Group of Legal Experts Report, above n 27.

51 This is typical of civil law jurisdictions such as Brazil, Egypt, France, Japan, Mexico, Namibia, the Netherlands, and Russia. See discussion by A Byrnes and C Renshaw "Within the State" in D Moeckli, S Shah and S Sivakumaran (eds) *International Human Rights Law* (Oxford University Press, Oxford, 2014) 458 at 461.

52 This is typical of common law systems such as the Commonwealth countries of Australia, New Zealand, and the United Kingdom. See Byrnes and Renshaw, above n 51, at 464.

53 It should be noted that the monist/dualist dichotomy is not always applicable, and the status of international agreements in domestic law can be more uncertain. This is the case for another top TCC, Ethiopia: see GA Woldemariam "The Place of International Law in the Ethiopian Legal System" (2016) *Ethiopian Yearbook of International Law* 61.

54 Above n 34. Although the 1986 Vienna Convention is not in force, its provisions closely follow those in the 1969 Convention, which has been argued as representing customary international law, see: J Klabbers *International Law* (Cambridge University Press, Cambridge, 2013) at 42.

55 1986 Vienna Convention, art 2.

At first glance, the MOU would fall within the scope of the Convention, assuming that it is at least an international agreement governed by international law. The MOU is in written form and is between a state and an international organisation.

The content of the MOU may also point to an intention to conclude a treaty. When looking at the particular form of the Model MOU it arguably looks like a treaty. According to Anthony Aust, there are particular key indicators that support a claim that an MOU is in fact a treaty:[56] firstly, the use of mandatory and treaty-like language. The MOU uses obligatory language throughout its provisions, such as "shall", instead of discretionary terms, such as "may".[57] The MOU also refers to "articles" rather than the less formal term "sections". This seems to be a deliberate change from the previous 1991 Model TCA, which referred to numbered sections only. Additionally, the preamble concludes with the phrase "[the parties] agree as follows".[58] These terms are more often associated with treaties rather than informal documents, which typically state that the parties "understand" or "decide".[59] Secondly, there are certain provisions that are typically found in treaties. The MOU has provisions governing the amendment of the MOU,[60] the settlement of disputes,[61] and the termination of the MOU.[62] Such provisions can, however, also be found in non-binding MOUs, so their presence on their own cannot be determinative.[63] Moreover, the MOU has an "entry into force" article.[64] Thirdly, the MOU is effective upon the signature of representatives of the government and the UN. The act of signing such an instrument can be evidence of consent to be bound by the terms therein.[65]

Although these attributes are not determinative as to status on their own, together they provide good evidence that the MOU may have been drafted with the intention that it be a treaty. Other indicators may come from the subsequent behaviour of both parties.

(ii) Subsequent behaviour - is the MOU a treaty from the perspective of the UN?

The UN considers MOUs concluded with TCCs to be legally binding documents, and it is explicitly stated as such in the *Manual on Policies and Procedures*

56 See Aust, above n 40, at 33–36. Anthony Aust is one of the leading authorities on contemporary treaty conception in international law.
57 Mandatory language had been used in the previous versions of these agreements.
58 2007 MOU, preamble.
59 Aust, above n 40, at 427.
60 2007 MOU, art 12.
61 At art 13.
62 At art 15.
63 Aust, above n 40, at 46.
64 2007 MOU, art 14; See also, Klabbers *The Concept of Treaty in International Law*, above n 41, at 75.
65 Aust, above n 40, at 96; see also 1986 Vienna Convention, arts 11–12; however, the Model MOU's entry in force clause does not state that the parties are to be bound by signature, see 2007 MOU, art 14.

Concerning the Reimbursement and Control of Contingent-Owned Equipment of Troop/Police Contributors Participating in Peacekeeping Mission.[66] Additionally, some of the concluded MOUs are registered with the Secretariat of the UN and published in the *United Nations Treaty Series.* [67] When it is the Secretariat that registers an instrument, there will be a determination made as to whether that document is in fact a treaty.[68] Therefore, the registration may provide good evidence that the MOUs are in fact treaties, at least from the perspective of the UN. However, this practice has been inconsistent with peacekeeping-related MOUs, and registration alone cannot be said to be determinative.[69] As Aust points out, many instruments have been wrongly registered in the past.[70] Nevertheless, the fact that they are then published in the *United Nations Treaty Series* (and thus available to all member states) may mean that TCCs failing to object to the MOU's treaty status may preclude later denial to its status.[71] This would be more cogent if the matter ever arose before the International Court of Justice (ICJ), which has not yet happened. Additionally, in another relevant publication, the *UN Treaty Handbook,* the peacekeeping MOUs are used as an example of MOUs that can be legally binding.[72]

Other indications that the MOU may be a treaty come from various statements made in UN reports or by the Secretary-General. The Secretary-General noted in 1997 that the MOU "entails legally binding rights and obligations and, once concluded, is legally binding on the parties".[73] Likewise, Prince Zeid referred to the MOU giving rise to certain obligations on states and indicated the binding nature of the document.[74] The same reports noted that certain legislative changes

66 *Manual on Policies and Procedures Concerning the Reimbursement and Control of Contingent-Owned Equipment of Troop/Police Contributors Participating in Peacekeeping Mission,* above n 1, at 8.

67 See for example *Memorandum of Understanding between the United Nations and the Government of Romania Contributing Resources to the United Nations Special Police Unit in Kosovo* 2421 UNTS 293 (opened for signature 11 February 2001, entered into force 20 February 2002); *Memorandum of Understanding between the United Nations and the Government of New Zealand Contributing Resources to the United Nations in East Timor (DPKO/UNTAET/NZ/04)* 2152 UNTS 3 (opened for signature 27 April 2001, entered into force with retroactive effect 21 February 2000); *Memorandum of Understanding between the United Nations and the People's Republic of Bangladesh Contributing Resources to the United Nations Mission for the Referendum in Western Sahara (MINURSO)* 2716 UNTS 139 (opened for signature 10 December 2010, entered into force with retroactive effect 1 November 2010).

68 DN Hutchinson "The Significance of the Registration of an International Agreement in Determining Whether or Not It Is a Treaty" in S Davidson *The Law of Treaties* (Ashgate, Aldershot, 2004) 133 at 139. See also Klabbers *The Concept of Treaty in International Law,* above n 41, at 79–84.

69 Klabbers *The Concept of Treaty in International Law,* above n 41, at 142.

70 Aust, above n 40, at 36.

71 Hutchinson, above n 68, at 272–273.

72 "Glossary" *UN Treaty Handbook* (Prepared by the Treaty Section of the Office of Legal Affairs, UN Publications, 2006) at 61.

73 *Reform of the Procedures for Determining Reimbursement to Member States for Contingent Owned Equipment,* above n 23, at [2].

74 See for example Zeid Report, above n 7, at [80].

were required to implement the MOU. However, the need to undertake legislative changes to incorporate the terms of an MOU (or treaty) will depend on the constitutional framework of each individual state. As such, these statements may be unnecessarily expansive. As stated previously, before the 2007 amendments, the UN codes of conduct and the S-G Bulletin were not considered binding on all categories of personnel, specifically military contingents.[75] This was particularly concerning to Prince Zeid, who recommended their implementation in the MOU for the very purpose of binding TCCs to incorporate the standards into their own military codes of conduct.[76] The fact that the MOU was seen to have such an effect supports the argument that it is a treaty.

(iii) Subsequent behaviour - is the MOU a treaty from the perspective of states?

The Special Committee on Peacekeeping Operations met in 2006 and 2007 to discuss redrafting the Model MOU.[77] The Committee included representatives from prominent TCCs such as Bangladesh, India, and Pakistan,[78] as well as representatives from top financing states such as France, Japan, and the United States.[79] These sessions of the Special Committee were closed to the public.[80] With no information on the Committee's deliberations and in the absence of statements from TCCs, it is difficult to ascertain how states view the MOU's legal status.

(iv) The annexed documents - the extent to which sexual exploitation and abuse are incorporated

There are three documents relevant to sexual exploitation and abuse that collectively form part of the zero-tolerance policy; they are two UN codes of conduct (*We Are United Nations Peacekeeping Personnel* and *Ten Rules: Code of Personal Conduct for Blue Helmets*)[81] and the S-G

75 At [20]; Second Group of Legal Experts Report, above n 27, at [37].

76 See generally Second Group of Legal Experts Report, above n 27; see also Zeid Report, above n 7, at [25].

77 *Report of the Special Committee on Peacekeeping Operations and Its Working Group* GA, A/61/19/Rev.1 (2007) at [14] and Annex "Composition of the Special Committee on Peacekeeping Operations at Its 2007 Session".

78 *Report of the Special Committee on Peacekeeping Operations and Its Working Group* (2005), above n 23; Department of Peacekeeping Operations "Ranking of Military and Police Contributions to UN Operations" (August 2015) available online: <www.un.org>.

79 *Report of the Special Committee on Peacekeeping Operations and Its Working Group* (2005), above n 23; United Nations Peacekeeping "Financing Peacekeeping" (August 2015) available online: <www.un.org>.

80 An Official Information Act (OIA) application was made by the author to the New Zealand Ministry of Foreign Affairs & Trade in 2014 in order to obtain information from the Special Committee's meetings on the draft MOU where New Zealand was included (in 2006 and 2007). However, most of that information has been rendered classified.

81 UN Conduct and Discipline Unit *Ten Rules: Code of Personal Conduct for Blue Helmets* (1999) <http://cdu.unlb.org>; UN Conduct and Discipline Unit *We Are United Nations Peacekeeping Personnel*<http://cdu.unlb.org>.

Bulletin.[82] The main text of the MOU does not mention sexual exploitation and abuse. Instead, the three policy documents are incorporated across two annexed documents: Annex H (*We Are United Nations Peacekeeping Personnel*) and Annex F (*Definitions*).

Annex H combines the two UN codes of conduct. It makes simple reference to "sexual exploitation and abuse". Additionally, it covers the prohibition of sexual activity with minors. It also makes clear that there will be enforcement action taken against those that contravene the codes. However, Annex H does not make direct reference to the S-G Bulletin, which is the most detailed policy document regarding sexual exploitation and abuse.

Annex F does make direct reference to sexual exploitation and abuse as forming part of the definition of "serious misconduct". Both sexual abuse and sexual exploitation are further defined separately in Annex F as having the exact same meaning as in the S-G Bulletin, therefore filling any gap provided by the standards in Annex H. There are references made to "serious misconduct" in the main text of the MOU, including article 7 *quater* (investigations), article 7 *quinquiens* (exercise of jurisdiction by the government), and article 7 *sexiens* (accountability). Consequently, standards related to sexual exploitation and abuse are incorporated into the MOU, although this is through the use of annexed documents. As such, it is necessary to turn to the issue of legal status of the annexed documents themselves.

It has been asserted that not all documents annexed to the MOU are legally binding.[83] In the Zeid Report, it was noted that mission-specific *Guidelines to Troop-Contributing Countries* were not binding, although they were subsequently attached to the MOU.[84] These guidelines were contrasted with rules, where it was explained that the latter were of greater legal status than mere guidelines.[85] This reasoning would suggest that whether or not those documents attached to the MOU are legally binding depends on the legal status of the individual documents. The UN codes are more likely to represent policy documents rather than documents having any binding force. Therefore, it would seem on the above reasoning that although *We Are United Nations Peacekeepers* is attached to the MOU, it is not legally binding in the same way as the MOU itself. Moreover, Annex F would similarly not be legally binding, because alone, it is a mere glossary of terms.

According to Anthony Aust, unless there is a provision stating that the annexes are integral to the treaty, the presumption is that they are not binding.[86] Article two of the MOU states, "this document, including all of its annexes, constitutes the entire memorandum of understanding". This is a strong indication that the annexes, including the definitions in Annex F, form part of the MOU and therefore part of the "treaty". However, the statements about the non-binding nature

82 See above n 26.
83 See Zeid Report, above n 7, at [20]; Deen-Racsmany, above n 16, at 331.
84 See for example 2007 MOU, Annex G.
85 Zeid Report, above n 7, at [20].
86 Aust, above n 40, at 436–437.

of the *Guidelines to Troop-Contributing Countries* are not easily reconciled with a conclusion that the annexes are binding.

Assuming that Annexes H and F form part of the content of the MOU (and that the MOU is a treaty), then TCCs are arguably bound by them. This would then transform these documents from policy into legal documents, giving rise to legal obligations. One of those obligations would be to ensure relevant pre-deployment training in the standards and to incorporate them into national military codes, as provided in article 7 *bis.* [87] The reference in Annex H to accountability for contravention of standards, including sexual exploitation and abuse, may provide further obligations – particularly when read together with other provisions of the MOU, such as article 7 *quinquiens* (discussed below).

Provisions of the 2007 MOU

Proceeding on the assumption that the MOU is in fact a treaty, it is necessary then to examine the terms of the MOU and consider whether there are binding obligations on TCCs to exercise their criminal jurisdiction. There are three provisions of the current Model MOU that directly apply to this inquiry: articles 7 *quinquiens* (exercise of jurisdiction by the government), 7 *quater* (investigations), and 7 *sexiens* (accountability). These provisions provide the basis for a framework that is anchored to the primary role of TCCs.

(i) Article 7 quinquiens

The first article to examine concerns the issue of formal assurances obtained from TCCs that they will exercise their criminal jurisdiction. Article 7 *quinquiens* reads:[88]

> Military members and any civilian members subject to national military law of the national contingent provided by the Government are subject to the Government's exclusive jurisdiction in respect of any crimes or offences that might be committed by them while they are assigned to the military component of [UNPKO]. The Government assures the UN that it shall exercise such jurisdiction with respect to such crimes or offences.

An assurance that the TCC will exercise its criminal jurisdiction is not an assurance of prosecution. The decision as to whether or not to prosecute is a matter of state sovereignty (prosecutorial discretion), which has not been interfered with by the provision of such assurances.[89] So what does the formal assurance mean? The assurance is firstly directed at the UN itself; the TCC does not assure the host

87 This also may be implied from the purpose section of the 2007 MOU, see art 3 "... and to specify United Nations standards of conduct for personnel provided by the Government".

88 2007 MOU, art 7 *quinquiens* [7.22]-[7.23].

89 Zeid Report, above n 7, at [80].

state or victims that it will provide justice. This is consistent with the complete silence of the MOU regarding victims and a lack of consideration of the host state. Secondly, the provision is one sided; the TCC assures the UN that it will exercise its jurisdiction, but the provision does not explicitly authorise the UN to enforce this. Therefore, article 7 *quinquiens,* if it can be construed as an obligation to exercise criminal jurisdiction, does not satisfy the principle of host state ownership. Furthermore, there can be no guarantee that justice will be seen to be done. There is no explicit authority for the UN to take leadership within this provision, either.

Before the amendments in 2007, some scholars[90] and authors of UN reports[91] lamented the absence of these assurances in practice. Although the early TCAs made similar provision for assurances, the 1997 redrafting dropped this requirement. The withdrawal of the assurance clause represented practice at the time; formal assurances were not actively sought from TCCs, despite the fact that they were still required by the SOFA.[92] It was argued that a re-introduction of the provision would place more pressure on TCCs to hold their military forces to account.[93] Whether or not this translates into a binding obligation is unclear.

The principles of treaty interpretation may be helpful for the purposes of this inquiry. Article 31 of the 1986 Vienna Convention states the general rule of treaty interpretation, which is simply to interpret the text in good faith according to the ordinary meaning of the words in their context and "in light of its object and purpose".[94] Starting with the ordinary meaning of the words alone, is an "assurance" an agreement to be bound to exercise criminal jurisdiction or is it a mere expectation? The 1991 TCA did not make reference to an assurance but rather that the national government "agrees" to exercise criminal jurisdiction.[95] Arguably, to agree to exercise jurisdiction seems to indicate the involvement of both parties in reaching that decision in drafting the TCA – that the UN expects the TCC to exercise its jurisdiction and that the state has agreed to do so. When the similar provision was put back into the Model MOU, the word used was not "agree", but the TCC "assures" that it will exercise jurisdiction. Is this signifying something less than an agreement or is it an equivalent term? The absence of "assures" from the *Definitions* (Annex F) suggests that it does not have any special meaning.[96]

90 For example, A Miller "Legal Aspects of Stopping Sexual Exploitation and Abuse in UN Peacekeeping Operations" (2006) 39 *Cornell International Law Journal* 71; M Nuldo "The United Nations Responses to the Sexual Abuse and Exploitation of Women and Girls by Peacekeepers during Peacekeeping Missions" (2009) 27 *Berkeley Journal of International Law* 127.
91 For example, Zeid Report, above n 7.
92 Deen-Racsmany, above n 16, at 329.
93 Zeid Report, above n 7.
94 It has been established that these principles reflect customary international law. See *Case Concerning Sovereignty over Pulau Ligitan and Pulau Sipadan (Indonesia/ Malaysia) (Merits)* [2002] ICJ Rep 625 at 23–24.
95 1991 TCA, above n 22, at VIII [25].
96 1986 Vienna Convention, art 31(4).

A provision such as article 7 *quinquiens* was supported by both the Zeid Report[97] and the Group of Legal Experts Report.[98] In fact, the Group of Legal Experts recommended that contribution should only be made on the basis that formal assurances will be made, and that this should be required under the MOU.[99] However, it has been argued that the wording that eventually made the amendment is not such a key provision; for example, Deen-Racsmany labels the article a "watered down" version of the 1991 TCA.[100] Although it should be remembered that, despite the strong wording in 1991, formal assurances were not often sought; therefore, the provision was not reflected in practice.

The principles of treaty interpretation dictate that the ordinary meaning must be read in light of the context and the object and purpose of the treaty itself. The object and purpose may be inferred from the text of the treaty (such as the preamble and even its annexes) and by reading the treaty as a whole.[101] The TCA and the 1991 MOU were created undoubtedly for the purpose of supplying troops and equipment to UN peacekeeping operations. However, the amended MOU has the additional articles detailing the accountability of troops. These additions are detailed and considered; the majority of the Model MOU is now taken up with accountability provisions. Such a change must have an impact on the object and purpose of the MOU.

The purpose section of the MOU includes: "to specify UN standards of conduct for personnel provided by the Government".[102] This phrase represents a change from a previous draft, which was much more specific and more clearly indicated that improved accountability of peacekeeping personnel was a central issue.[103] The purpose is now limited to the UN standards of conduct. However, Deen-Racsmany notes that this should not alter the general impression of the previous wording, because when read within the context of the other changes made, it is clear that accountability is still part of the purpose of the MOU.[104] I generally agree with this proposition. It is noted in Annex H that criminal accountability is expected from TCCs where their national contingents breach the standards that translate into crimes in their domestic law.[105]

97 Zeid Report, above n 7, at [80].
98 Second Group of Legal Experts Report, above n 27, at [18(i)].
99 At [18(i)].
100 Deen-Racsmany, above n 16, at 339.
101 F Jacobs "Varieties of Approach to Treaty Interpretation: With Special Reference to the Draft Convention on the Law of Treaties before the Vienna Diplomatic Conference" in S Davidson (ed) *The Law of Treaties* (Ashgate, Aldershot, 2004) 297 at 298.
102 2007 MOU, art 2.
103 "… and to provide for the maintenance of discipline and good order among such personnel and the investigation of, and accountability for, violations" *Revised Draft Model Memorandum of Understanding between United Nations and [Participating State] Contributing Resources to [the United Nations Peacekeeping Operation]* GA, A/61/494 (2006) at 4.
104 Deen-Racsmany, above n 16, at 335, footnote 76.
105 2007 MOU, Annex H.

Arguably, the additional provisions[106] all have a similar theme: to improve accountability of peacekeeping personnel (but not to improve the accountability of states themselves). Additionally, these recommendations were made specifically with sexual exploitation and abuse in mind. They are also the most detailed provisions. Together with the purpose and Annex H, this could suggest that the object and purpose include holding contingent members to account for their criminal acts. On the above reasoning, the requirement that a TCC assures the UN that its government will exercise criminal jurisdiction can be interpreted as an obligation to do so.

As part of the preparatory work on the amended MOU, the Secretary-General issued a commentary on the new provisions.[107] Commenting on article 7 *quinquiens*, the Secretary-General noted simply that the provision gives effect to the requirement under article 48 of the Model SOFA (that the TCC should provide an assurance it will exercise criminal jurisdiction).[108] However, the draft article 7 *quinquiens* the Secretary-General commented on is different to the version that was finally accepted, with the original version having much stronger and obligatory wording (such as "the Government *will* exercise ... jurisdiction").[109] It is difficult to assess whether the omission of the obligatory language means that the current version has been watered down in its effect, since the reasoning behind the change has not been publically released.

Overall, the meaning of article 7 *quinquiens* is unclear because there is limited information about the intention of both parties. Information that is available, such as the official recommendations, comes from the pre-drafting stages. There is enough evidence to suggest that the UN expects that the TCC will exercise criminal jurisdiction and they may be obligated by article 7 *quinquiens*. However, there is further evidence to counter this proposition, as seen by comparing the previous draft of the provision and the similar yet more strongly worded provision under the 1991 TCA. Nevertheless, reading the MOU as a whole, it would seem that the ordinary meaning of article 7 *quinquiens*, taking into consideration the additional and detailed provisions made in 2007, suggests that an assurance is likely an obligation on the TCC to exercise its criminal jurisdiction. But this still leaves the question of what amounts to the exercise of criminal jurisdiction under the MOU.

(ii) Other obligations?

Article 7 *quater* is a particularly lengthy provision governing the investigation of contingent members for misconduct and serious misconduct. Although it is reiterated several times that the TCC has the exclusive jurisdiction in such

106 Namely arts 7 *bis*,7 *ter*, 7 *quater*, 7 *quinquiens* and 7 *sexiens*.
107 *Revised Draft Model Memorandum of Understanding*, above n 103.
108 At 12.
109 At 56, emphasis added.

investigations,[110] the provision attempts to increase cooperation between the TCC and the UN in certain circumstances. For instance, where the national government fails to initiate a preliminary investigation when it has received a complaint, the UN's investigative arm, the Office of Internal Oversight Services (OIOS), will take over this task.[111] The UN will be limited to an administrative investigation.[112] This is where information is gathered (for example, contact details of witnesses) and held by the OIOS until a formal criminal investigation can be undertaken by the relevant TCC's national investigation teams.[113] It is still up to the TCC to make a decision whether to investigate or not.[114]

If requested by the government, the UN has agreed to assist the national investigation officers in several different ways.[115] The OIOS will attempt to work with members of the national investigative team as much as possible to this end. Nevertheless, article 7 *quater* emphasises several times that it is the representatives of the TCC that are in charge of investigations.[116] The UN provides support only. The provision also draws attention to the sovereign right of the TCC to investigate its national contingent members.[117] Since May 2015, the UN has encouraged a six-month time limit to conduct formal investigations, without any additional enforcement mechanism in place to make sure TCCs adhere to the time limit or otherwise exercise their criminal jurisdiction outside the MOU.[118] With the total absence of victims and the host state from the agreement, there are no enforcement mechanisms available for them, either.

There appears to be no indication of an obligation to investigate per se within article 7 *quater*, at least on the TCC. The provision instead seems to focus more on the role of the UN and its own obligations, particularly in relation to the information it collects in its administrative investigations. Such information must return to the TCC. This is important for the TCC to adhere to the requirements under articles 7 *ter* (discipline) and 7 *quinquiens* (exercise of criminal jurisdiction).[119] Moreover, any support the UN gives is subject to the decisions of the

110 2007 MOU, art 7 *quater* at [7.10] and [7.20].
111 2007 MOU, art 7 *quater* at [7.13].
112 This will not include the interviewing of witnesses for example, see 2007 MOU, Annex F at [30].
113 2007 MOU, art 7 *quater at* [7.16, 7.17] and Annex F [33]; see also TA Shockley "The Investigation Procedures of the United Nations Office of Internal Oversight Services and the Rights of the United Nations Staff Member: An Analysis of the United Nations Judicial Tribunals' Judgments on Disciplinary Cases in the United Nations" (2015) 27 *Pace International Law Review* 468 at 485.
114 2007 MOU, art 7 *quater* at [7.15].
115 At art 7 *quater* at [7.17, 7.18].
116 At art 7 *quater* at [7.10, 7.20].
117 At art 7 *quater* at [7.21].
118 UN Conduct and Discipline Unit "Fact Sheet on Sexual Exploitation and Abuse" (3 September 2015) available online: <http://cdu.unlb.org>.
119 See *Revised Draft Model Memorandum of Understanding*, above n 103, at 10.

national investigative teams.[120] However, in turn the government is required to make sure contingent commanders cooperate with any UN investigation.[121]

The only obligatory language used in article 7 *quater* that relates to the TCC concerns informing the UN of *prima facie* cases received by them and forwarding the case to the appropriate national authorities:[122]

> In the event that the Government has *prima facie* grounds indicating that any member of its national contingent has committed an act of serious misconduct it shall without delay inform the United Nations and forward the case to its appropriate national authorities for the purposes of investigation.

Prince Zeid noted that the provisions, when read together, obliged the TCC to submit the case to the appropriate national authorities.[123]

Submitting a case to the appropriate national authorities seems to be the first step in the exercise of criminal jurisdiction under article 7 *quinquiens.* [124] If the outcome of a UN investigation or that of the government reveals that the allegations were well founded, then the case must be "forwarded to [the TCC's] appropriate authorities for due action".[125] Such action would include initiating formal investigation (if the allegation is well founded under a UN administrative investigation) or deciding whether or not to prosecute.[126] Therefore, this step seems to be an obligation under the MOU. However, the provisions governing what the TCC is expected to do after this step is taken seem to defer to the sovereign right of the TCC to make such decisions. It is up to the prosecutorial discretion of that TCC.

Although there is an attempt to increase cooperation between TCCs and the UN, the primary role within this framework remains secured to TCCs. There is no guarantee that justice will be seen to be done, because TCCs are not obligated to investigate and prosecute, rather only to forward the case to the appropriate national authorities. The UN has some leadership within these provisions to initiate administrative investigations where a TCC has failed to do so, although this does not amount to formal criminal investigation (which is needed to bring forward prosecution and punishment for sexual exploitation and abuse). These provisions do not provide any mechanisms for the UN, victims, or the host state to enforce compliance or gain access to justice.

120 2007 MOU, arts 7 *quater* at [7.10,] and [7.20].
121 At art 7 *quarter* at [7.14]; *Revised Draft Model Memorandum of Understanding*, above n 103, at 10.
122 2007 MOU, art 7 *quater* at [7.11].
123 Zeid Report, above n 7, at [80].
124 *Revised Draft Model Memorandum of Understanding*, above n 103, at 13.
125 2007 MOU, art 7 *sexiens* at [7.24].
126 *Revised Draft Model Memorandum of Understanding*, above n 103, at 15.

The MOU as a treaty

There are several consequences that flow from the MOU being interpreted as a treaty. Because an MOU is signed between the UN and each TCC, its provisions may have cogent normative value; for example, the binding agreement detailing obligations on TCCs to exercise criminal jurisdiction by forwarding a case to the national authorities carries more normative weight if the MOU is considered a treaty. The normative value of these obligations is important if the UN wants to use coercive or noncoercive measures against TCCs for failing to discharge such obligations Additionally, if it is at least arguable that the above observations are correct then the principle of *pacta sunt servanda* will apply.[127] Article 26 of the 1986 Vienna Convention states that "every treaty in force is binding on the parties and must be performed by them in good faith". Therefore, if there was evidence to suggest that the TCC was not submitting cases to its national authorities then this may amount to a breach of treaty obligations.

A breach of the MOU

Pending a breach of a treaty, there can be various consequences that flow from this. Among these is the unilateral termination of the treaty. A treaty may be terminated or its operation suspended by one party in certain circumstances; these include a fundamental change in circumstances,[128] impossibility of performance,[129] and material breach.[130] The most relevant applicable circumstance is material breach.[131]

A material breach is defined under article 60(3) of the 1986 Vienna Convention as the following:

a a repudiation of the treaty not sanctioned by the present Convention; or
b the violation of a provision essential to the accomplishment of the object and purpose of the treaty.

The ICJ has used much stronger language in relation to this section, stating that for a breach to be considered "material" it must be "of a deliberate and persistent violation of obligations which destroys the very object and purpose of that relationship".[132] Article 60(3) seems to set a deceivingly high threshold as noted

127 This principle is a well-established customary norm. See *Nuclear Test Cases (Australia v France)* [1974] ICJ Rep 253; *(New Zealand v France)* [1974] ICJ Rep 475.
128 1986 Vienna Convention, art 62.
129 At art 61.
130 At art 60.
131 Impossibility of performance relates directly to the object of the treaty; in peacekeeping this would be the operation itself.
132 *Legal Consequences for States of the Continued Presence of South Africa in Namibia (South West Africa) notwithstanding Security Council Resolution 276 (Advisory Opinion)* [1971] ICJ Rep 16 at 47.

by the lack of successful claims before the ICJ.[133] As argued above, the object and purpose may include holding contingent members to account for their criminal acts. Failing to at least forward a case to the appropriate national authorities could qualify as a material breach. It would directly hinder the process of accountability of contingent members.

For the termination of a treaty, there are certain procedures that both parties must follow. Articles 65–67 of the 1986 Vienna Convention cover such procedures. The TCC should first be notified of the proposed breach and be given a period of time to object. The Vienna Conventions prioritise peaceful means to resolve such issues, such as negotiations between the parties and arbitration. Thus, the dispute resolution mechanism in the MOU itself should be initiated first.

The Model MOU has its own dispute resolution mechanism that should be the first point of call. Therefore, it is necessary to briefly examine article 13. There are three levels of dispute resolution envisioned by the Model MOU: the first two consisting of negotiation between the parties and the third by way of binding arbitration before the ICJ.[134] Either party may initiate the mechanism; thus, it would be available to the UN if it was considered that TCCs were not adhering to the requisite obligations. Cooperation with the mechanism relies on the will of each state.[135] The arbitration mechanism has never been used.

If the UN terminates the MOU in response to a failure to exercise jurisdiction, this does send a strong signal of leadership in enforcing the zero-tolerance policy. It should be noted that the removal of problematic contingents has already been authorised by the Security Council in Resolution 2272,[136] which refers to obligations beyond what is detailed in the MOU and does not refer to the MOU itself. To action the authorised removal of troops in this Resolution, the Secretary-General would be required to terminate or amend the MOU. In doing so, the MOU's dispute resolution mechanism is ignored. Chapter three will analyse the Resolution further, but for the purposes of this section it is sufficient to suggest that as authorisation flows from the Security Council, termination of the MOU by the Secretary-General without going through the dispute resolution process may still support the argument that the MOU is in fact a treaty.

Although removing contingents sent by states that have failed to exercise criminal jurisdiction over acts of sexual abuse within their ranks will remove any offenders from the host state, the international community may still not see justice being done. The removal of troops is not a guarantee or an

133 G Triggs *International Law: Contemporary Principles and Practices* (2nd ed, LexisNexis Butterworths, Chatswood, 2011) at 133.

134 See 2007 MOU, art 13 at 13.1–13.2.

135 2007 MOU, art 13 states that both parties must agree on an arbitrator. An unwilling state may not agree and thus be limited to continued negotiations between the UN and the TCC.

136 *Security Council Resolution 2272* SC Res, S/Res/2272 (2016).

indication that the TCC will then go on to exercise jurisdiction over perpetrators. Again, there are no enforcement mechanisms available to the UN, victims, or the host state in such cases. Such an outcome does not fill the accountability gap and is thus unacceptable as a solution.

Conclusion

A strong argument can be made that the MOU is in fact a treaty. Evidence of an intention to conclude a treaty may be found by looking at the form of the MOU: it uses treaty-like and obligatory language; it represents what the parties "agree"[137] rather than merely "decide"; and its provisions reflect those commonly found in treaties, such as an "entry into force" article. The fact that an MOU has been chosen over a formal treaty structure may be due to the practical benefits of avoiding costly ratification procedures. Furthermore, subsequent behaviour and statements by UN officials suggest that, at least from the perspective of the UN, the MOU is a treaty. It is unclear how states themselves view the MOU.

Incorporation of the standards relating to sexual exploitation and abuse has been primarily achieved through the use of documents annexed to the MOU. There is a grey area associated with the legal status of the annexed materials. However, Annexes H (*We Are United Nations Peacekeepers*) and F (*Definitions*) form part of the content of the MOU, because if they were not binding then it would be inconsistent with the reasons behind the Group of Legal Experts' recommendations to attach the standards to the MOU rather than the *Guidelines to Troop-Contributing Countries.*

The provisions of the MOU reveal obligations on TCCs to submit cases to appropriate national authorities. Despite an assurance that TCCs will exercise their criminal jurisdiction, there is no obligation in the MOU to investigate or prosecute.

If it were assumed that article 7 *quinquiens* gave rise to a legal obligation on the TCC to exercise criminal jurisdiction and they failed to do so, then this may be a material breach for the purposes of termination of the MOU. Termination would most definitely achieve the withdrawal of troops. However, this does not fill the accountability gap as it does not guarantee that justice will be done once troops leave.

Overall, the MOU centralises the role of TCCs and renders invisible the victims and the host state. There are no additional enforcement mechanisms available to ensure that justice will be done, and it provides the very accountability gap that allows for impunity. Obligations for TCCs to take further positive steps in response to sexual exploitation and abuse may be found elsewhere, such as in international human rights law.

137 2007 MOU, Preamble.

References

F Akada "The Enforcement of Military Justice and Discipline in External Military Operations: Exploring the Fault Lines" (2008) 47 *Military Law and the Law of War Review* 253

A Aust *Modern Treaty Law and Practice* (2nd ed, Cambridge University Press, Cambridge, 2007)

M Brandon "Analysis of the Terms 'Treaty' and 'International Agreement' for the Purposes of Registration under Article 102 of the United Nations Charter" (1953) *The American Journal of International Law* 49

A Byrnes and C Renshaw "Within the State" in D Moeckli, S Shah and S Sivakumaran (eds) *International Human Rights Law* (Oxford University Press, Oxford, 2014)

Case Concerning Sovereignty over Pulau Ligitan and Pulau Sipadan (Indonesia/Malaysia) (Merits) [2002] ICJ Rep 625

Z Deen-Racsmany "The Amended UN Model Memorandum of Understanding: A New Incentive for States to Discipline and Prosecute Military Members of National Peacekeeping Contingents?" (2011) 16 *Journal of Conflict and Security Law* 321

D Door and K Schmalenbach *Vienna Convention on the Law of Treaties* (Springer, Berlin, 2011)

Exchange of Letters Constituting an Agreement Concerning the Service with the United Nations Emergency Force of the National Contingent Provided by the Government of Finland 271 UNTS 135 (1957)

D Fleck and M Saalfeld "Combining Efforts to Improve the Legal Status of UN Peacekeeping Forces and Their Effective Protection" (1994) *International Peacekeeping* 82

D Fleck "Introduction" in D Fleck (ed) *The Handbook of the Law of Visiting Forces* (Oxford University Press, Oxford, 2001)

D Fleck "Securing Status and Protection of Peacekeepers" in R Arnold and GA Knoops (eds) *Practice and Policies of Modern Peace Support Operations under International Law* (Transnational Publishers, New York, 2006)

D Fleck *The Handbook of the Law of Visiting Forces* (Oxford University Press, Oxford, 2001)

General Assembly Resolution GA Res, A/Res/998 (ES-I) (1956)

General Assembly Resolution GA Res, A/Res/1000 (ES-I) (1956)

D Hammarskjold *Summary Study of the Experience Derived from the Establishment and Operation of the Force: Report of the Secretary-General* GA A/3943 XIII (1958)

DN Hutchinson "The Significance of the Registration of an International Agreement in Determining Whether or Not It Is a Treaty" in S Davidson (ed) *The Law of Treaties* (Ashgate, Aldershot, 2004)

F Jacobs "Varieties of Approach to Treaty Interpretation: With Special Reference to the Draft Convention on the Law of Treaties before the Vienna Diplomatic Conference" in S Davidson (ed) *The Law of Treaties* (Ashgate, Aldershot, 2004)

J Klabbers *International Law* (Cambridge University Press, Cambridge, 2013)

J Klabbers *The Concept of Treaty in International Law* (Kluwer Law International, Boston, 1996)

Legal Consequences for States of the Continued Presence of South Africa in Namibia (South West Africa) notwithstanding Security Council Resolution 276 (Advisory Opinion) [1971] ICJ Rep 16

C Lipson "Why Are Some International Agreements Informal?" (1991) 45 *International Organization* 495

Manual on Policies and Procedures Concerning the Reimbursement and Control of Contingent-Owned Equipment of Troop/Police Contributors Participating in Peacekeeping Missions (COE Manual) GA, A/c.5/69/18 (2014)

Memorandum of Understanding between the United Nations and the Government of New Zealand Contributing Resources to the United Nations in East Timor (DPKO/UNTAET/NZ/04) 2152 UNTS 3 (opened for signature 27 April 2001, entered into force with retroactive effect 21 February 2000)

Memorandum of Understanding between the United Nations and the Government of Romania Contributing Resources to the United Nations Special Police Unit in Kosovo 2421 UNTS 293 (opened for signature 11 February 2001, entered into force 20 February 2002)

Memorandum of Understanding between the United Nations and the People's Republic of Bangladesh Contributing Resources to the United Nations Mission for the Referendum in Western Sahara (MINURSO) 2716 UNTS 139 (opened for signature 10 December 2010, entered into force with retroactive effect 1 November 2010)

A Miller "Legal Aspects of Stopping Sexual Exploitation and Abuse in UN Peacekeeping Operations" (2006) 39 *Cornell International Law Journal* 71

Model Agreement between the United Nations and Member States Contributing Personnel and Equipment to United Nations Peace-Keeping Operations GA, A/46/1991 (1991)

Model Status of Forces Agreement between the United Nations and Host Countries GA, A/45/594 (1990)

Nuclear Test Case (Australia v France) [1974] ICJ Rep 253

Nuclear Test Case (New Zealand v France) [1974] ICJ Rep 475

M Nuldo "The United Nations Responses to the Sexual Abuse and Exploitation of Women and Girls by Peacekeepers during Peacekeeping Missions" (2009) 27 *Berkeley Journal of International Law* 127

M Odello "Tackling Criminal Acts in Peacekeeping Operations: The Accountability of Peacekeepers" (2010) 15 *Journal of Conflict & Security Law* 347

R Opie "Human Rights Violations by Peacekeepers: Finding a Framework for Attribution of Responsibility" (2006) *New Zealand Law Review* 1

Reform of the Procedures for Determining Reimbursement to Member States for Contingent-Owned Equipment GA, A/51/967 (1997)

Report of the Advisory Committee on Administrative and Budgetary Questions GA, A/61/646 (1996)*Report of the Group of Legal Experts on Ensuring the Accountability of United Nations Staff and Experts on Mission with Respect to Criminal Acts Committed in Peacekeeping Operations* GA A/60/980 (2006)

Report of the Group of Legal Experts on Making the Standards Contained in the Secretary-General's Bulletin Binding on Contingent Members and Standardising the Norms of Conduct so That They Are Applicable to All Categories of Peacekeeping Personnel GA, A/61/645 (2006)

Report of the Special Committee on Peacekeeping Operations and Its Working Group GA, A/59/19/Rev. 1 (2005)

Report of the Special Committee on Peacekeeping Operations and Its Working Group GA, A/61/19/Rev.1 (2007)

Revised Draft Model Memorandum of Understanding between United Nations and [Participating State] Contributing Resources to [the United Nations Peacekeeping Operation] GA, A/61/494 (2006)

C Ryngaert *Jurisdiction in International Law* (Oxford University Press, Oxford, 2008)

Secretary-General *A Comprehensive Strategy to Eliminate Future Sexual Exploitation and Abuse in United Nations Peacekeeping Operations* A/59/710 (2005) prepared by Prince Zeid Ra'ad Zeid Al-Hussein

Security Council Resolution 1528 SC Res, S/Res/1528 (2004)

Security Council Resolution 1542 SC Res, S/Res/1542 (2004)

Security Council Resolution 2272 SC Res, S/Res/2272 (2016)

TA Shockley "The Investigation Procedures of the United Nations Office of Internal Oversight Services and the Rights of the United Nations Staff Member: An Analysis of the United Nations Judicial Tribunals' Judgments on Disciplinary Cases in the United Nations" (2015) 27 *Pace International Law Review* 468

G Simm "International Law as a Regulatory Framework for Sexual Crimes Committed by Peacekeepers" (2012) 16 *Journal of Conflict & Security Law* 473

G Simm *Sex in Peace Operations* (Cambridge University Press, Cambridge, 2013)

G Triggs *International Law: Contemporary Principles and Practices* (2nd ed, LexisNexis Butterworths, Chatswood, 2011)

UN Conduct and Discipline Unit Ten Rules: Code of Personal Conduct for Blue Helmets (1999) <http://cdu.unlb.org>

UN Conduct and Discipline Unit We Are United Nations Peacekeeping Personnel <http://cdu.unlb.org>

United Nations Secretary-General's Bulletin *Special Measures for Protection from Sexual Exploitation and Sexual Abuse* SG B, ST/SGB/2003/13 (2003)

UN Treaty Handbook (Prepared by the Treaty Section of the Office of Legal Affairs, UN Publications, 2006)

Vienna Convention on the Law of Treaties 1155 UNTS 331 (opened for signature 1969, entered into force 1980)

Vienna Convention on the Law of Treaties between States and International Organisations or between International Organisations 1986 (opened for signature 21 March 1986, not yet in force)

GA Woldemariam "The Place of International Law in the Ethiopian Legal System" (2016) *Ethiopian Yearbook of International Law* 61

2 International Human Rights

This chapter will investigate the extent to which there are positive obligations on states to criminalise, investigate, prosecute, and punish sexual exploitation and abuse under international human rights law. Moreover, whether there are requirements for states to assert extraterritorial jurisdiction will also be examined. A focus on international human rights law is preferred over international humanitarian law[1] for two key reasons: firstly, peacekeepers are not always operating as combatants for the continued application of humanitarian law, and human rights law will apply in both peacetime and armed conflict.[2] Secondly, due to the opportunistic nature of the behaviour, peacekeepers are not likely to commit sexual exploitation and abuse within the scope of official state actions, and human rights law will apply to violations committed by both state and non-state actors.[3]

To clarify the existence of such obligations, this chapter will break up discussion between sexual abuse on the one hand and sexual exploitation on the other. Sexual abuse concerns conduct such as rape, sexual violence, and sexual activity with children, and so might be covered by human rights instruments dealing with torture, or other cruel, inhuman, and degrading treatment, and violence against children. Therefore, the first section will examine the Convention against Torture

1 The obligation on states to respond to crimes committed by their troops during armed conflict may apply under international humanitarian law and has been discussed at length elsewhere. See for example R Murphy "United Nations Military Operations and International Humanitarian Law: What Rules to Apply to Peacekeepers?" (2003) 14 *Criminal Law Forum* 153; J Saura "Lawful Peacekeeping: Applicability of International Humanitarian Law to United Nations Peacekeeping Operations" (2006–2007) 58 *Hastings Law Journal* 479; and D Shraga "UN Peacekeeping Operations: Applicability of International Humanitarian Law and Responsibility for Operations-Related Damage" (2000) 94 *The American Journal of International Law* 406. See also United Nations Secretary-General's Bulletin *Observance by UN Forces of International Humanitarian Law* SG B, ST/SGB/1999/13 (2006).

2 *Legality of the Threat or Use of Nuclear Weapons Advisory Opinion*, ICJ Reports 1996, 226 at [25]; *Legal Consequences of the Construction of a Wall in the Occupied Palestinian Territory Advisory Opinion*, ICJ Reports 2004, 178 at [106].

3 P Alston and R Goodman *International Human Rights* (Oxford University Press, Oxford, 2013) at 58–59; R Burke *Sexual Exploitation and Abuse by UN Military Contingents: Moving Beyond the Current Status Quo and Responsibility under International Law* (Leiden, Brill, 2014) at 331.

(CAT)[4] and the International Covenant on Civil and Political Rights (ICCPR)[5] for relevant obligations to respond to rape and sexual violence. Secondly, this chapter will explore the Convention on the Rights of the Child (CRC)[6] and its Optional Protocol for state duties to investigate and prosecute sexual activity with children.

As sexual exploitation concerns survival sex, the third section will discuss whether the violence against women framework provides for state obligations. This discussion will draw on the jurisprudence of the treaty body responsible for the Convention on the Elimination of All Forms of Discrimination against Women (CEDAW).[7] The fourth section will illustrate the gap in current international human rights law with respect to male victims of sexual exploitation.

Essentially, this chapter will show that there are obligations relating to sexual abuse that may be attached to human rights standards dealing with rape, sexual violence, and sexual activity with children. However, while sexual exploitation may be interpreted as violence against women under international human rights law, this chapter will argue that state obligations to respond to survival sex do not currently exist.

Torture and other cruel, inhuman, or degrading treatment

Rape and sexual violence have been treated as torture or other cruel, inhuman, or degrading treatment by a number of international human rights mechanisms, such as the Committee against Torture,[8] the Inter-American Commission on Human Rights,[9] and the European Court of Human Rights.[10] Similarly, it is possible that

4 *Convention against Torture and Other Cruel, Inhuman or Degrading Treatment or Punishment* 1465 UNTS 85 (opened for signature 10 December 1984, entered into force 26 June 1987) [CAT].

5 *International Covenant on Civil and Political Rights* 999 UNTS 171 (opened for signature 16 December 1966, entered into force 23 March 1976) [ICCPR].

6 *Convention on the Rights of the Child* 1577 UNTS 3 (opened for signature 20 November 1989, entered into force 2 September 1990) [CRC].

7 *Convention on the Elimination of All Forms of Discrimination against Women* 1249 UNTS 13 (opened for signature 18 December 1979, entered into force 3 September 1981) [CEDAW].

8 Based on art 1 of CAT; Committee against Torture *VL v Switzerland* Commission No. 262/2005, CAT/37/D/262/2005 (2007). See also Concluding Observations by the Committee, which has addressed rape and sexual violence generally as violence against women under the Convention's definitions of torture (art 1) and cruel, inhuman, or degrading treatment (art 16). Examples are Committee against Torture *Concluding Observations on the combined fifth and sixth periodic reports of Peru, adopted by the Committee at its forty-ninth session* CAT/C/PER/CO/5–6 (2013) at [14]; Committee against Torture *Concluding Observations of the Committee against Torture: Ghana* CAT/C/GHA/CO/1 (2011) at [22].

9 Based on the *Inter-American Convention on the Prevention, Punishment and Eradication of Violence against Women [Convention of Belém do Pará]* (opened for signature 9 June 1994, entered into force 5 March 1995).

10 Based on art 3, *European Convention for the Protection of Human Rights and Fundamental Freedoms* ETS 3 (opened for signature 14 November 1950, entered into force 3 September 1953); see also *Aydin v Turkey* (1998) 25 EHRR 251 (ECHR).

sexual abuse (rape and sexual violence) committed by peacekeepers could be considered as torture or inhuman treatment in certain circumstances. It is important to be aware, however, that there are specific requirements for the definition of torture which may not be met in all instances of sexual abuse in the peacekeeping context.

For the purposes of this chapter, the definition of torture will be drawn from article one of CAT:

> … "torture" means any act by which severe pain or suffering, whether physical or mental, is intentionally inflicted on a person for such purposes as obtaining from him or a third person information or a confession, punishing him for an act he or a third person has committed or is suspected of having committed or intimidating or coercing him or a third person or for any other reason based on discrimination of any kind, when such pain or suffering is inflicted by or at the instigation of or with the consent or acquiescence of a public official or other person acting in an official capacity.

Although "severe pain or suffering" is a high threshold, rape has been held to meet this requirement.[11] Often it is dependent on the circumstances, such as the duration of the act/s, the effects both mentally and physically, and whether the other components of the definition are met.[12] The gendered context of peacekeeping may also invite a gender-sensitive approach to determining pain and suffering.[13]

A second requirement is that the infliction is for one of the prohibited purposes listed in article one. For example, if rape or sexual violence is used to punish, intimidate, and humiliate, or is otherwise directed towards a woman because she is a woman (discrimination), then these will be considered prohibited purposes under CAT.[14] The third relevant requirement is that the acts are committed by a public official or with consent or acquiescence of the public official.

11 K Fortin "Rape as Torture: An Evaluation of the Committee against Torture's Attitude to Sexual Violence" (2008) 4 *Utrecht Law Review* 145 at 149; *VL v Switzerland*, above n 8; J Marshall "Positive Obligations and Gender-Based Violence: Judicial Developments" (2008) 10 *International Community Law Review* 143 at 146; DS Mitchell "The Prohibition of Rape in International Humanitarian Law as a Norm of *jus cogens:* Clarifying the Doctrine" (2004–2005) 15 *Duke Journal of Comparative and International Law* 219 at 251–256; and N Ousman *Contribution of the Special Court for Sierra Leone to the Development of International Humanitarian Law* (Duncker & Humlot, Berlin, 2013) at 117–118.

12 *Moldovan v Romania* [2003] ECHR 485 at [100] regarding art 3 of the *European Convention for the Protection of Human Rights.*

13 M Nowak *Report of the Special Rapporteur on Torture and Other Cruel, Inhuman or Degrading Treatment or Punishment* HRC, A/HRC/7/3 (2008) at [36].

14 NS Rodley *Question of the Human Rights of All Persons Subjected to Any Form of Detention or Imprisonment, in Particular: Torture and Other Cruel, Inhuman or Degrading Treatment or Punishment* E/CN.4/1994/31 (1994) at [431]; *Prosecutor v Zejnil Delalic, Zdravko Mucic, Hazim Delic and Esad Landzo (Judgment)* ICTY Trial Chamber IT-96–21-T, 16 November 1998 at [493].

Mindful that the application of torture is in many ways continuously evolving,[15] there may be circumstances in which sexual abuse in the peacekeeping context could fulfil the above requirements for torture. Given the differential power dynamic between peacekeepers and local people, the particular vulnerability of victims might support its application.[16] Moreover, if sexual abuse by peacekeepers is not found to meet the threshold of severity under article one, or if the purposive element is found lacking, such conduct may nevertheless be considered cruel, inhuman, or degrading treatment under article 16.[17]

CAT operates alongside the general prohibition of torture and inhuman treatment in article seven of the ICCPR. Out of the 123 states which currently contribute military and police to peacekeeping,[18] 110 have ratified CAT and 115 have ratified the ICCPR.[19] Furthermore, the prohibition of torture is considered customary international law.[20] Consequently, both CAT and the ICCPR are relevant here.

As with many human rights treaties, article two of the ICCPR has a general obligation to respect and ensure rights under the Covenant. The duty to ensure has been understood as placing positive obligations on states parties to prevent violations and investigate and prosecute violators.[21] Specifically, the Human Rights Committee (HRC) has interpreted article two so as to include a duty on states to bring those responsible to justice.[22] However, these words do not strictly refer to punishment in criminal law. Instead the interpretation of "justice" changes depending on the nature of the right violated.[23] Generally, how violators are brought to justice is left to the discretion of states parties.[24] However, the HRC has noted that only criminal

15 JE Méndez and A Nicolescu "Evolving Standards for Torture in International Law" in M Basoglu (ed) *Torture and Its Definition in International Law: An Interdisciplinary Approach* (Oxford, Oxford University Press, 2017) at 220.

16 The status of the victim, or powerlessness and vulnerability, has been argued as a factor in considering the application of the definition to acts of female genital mutilation and could similarly be persuasive here. See *Report of the Special Rapporteur on Torture and Other Cruel, Inhuman or Degrading Treatment or Punishment* (2008), above n 13; See also Human Rights Committee *General Comment 28* CCPR/C/21/Rev.1/Add.10 (2000).

17 Méndez and Nicolescu, above n 15, at 219.

18 The top four TCCs contribute the majority of troops. These are Ethiopia, India, Pakistan, and Bangladesh.

19 Those TCCs that have not ratified CAT are India, United Republic of Tanzania, Malaysia, Gambia, Zimbabwe, Bhutan, Brunei, Samoa, Iran, Myanmar, Papua New Guinea, Solomon Islands, and Jamaica. Those TCCs that have not ratified the ICCPR include China, Malaysia, Fiji, Bhutan, Brunei, Myanmar, Qatar, and Solomon Islands.

20 See *The Prosecutor v Furundzija (Judgment)* IT-95-17/I-T. Trial Chamber, 10 December 1998, at [153].

21 *Velasquez Rodriguez v Honduras (Judgment)* (1989) Inter-American Court of Human Rights (Ser C) No 42 at [166]-[167].

22 Human Rights Committee *Minanga v Zaire* Communication No. 366/1989, CCPR/C/49/D/366/1989 (1993) at [7].

23 A Seibert-Fohr *Prosecuting Serious Human Rights Violations* (Oxford University Press, Oxford, 2009) at 13.

24 At 13.

punishment may suffice in certain circumstances, for example, for acts of torture.[25] To "make remedies effective" in terms of article two, the HRC has signified the importance of investigation.[26] This line of reasoning has been applied to all forms of serious human rights violations, which again includes torture.[27]

According to the HRC, upon a positive outcome of investigation, adequate punishment is required, which may imply a duty to prosecute.[28] Moreover, the HRC has indicated in its General Comments and in various Concluding Observations that prosecution and punishment (following a conviction) are indeed expected in cases of torture.[29] In sum, for states to fulfil their obligations under articles two and seven of the ICCPR, states must criminalise, investigate, prosecute, and punish acts of torture or other cruel, inhuman, or degrading treatment.[30]

The Committee against Torture considered domestic prosecution of the acts described in articles one and sixteen[31] under CAT as essential for protection.[32] Moreover, a failure by the state to exercise due diligence to investigate, prosecute, and punish acts of torture committed by state or private actors will be a breach of

25 Human Rights Committee *General Comment No 31: The Nature of the General Legal Obligation Imposed on States Parties to the Covenant* CCPR/C/21/Rev.1/Add.13 (2004) [HRC General Comment No 31] at [16] and [18].

26 Seibert-Fohr, above n 23, at 35; Human Rights Committee *General Comment No 20: Article 7 (Prohibition of Torture, or Other Cruel, Inhuman or Degrading Treatment or Punishment)* Adopted at the Forty-Fourth Session (1992) [HRC General Comment No 20] at [11]-[12].

27 HRC General Comment No 20, above n 26, at [11]-[12].

28 Seibert-Fohr, above n 23, at 46.

29 Human Rights Committee *Concluding Observations on the initial Report of Indonesia* CCPR/C/IDN/CO/1 (2013) at [14]; Human Rights Committee *Concluding Observations on Kuwait* CCPR/C/KWT/CO/2 (2011) at [16]; HRC General Comment No 20, above n 26, at [14].

30 Similar findings have been made under regional instruments – for example, the *Inter-American Convention on Human Rights* based on art 5(2): *American Convention on Human Rights "Pact of San Jose, Costa Rica"* OAS (opened for signature 22 January 1969, entered into force 18 July 1978).

31 CAT, art 1 is included in text above and art 16(1) reads: "Each State Party shall undertake to prevent in any territory under its jurisdiction other acts of cruel, inhuman or degrading treatment or punishment which do not amount to torture as defined in article 1, when such acts are committed by or at the instigation of or with the consent or acquiescence of a public official or other person acting in an official capacity. In particular, the obligations contained in articles 10, 11, 12 and 13 shall apply with the substitution for references to torture of references to other forms of cruel, inhuman or degrading treatment or punishment."

32 Based on CAT, arts 1, 2, 12, and 16. See for example Committee against Torture *Concluding Observations on the combined fifth and sixth periodic reports of Guatemala adopted by the Committee at its fiftieth session* CAT/C/GTM/CO/5–6 (2013) at [13 (b)]; Committee against Torture *Concluding Observations on the second periodic report of the Plurinational State of Bolivia as approved by the Committee at its fiftieth session* CAT/C/BOL/CO/2 (2013) at [15a]; and Committee against Torture *Concluding Observations of the Committee against Torture: Sri Lanka* CAT/C/LKA/CO/3–4 (2011) at [22].

their obligations under CAT.[33] Asserting extraterritorial jurisdiction over torture crimes is also expected where military members operate abroad.[34]

Sexual activity with children

Sexual activity with children (including child prostitution) is sexual abuse under the UN zero-tolerance policy. The CRC, one of the UN's core human rights treaties, is specifically relevant here. Of the current TCCs, 121 have ratified the CRC, including those states which contribute the majority of troops to peacekeeping (Ethiopia, India, Pakistan, and Bangladesh).[35]

The CRC primarily focuses on preventative measures rather than punishment. Explicit obligations involving state enforcement against rights-abusers are limited to article 32, which concerns exploitation of children in employment. The wording of article 32 is similar to article 10(3) of the *International Covenant on Economic, Social and Cultural Rights* (ICESCR), with references made to protection from exploitative work that may negatively interfere with the "child's health or physical, mental, spiritual, moral or social development".[36] It is arguable that such phrasing could include child prostitution or sex work; one example would be that child prostitution exposes children to the increased possibility of contracting HIV, which is a major health risk.[37] Moreover, article ten of ICESCR has been interpreted widely as comprising violence against children, including sexual abuse or exploitation.[38] Concluding Observations of the Committee on the Rights of the Child reveal a similar interpretation of the CRC, implying a duty on states parties to protect children from all forms of sexual exploitation and abuse.[39]

The obligations for states parties under the CRC's article 32 provide that:

33 Committee against Torture *General Comment No 2: Implementation of Article 2 by States Parties* CAT/C/GC/2 (2008) at [18].

34 See CAT, art 7(1); HRC General Comment No 31, above n 25, at [80]; Seibert-Fohr, above n 23, at 159.

35 Those TCCs that have not ratified the CRC are the United States and Iran.

36 *International Covenant on Economic, Social and Cultural Rights* 993 UNTS 3 (opened for signature 18 December 1979, entered into force 3 September 1981) [ICESCR].

37 See for example BM Willis and BS Levy "Child Prostitution: Global Health Burden, Research Needs, and Interventions" (2002) 359 *The Lancet: Public Health* 1417.

38 See for example Committee on Economic, Social and Cultural Rights *Concluding Observations on the combined third and fourth periodic reports of Jamaica adopted by the Committee at its fiftieth session* E/C.12/JAM/CO/3-4 (2013) at [20]; Committee on Economic Social and Cultural Rights *Concluding Observations on the initial to third reports of the United Republic of Tanzania adopted by the Committee at its forty-ninth session* E/C.12/TZA/CO/1-3 (2012) at [13].

39 See for example, Committee on the Rights of the Child *Concluding Observations: Guinea-Bissau* CRC/C/GNB/CO/2-4 (2013) at [38]-[39]; Committee on the Rights of the Child *Concluding Observations: Afghanistan* CRC/C/AFG/CO/1 (2011) at [71(e)]; and Committee on the Rights of the Child *Concluding Observations: Montenegro* CRC/C/MNE/CO/1 (2010) at [67].

> 2. States Parties shall take legislative, administrative, social and educational measures to ensure the implementation of the present article.... States Parties shall in particular:
>
> ...
>
> (c) Provide for appropriate penalties or other sanctions to ensure the effective enforcement of the present article.

The provision requires states to make the necessary changes to their national law to incorporate penalties for the exploitation of children in employment. The article does not explicitly provide for states to investigate and prosecute offenders. However, according to the Committee on the Rights of the Child, states are nevertheless expected to actively respond to sexual exploitation and abuse of children that occurs within their territory.[40] Positive steps expected from states parties will include exercising their criminal jurisdiction over violators.[41] For example, buying sex from child prostitutes in the peacekeeping context would seem to require positive action from the TCC, such as investigation and prosecution under article 32 of the CRC. Arguably, states that do not react to such abuse in the prescribed ways will breach the spirit of the CRC.

Additionally, the *Optional Protocol to the CRC on the Sale of Children, Child Prostitution and Child Pornography* (OP-SC)[42] seeks to expand the duties under a number of the CRC's provisions in certain areas, including articles 32 and 34. The OP-SC focuses on the criminalisation and enforcement of certain offences. As this is specific to child prostitution, it is relevant to examine obligations on states to investigate and prosecute. Article three requires states to make the following an offence under their domestic criminal law in relation to child prostitution: "the offering, obtaining, procuring or providing a child for child prostitution as defined in article 2".[43] In fulfilment of their obligations under the OP-SC, states are expected to assert extraterritorial jurisdiction over these offences.[44]

40 See for example Committee on the Rights of the Child *Concluding Observations: Rwanda* CRC/C/RWA/CO/3-4 (2013) at [30]; Committee on the Rights of the Child *Concluding Observations: Slovenia* CRC/C/SVN/CO/3-4 (2013) at [42].

41 Such as to "prohibit all violence against children" and "take measures to prosecute perpetrators of sexual exploitation of children" see examples *Concluding Observations: Rwanda,* above n 40, at [30(a)]; *Concluding Observations: Afghanistan*, above n 39, at [71(e)]; and *Concluding Observations: Montenegro* above n 39, at [38(a)(i)].

42 *Optional Protocol to the CRC on the Sale of Children, Child Prostitution and Child Pornography* 2171 UNTS 227 (opened for signature May 25 2000, entered into force January 18 2002) [OP-SC].

43 At art 3(1)(b).

44 Committee on the Rights of the Child *Consideration of reports submitted by States Parties under article 12. Paragraph 1, of the Optional Protocol to the Convention on the Rights of the Child on the Sale of Children, Child Prostitution and Child Pornography, Concluding Observations: Argentina* CRC/C/OPSC/ARG/CO/1 (2010) at [32]; Committee on the Rights of the Child *Consideration of reports submitted by States Parties under article 12. Paragraph 1, of the Optional Protocol to the Convention on the*

The Protocol itself does tend to focus on the movement of children for the stated purposes rather than on those who buy sex from child prostitutes, being primarily influenced by state obligations to prevent the transnational trafficking of children and child pornography.[45] The requirement to criminalise certain conduct implies that states parties should also actively investigate and prosecute offenders.[46] Additionally, the Third World Congress against Sexual Exploitation of Children and Adolescents in 2008 noted that in order to implement the OP-SC, states were urged to address the issue of demand by criminalising the buying of sex from children.[47] The act of buying sex from children is of most concern under the SG Bulletin's prohibitions, rather than who is supplying the children. Thus, the above seems to suggest positive action is required from TCCs to criminalise buying sex from child prostitutes (and, by implication, to extend their jurisdiction in order to cover their peacekeeping personnel acting abroad).

However, upon examining the work of the Committee on the Rights of the Child, it seems that addressing demand in criminal law is not generally expected from states parties.[48] Instead, emphasis has been placed on education and research in identifying the causes of child prostitution and trafficking.[49] Moreover, the Special Rapporteur on the Sale of Children has urged states to address demand through implementation of awareness-raising measures, rather than through criminalisation.[50] In sum, there seems to be no general or explicit duty stemming

Rights of the Child on the Sale of Children, Child Prostitution and Child Pornography, Concluding Observations: Colombia CRC/C/OPSC/COL/CO/1 (2010) at [25].

45 See generally United Nations Children's Fund *Handbook on the Optional Protocol on the Sale of Children, Child Prostitution and Child Pornography* (Innocenti Research Centre, Florence, 2009).

46 This was also supported by several statements to this effect in the Third World Congress against Sexual Exploitation of Children and Adolescents *The Rio de Janeiro Declaration and Call for Action to Prevent and Stop Sexual Exploitation of Children and Adolescents* (2008) at Preamble [4] and [A13].

47 At [C14].

48 See for example Committee on the Rights of the Child *Concluding Observations on the initial report of Paraguay submitted under article 12 of the Optional Protocol to the Convention on the Rights of the Child on the Sale of Children, Child Prostitution and Child Pornography, adopted by the Committee at its sixty-fourth session* CRC/C/OPSC/PRY/CO/1 (2013) at [23(b)]; Committee on the Rights of the Child *Concluding Observations on the initial report of Burkina Faso submitted under article 12 of the Optional Protocol to the Convention on the Rights of the Child on the Sale of Children, Child Prostitution and Child Pornography, adopted by the Committee at its sixty-second session* CRC/C/OPSC/BFA/CO/1 (2013) at [25].

49 *Concluding Observations on the initial report of Paraguay,* above n 48, at [23]; *Concluding Observations on the initial report of Burkina Faso,* above n 48, at [25].

50 See *Report of the Special Rapporteur on the Sale of Children, Child Prostitution and Child Pornography, Najat Maalla M'Jid* A/HRC/22/54 (2012) at [95(b)]; see also the General Assembly Resolution that urges states to address the demand for child prostitution and trafficking without explicitly referring to criminal measures: *General Assembly Resolution on the Rights of the Child* GA Res, A/RES/66/141 (2012) at [20].

from the OP-SC for states to criminalise, investigate, and/or prosecute the purchase of sex from child prostitutes. Nevertheless, child prostitution (as well as other forms of sexual activity with children) does fall into the general category of sexual exploitation and abuse as defined by the Committee under the CRC itself.[51]

Like the ICCPR, the CRC has a "respect and ensure" provision.[52] As such, it is arguable that, to ensure those relevant rights under the CRC (notably articles 32 and 34), states would need to address the demand side of child prostitution and pursue individuals that sexually exploit children. One of the steps states could take to respect and ensure these rights is to criminalise, investigate, and ultimately punish those activities. Furthermore, this is supported by several statements made by the Commission detailing the need to criminalise violence against children, which includes all forms of sexual abuse and exploitation.[53]

Unlike the OP-SC, the CRC itself is silent on the issue of asserting jurisdiction over crimes such as violence against children or sex offences committed abroad. Such an interpretation is deplorable when considering the perspective of victims and their communities; because host state jurisdiction has been waived under the SOFA, there is total reliance on TCCs to respond to sexual abuse of children committed by their military personnel. If TCCs do not assert jurisdiction, and are not required to do so under the CRC, then this is an unacceptable gap. However, in order to adhere to the obligation to "respect and ensure" rights under the CRC, it would be necessary for states to assert extraterritorial jurisdiction over acts of violence against children. The lack of extraterritorial jurisdiction for child sexual exploitation and abuse is perhaps the current situation for many TCCs, and this could in fact be a breach of the CRC "respect and ensure" provision.

Violence against women

I have examined in detail elsewhere[54] the extent to which states have obligations to respond to sexual exploitation under the violence against women framework. For the purposes of this chapter it is necessary to give an overall summary of these obligations.

Violence against women is understood as being contextual, arising out of social, cultural, and economic inequalities.[55] Within patriarchy these inequalities

51 See for example Commission on the Rights of the Child *Concluding Observations on the combined third and fourth periodic reports of Canada, adopted by the Committee at its sixty-first session* CRC/C/CAN/CO/3–4 (2012) at [49(b)]; *Concluding Observations: Montenegro,* above n 39, at [38(a)].

52 See CRC, art 2(1).

53 See above n 39 and accompanying text.

54 C Mudgway "Sexual Exploitation by UN Peacekeepers: The 'Survival Sex' Gap in International Human Rights Law" (2017) 21 *The International Journal of Human Rights* 1453.

55 Report of the Secretary-General *In-Depth Study on All Forms of Violence against Women* A/61/122/Add.1 (2006) at [65]–[92].

foster systematic power imbalances between men and women, with abuse and exploitation as a result.[56] The *UN Declaration on the Elimination of Violence against Women* (DEVAW) provides the leading definition and includes all forms of violence (physical, sexual, emotional, and psychological).[57] Such an understanding of violence against women is directly applicable to peacekeeping; not only do victims of sexual exploitation and abuse suffer physical, emotional, and psychological harm, the abuse is committed within a gendered context and differential power dynamics.[58] Therefore, the concept of violence against women can encompass both sexual abuse (rape and sexual violence) and sexual exploitation (survival sex).

Violence against women is addressed across many different international instruments, both binding and non-binding. Beginning with the non-binding, yet highly influential, documents, DEVAW notes that states should act with "due diligence to present, investigate … and punish" acts of violence against women. To facilitate this, states should "develop penal civil, labour and administrative sanctions in domestic legislation". DEVAW defers to existing domestic arrangements of states and does not require criminalisation or a criminal response to all acts of violence against women. Similarly, the Beijing Declaration and Platform for Action also defers to state discretion as to how violence against women is sanctioned and redressed.[59] However, since the conclusion of these instruments, the General Assembly has strongly supported the development of legislation or other laws to make violence against women punishable under domestic criminal law.[60] This indicates a shift towards wider criminalisation of violence against women being expected from states.

Moving on to international treaties, the most relevant is CEDAW. It should be noted at the outset that while most current TCCs have ratified CEDAW,[61] many states have lodged reservations regarding the application of the Convention. This includes Bangladesh, which is one of the primary TCCs.[62] The Committee on the Elimination of Discrimination against Women (CEDAW Committee) has issued several General Recommendations that examine obligations on states parties arising out of the Convention. *General Recommendation 19* provides that violence

56 D Otto "Violence against Women: Something Other Than a Human Rights Violation?" (1993) 1 *Australian Feminist Law Journal* 159 at 161.

57 *United Nations Declaration on the Elimination of Violence against Women* GA Res, A/RES/48/104 (1993) art 1.

58 See related discussion in the Introduction.

59 Fourth World Conference on Women *Beijing Declaration and Platform for Action* A/CONF.177/20 (1995) and A/CONF.177/20/Add.1 (1995) [Platform for Action] at 124(b)-(c).

60 See at *General Assembly Resolution on Further Actions and Initiatives to Implement the Beijing Declaration and Platform for Action* GA Res, A/RES/S-23/3 (2000) at [66(c)]-[66(d)].

61 The only current TCC that has not ratified CEDAW is the United States.

62 "The Government of the People's Republic of Bangladesh does not consider as binding upon itself the provisions of article 2 … as they conflict with *Sharia* law based on Holy Quran and Sunna". See information available online: <www.treaties.un.org>.

against women is a form of discrimination under article one of CEDAW.[63] As such, article two provides that states must *inter alia* "adopt appropriate legislative and other measures including sanctions where appropriate, prohibiting all discrimination against women".[64] Expanding on these obligations, *General Recommendation 28* notes that "[s]tates parties have a due diligence obligation to prevent, investigate, prosecute and punish such acts of gender-based violence".[65] These duties are reiterated again in *General Recommendation 35* and continually throughout the jurisprudence of the CEDAW Committee.[66]

During the past decade, the CEDAW Committee has made reference to sexual exploitation and abuse by peacekeepers twice: in its Concluding Observations for Côte d'Ivoire in 2011 and for Haiti in 2016.[67] After numerous allegations of sexual abuse by military contingent members during the UN Operation in Côte d'Ivoire, the CEDAW Committee requested that the UN ensure that those personnel were returned to their home country for criminal investigation and

63 Committee on the Elimination of Discrimination against Women *General Recommendation 19* CEDAW/C/GC/19 (1992) at [6].

64 CDEAW, art 2(b) see also art 2(e).

65 Committee on the Elimination of Discrimination against Women *General Recommendation No. 28 on the Core Obligations of States Parties under Article 2 of the Convention on the Elimination of All Forms of Discrimination against Women* CEDAW/C/2010/47/GC.2 (2010) at [19].

66 Committee on the Elimination of Discrimination against Women *General Recommendation No. 35 on Gender-Based Violence against Women, Updating General Recommendation No. 19* CEDAW/C/GC/35 (2017) at [24(2)(b)]; Committee on the Elimination of Discrimination against Women *Angela González Carreño v Spain* CEDAW/C/58/D/47/2012 Communication No 47/2012 (2014) at [9.7] and [11(b)(ii)]; Committee on the Elimination of Discrimination against Women *Banu Akbak, Gülen Khan and Melissa Őzdemir v Austria* CEDAW/C/39/D/6/2005 Communication No 6/2005 (2007) at [12.1.2] and [12.3(a)]; Committee on the Elimination of Discrimination against Women *Hakan Goekce, Handan Goekce and Guelue Goekce v Austria* CEDAW/C/39/D/5/2005 Communication No 5/2005 (2007) at [12.3(a)]; Committee on the Elimination of Discrimination against Women *SVP v Bulgaria* CEDAW/C/53/D/31/2011 Communication No 31/2011 (2012) at [9.3]; Committee on the Elimination of Discrimination against Women *VK v Bulgaria* CEDAW/C/49/D/20/2008 Communication No 20/2008 (2011) at [9.3]; Committee on the Elimination of Discrimination against Women *Concluding Observations on the combined initial and second periodic reports of Afghanistan* CEDAW/C/AFG/CO/1-2 (2013) at [23(a)]; Committee on the Elimination of Discrimination against Women *Concluding Observations of the Committee on the Elimination of Discrimination against Women: Israel* CEDAW/C/ISR/CO/5 (2011) at [23(a)]; and Committee on the Elimination of Discrimination against Women *Concluding Observations of the Committee on the Elimination of Discrimination against Women: South Africa* CEDAW/C/ZAF/CO/4 (2011) at [31(c)].

67 Committee on the Elimination of Discrimination against Women *Concluding Observations of the Committee on the Elimination of Discrimination against Women: Côte d'Ivoire* CEDAW/C/CIV/CO/1-3 (2011); Committee on the Elimination of Discrimination against Women *Concluding Observations on the combined eighth and ninth periodic reports of Haiti* CEDAW/C/HTI/ CO/8-9 (2016).

prosecution.[68] The CEDAW Committee arguably assumes here that TCCs should have criminalised sexual abuse and that criminal investigation and punishment was the required response. However, allegations involved sexual abuse of children, rather than sexual exploitation (survival sex). In its Concluding Observations for Haiti, the CEDAW Committee referred to the prevalence of sexual exploitation and urged the Haitian government to protect women from being exploited by UN personnel.[69] No mention was made about obligations on TCCs to investigate or prosecute. Overall, these two examples show that perhaps there are positive obligations on TCCs to respond to sexual abuse, but the Convention is unclear whether the same could be said for sexual exploitation.

So far, treaty bodies have focused on requiring criminalisation of only what they consider "serious" forms of violence against women; for example, rape and domestic violence.[70] This further supports a divergence in international human rights law between "sexual abuse" on the one hand, requiring positive steps from TCCs to respond, and "sexual exploitation" on the other, where it is unclear any such obligations currently exist at all. This is notwithstanding the Special Rapporteur and the previous Secretary-General supporting criminalisation of all forms of violence against women.[71]

The CEDAW Committee's update to *General Recommendation 19*, released in 2017, provides that states are obligated to criminalise all forms of violence against women that "amount to a violation of … physical, sexual or psychological integrity".[72] This could be read as a clarification of how certain forms of violence are characterised as "serious", and is helpful in the peacekeeping context. Sexual exploitation and abuse could have the same character as described in the General Recommendation. Although it is a relatively new document, there may be an argument to suggest that such conduct is required to be criminalised by states parties. At this point in time, however, it remains unclear whether criminalisation of sexual exploitation is actually an obligation under the provisions of CEDAW.

68 *Concluding Observations of the Committee on the Elimination of Discrimination against Women: Côte d'Ivoire,* above n 67.

69 *Concluding Observations on the combined eighth and ninth periodic reports of Haiti,* above n 67, at [23]-[24(e)].

70 See for example Human Rights Committee *Concluding Observations on the fifth periodic review of Peru, adopted at its 107th session* CCPR/C/PER/CO/5 (2013) at [10]; Committee on Economic Social and Cultural Rights *Concluding Observations on the initial to third reports of the United Republic of Tanzania, adopted by the Committee at its forty-ninth session* E/C.12/TZA/CO/1–3 (2012) at [13]; *Concluding Observations of the Committee on the Elimination of Discrimination against Women: Côte d'Ivoire,* above n 67, at [30]; and Committee on the Elimination of Discrimination against Women *Concluding Observations of the Committee on the Elimination of Discrimination against Women: Kuwait* CEDAW/C/KWT/CO/3–4 (2011) at [31(b)].

71 *Report of the Special Rapporteur on Violence against Women, Its Causes and Consequences* GA, A/66/215 (2011) at [17]; *In-Depth Study on All forms of Violence against Women,* above n 55, at 86.

72 *General Recommendation 35*, above n 66, at [29(a)].

If forms of violence against women are criminalised in domestic legal frameworks, many instruments have referred to the application of the due diligence standard to describe state obligations. The Special Rapporteur has defined "due diligence" as the following:[73]

> … the due diligence responsibility comprises the obligation of states to: (a) prevent acts of violence against women; (b) investigate and punish all acts of violence against women; (c) protect women against acts of violence, and (d) provide remedy and reparation to victims of violence against women.

Despite its seeming clarity, there is still considerable debate about the specific scope and content of the due diligence standard in regards to violence against women.[74] As a result there are two broad ways to interpret the obligation of due diligence.

Firstly, the expansive interpretation of "due diligence" implies a duty to prosecute. The CEDAW Committee has required states to promptly and effectively investigate and prosecute any act of violence against women that is criminalised in domestic criminal law.[75] A failure to do so would therefore be a breach of the due diligence standard. Applying this expansive interpretation, it would appear that the due diligence standard goes beyond what is expected under the Memorandum of Understanding (MOU) in terms of exercising criminal jurisdiction. As noted in chapter one, prosecution by the TCC was not required in the MOU. However, prosecution and punishment following any conviction is necessary in order for states to meet the due diligence standard under international human rights law, particularly in relation to violence against women.

73 *Report of the Special Rapporteur on Violence against Women, Its Causes and Consequences* (2011), above n 71, at [50].

74 *Report of the Special Rapporteur on Violence against Women, Its Causes and Consequences, Integration of the Human Rights of Women and the Gender Perspective: Violence against Women, The Due Diligence Standard as a Tool for the Elimination of Violence against Women* ESC, E/CN.4/2006/61 (2006) at [14]; *Report of the Special Rapporteur on Violence against Women, Its Causes and Consequences* GA, A/HRC/29/27 (2015) at [63].

75 *Hakan Goekce, Handan Goekce and Guelue Goekce v Austria*, above n 66, at [12.1.2]; Committee on the Elimination of Discrimination against Women *RPB v The Philippines* CEDAW/C/57/D/34/2011 Communication No 34/2011 (2014) at [8.3]; See also *Concluding Observations of the Committee on the Elimination of Discrimination against Women: Côte d'Ivoire,* above n 67, at [31(c)]-[31(d)]; *Concluding Observations of the Committee on the Elimination of Discrimination against Women: Kuwait*, above n 70, at [31(b)]; Committee on the Elimination of Discrimination against Women *Concluding Observations of the Committee on the Elimination of Discrimination against Women: Bangladesh* CEDAW/C/BGD/CO/7 (2011) at [20(b)]. As the relevant monitoring body for CEDAW, the Committee's interpretation of its provisions as a duty to prosecute could be construed as an "authoritative interpretation". See M Scharf "The Letter of the Law: The Scope of the International Legal Obligation to Prosecute Human Rights" (1996) 59 *Law and Contemporary Problems* 41 at 48–50.

However, the second, narrow, interpretation suggests that due diligence must be limited by state sovereignty. In reality, the due diligence standard is unlikely to remove or interfere with prosecutorial discretion and would not imply a duty to prosecute. Additionally, due diligence is based on reasonableness; that is, states should take steps that are reasonable according to their legal framework and resources available to them in order to address violence against women.[76] This is a further limitation as states can invariably point to lack of resources as the reason for substandard attempts at implementation.

The exact scope and content of the due diligence standard is continually questioned by states and scholars and requires further development. An expansive interpretation would lead to an obligation on TCCs to investigate and prosecute their troops, but it might also be limited by state sovereignty and prosecutorial discretion. Therefore, any due diligence obligation related to violence against women may in reality be a similar obligation to that under the MOU – to submit the case to the appropriate national authorities.

Many treaties are silent on the subject of extraterritorial jurisdiction. Where jurisdiction is mentioned, obligations to assert extraterritorial jurisdiction are confined to violations committed within the territory of that state or simply within that state's jurisdiction.[77] However, the CEDAW Committee has suggested that states will be responsible for all human rights violations committed by nationals, even if they are committed against persons outside that state's territory.[78] Although not specifically required under any convention, it can be argued that for states to comply with the due diligence standard of their obligations, it is necessary to assert jurisdiction over their military contingents operating abroad. This argument is supported by the CEDAW Committee's comments in their Concluding Observations on Côte d'Ivoire, where TCCs were assumed to have jurisdiction over sexual abuse committed by their military personnel.[79]

From this section it can be concluded that there are obligations on states to criminalise, investigate, prosecute, and punish sexual abuse within the violence against women framework. However, these obligations are unlikely to exist for sexual exploitation. This conclusion is quite unsatisfactory. For victims of sexual exploitation, this gap in international human rights law may mean it is less likely that the perpetrator will be punished and that justice will be done. Considering the seriousness of sexual exploitation in the context of peacekeeping, and

76 *Report of the Special Rapporteur on Violence against Women, Its Causes and Consequences* GA, A/HRC/23/49 (2013) at [72]; AJ Sennett "*Lenahan (Gonzales) v United States of America:* Defining Due Diligence?" (2012) 53 *Harvard International Law Journal* 538 at 543.

77 ICCPR, art 2(1); CRC, art 2(1); CAT, art 10; Inter-American Convention on Human Rights, art 1(1).

78 CEDAW *General Recommendation 28*, above n 65, at [12].

79 *Concluding Observations of the Committee on the Elimination of Discrimination against Women: Côte d'Ivoire,* above n 67.

assuming its continued spotlight in international media reflects concern at this behaviour,[80] this gap is unacceptable.

Sexual exploitation and abuse of men

Generally, international human rights treaties and their corresponding monitoring bodies fail to recognise adult men as a class of victims of sexual violence.[81] It is possible that sexual abuse of men might be caught within the parameters of CAT and the ICCPR (as torture or inhuman treatment); however, the HRC often considers rape and sexual violence within the larger category of violence against women.[82] It could be argued that there are obligations on states to respond to sexual abuse against men under these treaties, but it generally remains unclear.

Although violence against women within human rights law has developed a framework that can capture sexual exploitation of women committed by peacekeepers, the same cannot be said for sexual exploitation of men. The phrase "gender-based violence" as used by the CEDAW Committee has become synonymous with "violence against women", to the exclusion of all other genders.[83] This is notwithstanding that violence against women has been understood within the structure of patriarchy and the lens of masculinity; both can support men as a class of victims.[84] Without explicit acknowledgement in international human rights law, male victims of sexual exploitation are entirely vulnerable. There are no obligations on TCCs to respond to this conduct at all.

80 See for example, Amnesty International "CAR: UN Troops Implicated in Rape of Girl and Indiscriminate Killings Must Be Investigated" (news release, 11 August 2015); T Esslemont "EXCLUSIVE – UN Peacekeepers Face New Sex Allegations in Central African Republic" *Trust* (11 November 2015) <www.trust.org>; S Ghosh "Are UN Peacekeepers Doing More Harm Than Good?" *Al Jazeera* (15 August 2015) <www.aljazeera.com>; K Willsher and S Laville "France Launches Criminal Inquiry into Alleged Sex Abuse by Peacekeepers" *The Guardian* (7 May 2015) <www.theguardian.com/world>.

81 E Gorris "Invisible Victims? Where Are Male Victims of Conflict-Related Sexual Violence in International Law and Policy?" (2015) 22 *European Journal of Women's Studies* 412; DA Lewis "Unrecognized Victims: Sexual Violence against Men in Conflict Settings under International Law" (2009) *Wisconsin International Law Journal* 1; L Stemple "Human Rights, Sex, and Gender: Limits in Theory and Practice" (2011) 31 *PACE Law Review* 824; and L Stemple "Male Rape and Human Rights" (2009) 60 *Hastings Law Journal* 605.

82 See for example Human Rights Committee *Concluding Observations of the Human Rights Committee: Cape Verde* CCPR/C/CPV/CO/1 (2012) at [9]; Human Rights Committee *Concluding Observations of the Human Rights Committee: Dominican Republic* CCPR/C/DOM/CO/5 (2012) at [11].

83 L Stemple "Human Rights, Sex, and Gender", above n 81, at 829–831; Lewis, above n 81, at 19. Although recently the CEDAW Committee have changed their terminology by using "gender-based violence against women" and this seems to open up the opportunity to talk about other forms of gender-based violence. See generally *General Recommendation 35*, above n 66.

84 Refer to discussion in the Introduction of this book under "Aims of this Book and Guiding Principles: Feminist Lens".

Conclusion

The aim of this chapter was to establish that there are human rights obligations on states to positively respond to sexual exploitation and abuse committed by their military contingent members. A number of provisions in human rights treaties require states to criminalise, or at least create a legal framework to address, conduct that would be considered sexual exploitation and abuse. This chapter has exposed significant gaps, however, with regard to sexual exploitation (survival sex). Both male and female victims of sexual exploitation are largely left unprotected by human rights law and without the ability to pursue justice.

Under the ICCPR and the CAT, acts of torture and other cruel, inhuman, and degrading treatment have been interpreted as including rape and other sexual violence against women. Although there are specific additional requirements, such as a prohibited purpose, there may be circumstances (however unlikely) in which sexual abuse by peacekeepers would fulfil the definition of either torture or inhuman treatment. Moreover, in order to realise these obligations, it would be necessary for states to establish extraterritorial jurisdiction over their military members operating abroad.

Under the CRC there is an obligation on states to actively address violence against children (sexual abuse). However, there appears to be no explicit obligation to criminalise. This may be because criminalising violence against children is simply assumed by the treaty, due to the egregious nature of the violation. Therefore, there are likely obligations on TCCs to investigate, prosecute, and punish sexual activity with children. Again, in order to fulfil the obligation to respect and ensure the rights under the CRC, it may be necessary for states to assert extraterritorial jurisdiction over such conduct.

The due diligence standard would suggest that if a particular form of violence against women is criminalised in domestic law then it must be investigated, the violator prosecuted, and, if convicted, punished. On an expansive interpretation, the due diligence standard goes beyond what is expected in the MOU between the UN and TCCs by requiring prosecution. In theory, where a TCC has criminalised a form of violence against women that fits within the concept of sexual exploitation and abuse by peacekeepers, then a failure to investigate and prosecute would give rise to state responsibility. However, this interpretation may be limited; in reality the national authorities must still retain prosecutorial discretion, whether to investigate or initiate prosecution. As a result, the due diligence standard may only require submission of the case to the appropriate national authorities on all cases of sexual abuse (required to be criminalised) and cases of sexual exploitation that happen to be criminalised under domestic law. Nevertheless, in order to fulfil the due diligence standard, assertion of extraterritorial jurisdiction is required over those forms of violence against women that are criminalised under a TCC's domestic law.

Overall, both chapters one and two have proved that certain obligations on TCCs to respond exist under the current international legal framework. A failure to take particular steps may lead to a breach of treaty obligations and give rise to state responsibility.

References

P Alston and R Goodman *International Human Rights* (Oxford University Press, Oxford, 2013)

American Convention on Human Rights "Pact of San Jose, Costa Rica" OAS (opened for signature 22 January 1969, entered into force 18 July 1978)

Amnesty International "CAR: UN Troops Implicated in Rape of Girl and Indiscriminate Killings Must Be Investigated" (news release, 11 August 2015)

Aydin v Turkey (1998) 25 EHRR 251 (ECHR)

R Burke *Sexual Exploitation and Abuse by UN Military Contingents: Moving Beyond the Current Status Quo and Responsibility under International Law* (Leiden, Brill, 2014)

Committee against Torture *Concluding Observations of the Committee against Torture: Ghana* CAT/C/GHA/CO/1 (2011)

Committee against Torture *Concluding Observations of the Committee against Torture: Sri Lanka* CAT/C/LKA/CO/3-4 (2011)

Committee against Torture *Concluding Observations on the combined fifth and sixth periodic reports of Guatemala adopted by the Committee at its fiftieth session* CAT/C/GTM/CO/5-6 (2013)

Committee against Torture *Concluding Observations on the combined fifth and sixth periodic reports of Peru, adopted by the Committee at its forty-ninth session* CAT/C/PER/CO/5-6 (2013)

Committee against Torture *Concluding Observations on the second periodic report of the Plurinational State of Bolivia as approved by the Committee at its fiftieth session* CAT/C/BOL/CO/2 (2013)

Committee against Torture *General Comment No. 2: Implementation of Article 2 by States Parties CAT/C/GC/2* (2008)

Committee against Torture *VL v Switzerland* Commission No. 262/2005, CAT/37/D/262/2005 (2007)

Convention against Torture and Other Cruel, Inhuman or Degrading Treatment or Punishment 1465 UNTS 85 (opened for signature 10 December 1984, entered into force 26 June 1987)

Committee on Economic, Social and Cultural Rights *Concluding Observations on the combined third and fourth periodic reports of Jamaica adopted by the Committee at its fiftieth session* E/C.12/JAM/CO/3-4 (2013)

Committee on Economic, Social and Cultural Rights *Concluding Observations on the initial to third reports of the United Republic of Tanzania adopted by the Committee at its forty-ninth session* E/C.12/TZA/CO/1-3 (2012)

Committee on the Elimination of Discrimination against Women *Angela González Carreño v Spain* CEDAW/C/58/D/47/2012 Communication No 47/2012 (2014)

Committee on the Elimination of Discrimination against Women *Banu Akbak, Gülen Khan and Melissa Özdemir v Austria* CEDAW/C/39/D/6/2005 Communication No 6/2005 (2007)

Committee on the Elimination of Discrimination against Women *Concluding Observations on the combined eighth and ninth periodic reports of Haiti* CEDAW/C/HTI/ CO/8-9 (2016)

Committee on the Elimination of Discrimination against Women *Concluding Observations on the combined initial and second periodic reports of Afghanistan* CEDAW/C/AFG/CO/1-2 (2013)

Committee on the Elimination of Discrimination against Women *Concluding Observations of the Committee on the Elimination of Discrimination against Women: Bangladesh* CEDAW/C/BGD/CO/7 (2011)

Committee on the Elimination of Discrimination against Women *Concluding Observations of the Committee on the Elimination of Discrimination against Women: Côte d'Ivoire* CEDAW/C/CIV/CO/1–3 (2011)

Committee on the Elimination of Discrimination against Women *Concluding Observations of the Committee on the Elimination of Discrimination against Women: Israel* CEDAW/C/ISR/CO/5 (2011)

Committee on the Elimination of Discrimination against Women *Concluding Observations of the Committee on the Elimination of Discrimination against Women: Kuwait* CEDAW/C/KWT/CO/3–4 (2011)

Committee on the Elimination of Discrimination against Women *Concluding Observations of the Committee on the Elimination of Discrimination against Women: South Africa* CEDAW/C/ZAF/CO/4 (2011)

Committee on the Elimination of Discrimination against Women *General Recommendation 19* CEDAW/C/GC/19 (1992)

Committee on the Elimination of Discrimination against Women *General Recommendation No. 28 on the Core Obligations of States Parties under Article 2 of the Convention on the Elimination of All Forms of Discrimination against Women* CEDAW/C/2010/47/GC.2 (2010)

Committee on the Elimination of Discrimination against Women *General Recommendation No. 35 on Gender-Based Violence against Women, Updating General Recommendation No. 19* CEDAW/C/GC/35 (2017)

Committee on the Elimination of Discrimination against Women *Hakan Goekce, Handan Goekce and Guelue Goekce v Austria* CEDAW/C/39/D/5/2005 Communication No 5/2005 (2007)

Committee on the Elimination of Discrimination against Women *RPB v The Philippines* CEDAW/C/57/D/34/2011 Communication No 34/2011 (2014)

Committee on the Elimination of Discrimination against Women *SVP v Bulgaria* CEDAW/C/53/D/31/2011 Communication No 31/2011 (2012)

Committee on the Elimination of Discrimination against Women *VK v Bulgaria* CEDAW/C/49/D/20/2008 Communication No 20/2008 (2011)

Committee on the Rights of the Child *Concluding Observations: Afghanistan* CRC/C/AFG/CO/1 (2011)

Committee on the Rights of the Child *Concluding Observations: Guinea-Bissau CRC/C/GNB/CO/2–4* (2013)

Committee on the Rights of the Child *Concluding Observations: Montenegro* CRC/C/MNE/CO/1 (2010)

Committee on the Rights of the Child *Concluding Observations on the combined third and fourth periodic reports of Canada adopted by the Committee at its sixty-first session* CRC/C/CAN/CO/3–4 (2012)

Committee on the Rights of the Child *Concluding Observations on the initial report of Burkina Faso submitted under article 12 of the Optional Protocol to the Convention on the Rights of the Child on the Sale of Children, Child Prostitution and Child Pornography, adopted by the Committee at its sixty-second session* CRC/C/OPSC/BFA/CO/1 (2013)

Committee on the Rights of the Child *Concluding Observations on the initial report of Paraguay submitted under article 12 of the Optional Protocol to the Convention on the*

Rights of the Child on the Sale of Children, Child Prostitution and Child Pornography, adopted by the Committee at its sixty-fourth session CRC/C/OPSC/PRY/CO/1 (2013)
Committee on the Rights of the Child *Concluding Observations: Rwanda* CRC/C/RWA/CO/3–4 (2013)
Committee on the Rights of the Child *Concluding Observations: Slovenia* CRC/C/SVN/CO/3–4 (2013)
Committee on the Rights of the Child *Consideration of reports submitted by States Parties under article 12. Paragraph 1, of the Optional Protocol to the Convention on the Rights of the Child on the Sale of Children, Child Prostitution and Child Pornography, Concluding Observations: Argentina* CRC/C/OPSC/ARG/CO/1 (2010)
Committee on the Rights of the Child *Consideration of reports submitted by States Parties under article 12. Paragraph 1, of the Optional Protocol to the Convention on the Rights of the Child on the Sale of Children, Child Prostitution and Child Pornography, Concluding Observations: Colombia* CRC/C/OPSC/COL/CO/1 (2010)
Convention on the Elimination of All Forms of Discrimination against Women 1249 UNTS 13 (opened for signature 18 December 1979, entered into force 3 September 1981)
Convention on the Rights of the Child 1577 UNTS 3 (opened for signature 20 November 1989, entered into force 2 September 1990)
T Esslemont "EXCLUSIVE – UN Peacekeepers Face New Sex Allegations in Central African Republic" *Trust* (11 November 2015) <www.trust.org>
European Convention for the Protection of Human Rights and Fundamental Freedoms ETS 3 (opened for signature 14 November 1950, entered into force 3 September 1953)
K Fortin "Rape as Torture: An Evaluation of the Committee against Torture's Attitude to Sexual Violence" (2008) 4 *Utrecht Law Review* 145
Fourth World Conference on Women *Beijing Declaration and Platform for Action* A/CONF.177/20 (1995) and A/CONF.177/20/Add.1 (1995)
General Assembly Resolution on Further Actions and Initiatives to Implement the Beijing Declaration and Platform for Action GA Res, A/RES/S-23/3 (2000)
General Assembly Resolution on the Rights of the Child GA Res, A/RES/66/141 (2012)
S Ghosh "Are UN Peacekeepers Doing More Harm Than Good?" *Al Jazeera* (15 August 2015) <www.aljazeera.com>
E Gorris "Invisible Victims? Where Are Male Victims of Conflict-Related Sexual Violence in International Law and Policy?" (2015) 22 *European Journal of Women's Studies* 412
Human Rights Committee *Concluding Observations of the Human Rights Committee: Cape Verde* CCPR/C/CPV/CO/1 (2012)
Human Rights Committee *Concluding Observations of the Human Rights Committee: Dominican Republic* CCPR/C/DOM/CO/5 (2012)
Human Rights Committee *Concluding Observations on Kuwait* CCPR/C/KWT/CO/2 (2011)
Human Rights Committee *Concluding Observations on the fifth periodic review of Peru, adopted at its 107th Session* CCPR/C/PER/CO/5 (2013)
Human Rights Committee *Concluding Observations on the initial report of Indonesia* CCPR/C/IDN/CO/1 (2013)Human Rights Committee *General Comment 28* CCPR/C/21/Rev.1/Add.10 (2000)
Human Rights Committee *General Comment No 20: Article 7 (Prohibition of Torture, or Other Cruel, Inhuman or Degrading Treatment or Punishment)* Adopted at the Forty-Fourth Session (1992)

Human Rights Committee *General Comment No 31: The Nature of the General Legal Obligation Imposed on States Parties to the Covenant* CCPR/C/21/Rev.1/Add.13 (2004)

Human Rights Committee *Minanga v Zaire* Communication No. 366/1989, CCPR/C/49/D/366/1989 (1993)

Inter-American Convention on the Prevention, Punishment and Eradication of Violence against Women [Convention of Belém do Pará] (opened for signature 9 June 1994, entered into force 5 March 1995)

International Covenant on Civil and Political Rights 999 UNTS 171 (opened for signature 16 December 1966, entered into force 23 March 1976)

International Covenant on Economic, Social and Cultural Rights 993 UNTS 3 (opened for signature 18 December 1979, entered into force 3 September 1981)

Legal Consequences of the Construction of a Wall in the Occupied Palestinian Territory Advisory Opinion, ICJ Reports 2004, 178

Legality of the Threat or Use of Nuclear Weapons Advisory Opinion, ICJ Reports 1996, 226

DA Lewis "Unrecognized Victims: Sexual Violence against Men in Conflict Settings under International Law" (2009) *Wisconsin International Law Journal* 1

J Marshall "Positive Obligations and Gender-Based Violence: Judicial Developments" (2008) 10 *International Community Law Review* 143

JE Méndez and A Nicolescu "Evolving Standards for Torture in International Law" in M Basoglu (ed) *Torture and Its Definition in International Law: An Interdisciplinary Approach* (Oxford University Press, Oxford, 2017)

DS Mitchell "The Prohibition of Rape in International Humanitarian Law as a Norm of *jus cogens*: Clarifying the Doctrine" (2004–2005) 15 *Duke Journal of Comparative and International Law* 219

Moldovan v Romania [2003] ECHR 485

C Mudgway "Sexual Exploitation by UN Peacekeepers: The 'Survival Sex' Gap in International Human Rights Law" (2017) 21 *The International Journal of Human Rights* 1453

R Murphy "United Nations Military Operations and International Humanitarian Law: What Rules to Apply to Peacekeepers?" (2003) 14 *Criminal Law Forum* 153

M Nowak *Report of the Special Rapporteur on Torture and Other Cruel, Inhuman or Degrading Treatment or Punishment* HRC, A/HRC/7/3 (2008)

Optional Protocol to the CRC on the Sale of Children, Child Prostitution and Child Pornography 2171 UNTS 227 (opened for signature May 25 2000, entered into force January 18 2002)

D Otto "Violence against Women: Something Other Than a Human Rights Violation?" (1993) 1 *Australian Feminist Law Journal* 159

N Ousman *Contribution of the Special Court for Sierra Leone to the Development of International Humanitarian Law* (Duncker & Humlot, Berlin, 2013)

Prosecutor v Zejnil Delalic, Zdravko Mucic, Hazim Delic and Esad Landzo (Judgment) ICTY Trial Chamber IT-96–21-T, 16 November 1998

Report of the Secretary-General *In-Depth Study on All Forms of Violence against Women* A/61/122/Add.1 (2006)

Report of the Special Rapporteur on the Sale of Children, Child Prostitution and Child Pornography, Najat Maalla M'Jid A/HRC/22/54 (2012)

Report of the Special Rapporteur on Violence against Women, Its Causes and Consequences GA, A/66/215 (2011)

Report of the Special Rapporteur on Violence against Women, Its Causes and Consequences GA, A/HRC/23/49 (2013)

Report of the Special Rapporteur on Violence against Women, Its Causes and Consequences GA, A/HRC/29/27 (2015)

Report of the Special Rapporteur on Violence against Women, Its Causes and Consequences, Integration of the Human Rights of Women and the Gender Perspective: Violence against Women, The Due Diligence Standard as a Tool for the Elimination of Violence against Women ESC, E/CN.4/2006/61 (2006)

NS Rodley *Question of the Human Rights of All Persons Subjected to Any Form of Detention or Imprisonment, in Particular: Torture and Other Cruel, Inhuman or Degrading Treatment or Punishment* E/CN.4/1994/31 (1994)

J Saura "Lawful Peacekeeping: Applicability of International Humanitarian Law to United Nations Peacekeeping Operations" (2006–2007) 58 *Hastings Law Journal* 479

M Scharf "The Letter of the Law: The Scope of the International Legal Obligation to Prosecute Human Rights" (1996) 59 *Law and Contemporary Problems* 41

A Seibert-Fohr *Prosecuting Serious Human Rights Violations* (Oxford University Press, Oxford, 2009)

AJ Sennett "Lenahan (Gonzales) v United States of America: Defining Due Diligence?" (2012) 53 *Harvard International Law Journal* 538

D Shraga "UN Peacekeeping Operations: Applicability of International Humanitarian Law and Responsibility for Operations-Related Damage" (2000) 94 *The American Journal of International Law* 406

L Stemple "Human Rights, Sex, and Gender: Limits in Theory and Practice" (2011) 31 *PACE Law Review* 824

L Stemple "Male Rape and Human Rights" (2009) 60 *Hastings Law Journal* 605

The Prosecutor v Furundzija (Judgment) IT-95–17/I-T. Trial Chamber, 10 December 1998

Third World Congress against Sexual Exploitation of Children and Adolescents *The Rio de Janeiro Declaration and Call for Action to Prevent and Stop Sexual Exploitation of Children and Adolescents* (2008)

United Nations Children's Fund *Handbook on the Optional Protocol on the Sale of Children, Child Prostitution and Child Pornography* (Innocenti Research Centre, Florence, 2009)

United Nations Declaration on the Elimination of Violence against Women GA Res, A/RES/48/104 (1993)

United Nations Secretary-General's Bulletin *Observance by UN Forces of International Humanitarian Law* SG B, ST/SGB/1999/13 (2006)

Velasquez Rodriguez v Honduras (Judgment) (1989) Inter-American Court of Human Rights (Ser C) No 42

BM Willis and BS Levy "Child Prostitution: Global Health Burden, Research Needs, and Interventions" (2002) 359 *The Lancet: Public Health* 1417

K Willsher and S Laville "France Launches Criminal Inquiry into Alleged Sex Abuse by Peacekeepers" *The Guardian* (7 May 2015) <www.theguardian.com/world>

3 State Responsibility

Now that the legal framework has been clarified, chapter three will turn to the first option for improving accountability for sexual exploitation and abuse. That option is the United Nations (UN) sanctioning troop-contributing countries (TCCs) that fail to exercise criminal jurisdiction based on obligations identified in chapters one and two. In this way, the UN may take direct leadership in responding to sexual exploitation and abuse. Having the UN take measures against noncompliant TCCs, however, does little to challenge the primary role of TCCs within the current framework, because it by default accepts their centrality.

This chapter examines circumstances under which measures can be implemented by the UN using the principles of state responsibility to support such measures.[1] The relevant instruments to work with for this purpose are the International Law Commission's *Articles on the Responsibility of States for Internationally Wrongful Acts* (ARSIWA)[2] and the *Articles on the Responsibility of International Organizations* (ARIO).[3] The ARIO was modelled on the ARSIWA and largely mirrors its provisions.[4] Both instruments have been noted by the

1 See for example Z Deen-Racsmany "The Amended UN Model Memorandum of Understanding: A New Incentive for States to Discipline and Prosecute Military Members of National Peacekeeping Contingents?" (2011) 16 *Journal of Conflict and Security Law* 32; EF Defeis "UN Peacekeepers and Sexual Abuse and Exploitation: An End to Impunity" (2008) 7 *Washington University Global Studies Law Review* 186; A Harrington "Victims of Peace: Current Abuse Allegations against UN Peacekeepers and the Role of the Law in Preventing Them in the Future" (2005) 12 *ILSA Journal of International & Comparative Law* 125; V Kent "Peacekeepers as Perpetrators of Abuse" 14 *African Security Review* 85; R Murphy *UN Peacekeeping in Lebanon, Somalia and Kosovo: Operational and Legal Issues in Practice* (Cambridge University Press, Cambridge, 2007); and M Odello "Tackling Criminal Acts in Peacekeeping Operations: The Accountability of Peacekeepers" (2010) 15 *Journal of Conflict & Security Law* 347.

2 *Responsibility of States for Internationally Wrongful Acts* GA Res, A/Res/56/83 (2001) [ARSIWA].

3 *Articles on the Responsibility of International Organizations* GA Res, A/66/10 (2011) [ARIO].

4 D Akande "International Organizations" in MD Evans (ed) *International Law* (4th ed, Oxford University Press, Oxford, 2014) 248, at 265.

General Assembly.[5] However, states have pointed out that in certain areas the ARIO represents law that is currently unclear; this is particularly true of article 17 (involving the responsibility of member states for the internationally wrongful acts of International Organisations [IOs]).[6] Therefore, it is important to note that the law on the responsibility of IOs is still developing, with the Articles being a guide as to its direction.[7]

For state responsibility to arise, there must first be an internationally wrongful act: that is, conduct or an omission of the state that is considered a breach of an international obligation owed by that state.[8] Chapters one and two identified several obligations on TCCs to respond to sexual exploitation and abuse. Firstly, the Model Memorandum of Understanding (MOU) requires TCCs to exercise criminal jurisdiction over serious misconduct that is considered criminal under domestic law. "Exercise of criminal jurisdiction" under the MOU merely obligates the TCC to submit cases to the appropriate national authorities. If the MOU is understood as a treaty, a failure to exercise jurisdiction will be a breach of an international obligation. Secondly, there are other obligations that arise under international human rights law. Where a TCC is party to the relevant international treaty, there are positive duties on states to respond to sexual exploitation and abuse committed by both private and public actors.[9] Those obligations linked to the exercise of criminal jurisdiction involve the criminalisation of torture (or cruel, inhuman, or degrading treatment), sexual activity with children, and some serious forms of violence against women. States are additionally obligated to investigate, prosecute, and, if convicted, punish violators. Potentially, if TCCs fail to take any one of these steps, they will be in breach of their international obligation to take positive action.

The sources of obligations identified above to exercise criminal jurisdiction over sexual exploitation and abuse represent primary rules of international law. A breach of an obligation of such primary rules will be an internationally wrongful act for the purposes of the ARSIWA.[10] Additionally, the internationally wrongful

5 For further discussion around the legal status of the Articles see J Crawford and S Olleson "The Character and Forms of International Responsibility" in MD Evans (ed) *International Law* (4th ed, Oxford University Press, Oxford, 2014) 443 at 444. See also, *General Assembly Resolution Responsibility of International Organizations* GA Res, A/Res/69/126 (2014).
6 See for example, General Assembly *Summary Record of the 18th Meeting* A/C.6/69/SR.18 (2015) at [47]-[80]
7 At [69].
8 ARSIWA, art 2.
9 Related to *Convention against Torture and Other Cruel, Inhuman or Degrading Treatment or Punishment* 1465 UNTS 85 (opened for signature 10 December 1984, entered into force 26 June 1987), *International Covenant on Civil and Political Rights* 999 UNTS 171 (opened for signature 16 December 1966, entered into force 23 March 1976), *Convention on the Rights of the Child* 1577 UNTS 3 (opened for signature 20 November 1989, entered into force 2 September 1990) and *Convention on the Elimination of All Forms of Discrimination against Women* 1249 UNTS 13 (opened for signature 18 December 1979, entered into force 3 September 1981).
10 ARSIWA, art 2(b).

act must be attributable to the state.[11] As the failure to exercise criminal jurisdiction is firmly attached to the state itself, it can be asserted that such a breach is attributable to the state.

Although this chapter will explore the consequences of state responsibility, it will not strictly apply the principles of state responsibility or the responsibility of IOs. Applying ARIO/ARSIWA strictly requires determining whether the UN is an injured or non-injured party.[12] Such a discussion is not useful or particularly relevant here, because the failure of states to discharge their obligations to respond to sexual exploitation and abuse causes harm to individuals, who do not see justice being done. Instead, the principles of state responsibility and IO responsibility are useful tools to support the use of coercive or noncoercive measures against noncompliant states.

Under the principles of state responsibility, there are multiple steps that are required from the state in breach and the IO invoking that responsibility. Using these principles as a guide to how the UN should respond to noncompliant states, the first option that will be briefly discussed is economic sanctions. The second is cessation, reparation, and promises of non-repetition. The third option is that of countermeasures. Within this section, Security Council Resolution 2272, which endorses the Secretary-General's decisions to remove entire contingents where a TCC fails to hold perpetrators accountable, will be analysed as a possible form of countermeasures.[13]

Essentially, this chapter will conclude that sanctioning noncompliant TCCs does not in and of itself guarantee that justice will be done. Simple removal of contingents through Resolution 2272 does not equate to the UN taking meaningful leadership; rather, they seem to be "washing their hands", as there is no formal follow-up to ensure investigation and prosecution take place once repatriation has been enforced. However, such measures draw attention to a general failure of states to respond to sexual exploitation and abuse. For the UN to sanction TCCs in this way signifies the seriousness of sexual exploitation and abuse and perhaps makes victims more visible to the international community. Nevertheless, it does not help in centralising the interests of victims themselves. Overall, this top-down approach is not sufficient to fill the accountability gap.

Economic sanctions

Some authors[14] have suggested the more serious measure of trade or other economic sanctions. Scholars such as Alexander Harrington argue that the threat of sanctions would be difficult for TCCs to ignore and would help compel states to prosecute those responsible for sexual exploitation and abuse to the full extent of their domestic criminal law.[15] The General Assembly may recommend economic

11 ARSIWA, art 2(a).
12 ARSIWA, arts 49(1); ARIO, arts 51(1).
13 *Security Council Resolution 2272* SC Res, S/Res/2272 (2016).
14 For example see Defeis, above n 1; and Harrington, above n 1.
15 Harrington, above n 1, at 147–148.

sanctions, and it is also within the power of the Security Council to impose them.[16] It is certainly not within the powers of the Secretary-General.[17] Furthermore, such measures are typically only implemented as a response to a breach or threat to international peace and security.[18] While the interpretation of whether an act (or omission) is a breach or threat to international peace and security has been broadly defined, it is unlikely that sexual exploitation or abuse by peacekeepers would qualify. Additionally, economic sanctions may have detrimental consequences for the TCCs, many of which are developing states. Moreover, there is no previous practice to suggest that the Security Council would impose sanctions for noncompliance by states. Therefore, imposing economic sanctions on TCCs for failing to exercise their criminal jurisdiction in relation to sexual exploitation and abuse is an unlikely option.

Cessation, reparation, assurances, and guarantees of non-repetition

According to the principles of state responsibility and the responsibility of IOs, one response to a state's wrongful act would be for the UN to demand cessation and non-repetition.[19] Cessation implies that a state is doing something in breach of its international obligations rather than omitting to fulfil its obligations. Therefore, requiring the TCC to stop failing to exercise criminal jurisdiction will not suffice. On the other hand, states are also under an obligation to provide assurances and guarantees of non-repetition. Here it can be argued that TCCs would need to assure that they will in future exercise criminal jurisdiction.

Additionally, the TCC would be under an obligation to make reparations. Reparations cannot be used to punish the state for the wrongful act; rather it is for mitigating or mending the damage done by the wrongful act (whether physical or moral damage).[20] There are three forms of reparations:[21] firstly, restitution, which requires states to re-establish the situation which existed before the wrongful act; secondly, compensation for the damage caused by the wrongful act that is not covered by restitution; and thirdly, satisfaction.

The most relevant form of reparation for an omission such as the failure to exercise criminal jurisdiction would be that of satisfaction. Restoring the situation before the wrongful act (restitution) would not address the issue of failure to exercise criminal jurisdiction. Moreover, compensation is for damage caused that is financially assessable. As the damage caused to the host state, or even the UN, is that of purely moral or political reputation, it is not necessarily financially assessable.[22] Satisfaction is about acknowledging the breach and expressing regret, and

16 See Charter of the United Nations, Chapter VII.
17 Or the Under Secretary-General which officially heads UN Peacekeeping Operations. See Charter of the United Nations, arts 97–101.
18 Charter of the United Nations, Chapter VII.
19 ARSIWA, arts 28–31; ARIO, arts 29–31.
20 J Klabbers *International Law* (Cambridge University Press, Cambridge, 2013) at 131.
21 See ARSIWA, arts 34–37; ARIO, arts 34–37.
22 Financially accessible harm to victims would not be relevant for purposes of state responsibility, as the Articles deal with states rather than individuals.

this may be achieved through an apology.[23] Therefore, satisfaction would be the best option of reparation; the TCC would be required to acknowledge the breach and issue a formal apology.[24]

Acknowledgement of the breach and a formal apology may not result in justice being seen to be done. However, these acts may have some element of engagement with the host state, as it would arguably receive an apology for failing to exercise criminal jurisdiction over sexual exploitation and abuse committed against a national. In this way, the interests of victims might be to some extent formally recognised. Moreover, by directing this outcome, the UN would be illustrating strong leadership in responding to sexual exploitation and abuse.

Countermeasures

Under the principles of state responsibility and the responsibility of IOs, countermeasures are restricted to lawful measures.[25] They must be used to induce the state to provide reparation for injury caused by the internationally wrongful act (cessation, reparation, or non-repetition).[26] Furthermore, countermeasures must be proportionate to the gravity of the internationally wrongful act.[27] According to ARSIWA/ARIO there are certain steps that must be taken before countermeasures may be taken; for example, the state or IO must do the following:[28]

a call on the responsible state, in accordance with article 43, to fulfil its obligations under part two;

b notify the responsible state of any decision to take countermeasures and offer to negotiate with that state.

Countermeasures will not be available if the dispute is pending before a "tribunal which has the authority to make decisions binding on the parties".[29] This would apply if the dispute resolution mechanism under the MOU was initiated or pending.[30] If countermeasures are taken without fulfilling the above requirements, then they themselves will be internationally wrongful acts.[31]

23 ARSIWA, art 37(2).

24 Reparations to individual victims and their communities will be discussed in chapter seven.

25 ARSIWA, art 54; ARIO, art 57.

26 At art 49.

27 At art 51.

28 At art 53(1)(a) and(b).

29 At art 53(3)(b).

30 *Manual on Policies and Procedures concerning the Reimbursement and Control of Contingent-Owned Equipment of Troop/Police Contributors Participating in Peacekeeping Missions (COE Manual)* GA, A/c.5/69/18 (2014) Ch 9 Memorandum of Understanding [2007 MOU] art 13.

31 N White and A Abass "Countermeasures and Sanctions" in MD Evans (ed) *International Law* (4th ed, Oxford University Press, Oxford, 2010) 531 at 534.

A noncoercive measure that has been suggested is to publicly name TCCs that fail to hold offenders to account.[32] Naming and shaming TCCs was supported initially by the Zeid Report, where it was noted that such action should be undertaken by the Secretary-General in his annual reports where TCCs fail to report outcomes of cases to the UN.[33] Since 2016, the Secretary-General has indeed included country-specific data on noncompliant TCCs.[34] Naming and shaming certainly puts a TCC on notice regarding their noncompliance and might be seen as a precursor to countermeasures. It remains to be seen how much impact this measure will have on the rates of TCC noncompliance. However, as a possible solution to the accountability gap, naming and shaming itself does not guarantee that justice will be done and reinforces the primary role of TCCs.

A coercive measure that has been taken up by the Security Council is withdrawing and blacklisting troops from TCCs that have not adequately responded to sexual exploitation and abuse allegations against their nationals. Security Council Resolution 2272 might be understood as countermeasures.

Security Council Resolution 2272

Withdrawal and blacklisting measures have been suggested by academics, and there has been long-term official support for these options from the UN Secretariat. In 2006, the Group of Legal Experts recognised that the UN maintains the ultimate sanction[35] of refusing to accept or seek troops from particular member states (without going into detail about which organ of the UN is officially capable to refuse such troops). However, scholars have cast doubt on whether such a course of action is wise, given the difficulties in persuading enough countries to contribute troops to peacekeeping operations.[36] Nevertheless, the Security Council issued Resolution 2272 in March, 2016, which endorsed and authorised the removal of entire contingents where there is "credible evidence" of widespread or systemic sexual exploitation and abuse or when TCCs have failed to hold their personnel accountable.[37] The first contingent of troops withdrawn and replaced under this authorisation was the one from the Democratic Republic of the Congo,

32 For example Kent, above n 1, at 90; C Leck "International Responsibility in United Nations Peacekeeping Operations: Command and Control Arrangements and the Attribution of Conduct" (2009) *Melbourne Journal of International Law* 346 at 356.

33 Secretary-General *A Comprehensive Strategy to Eliminate Future Sexual Exploitation and Abuse in United Nations Peacekeeping Operations* A/59/710 (2005) prepared by Prince Zeid Ra'ad Zeid Al-Hussein [Zeid Report] at [82].

34 Report of the Secretary-General *Special Measures for Protection from Sexual Exploitation and Abuse* GA, A/70/729 (2016).

35 *Report of the Group of Legal Experts on Making the Standards Contained in the Secretary-General's Bulletin Binding on Contingent Members and Standardising the Norms of Conduct so That They Are Applicable to All Categories of Peacekeeping Personnel* GA, A/61/645 (2006) [Second Group of Legal Experts Report] at [10].

36 See for example Deen-Racsmany, above n 1, at 342; Defeis, above n 1, at 209; and Harrington, above n 1, at 148.

37 *Security Council Resolution 2272*, above n 13, at [1] and [2].

after widespread allegations of sexual abuse against their troops in the Central African Republic (CAR) in 2017.[38]

Countermeasures must be used to induce compliance rather than punish the state for noncompliance. The coercive nature of blacklisting states and removing contingents means these actions could be argued to be punitive. Countermeasures must also be proportionate, which might also be problematic in terms of some of the measures suggested. For example, a withdrawal of an entire contingent in response to the TCC's failure to exercise criminal jurisdiction over one of its members may be seen as not proportionate. This could arguably be the same for blacklisting TCCs. However, evidence of continued lack of prosecution of a number of members of a contingent may then change the nature of the breach enough to make the countermeasure proportionate.

Nevertheless, the appropriate measures to be taken by the UN may depend on the particular circumstances surrounding the TCC's failure to exercise criminal jurisdiction over sexual exploitation and abuse by its contingent members. For example, the withdrawal of an entire contingent as a countermeasure to a single occasion when the TCC does not refer the case to the appropriate national authority may not be proportionate. The provisions themselves are broad enough to interpret a single omission to respond to sexual exploitation and abuse as enough to authorise the Secretary-General to remove entire contingents.[39] If this interpretation is correct, then the effect of this Resolution is to recognise the gravity of harm caused to a single victim, and this is significant for the overall recognition of the seriousness of sexual exploitation and abuse on the international stage. However, perhaps, the withdrawal of troops and blacklisting options are more appropriate as countermeasures for the continuous failure to exercise criminal jurisdiction. Determination of such a "magic number" of offences or victims may in itself be problematic; to a single victim of sexual exploitation who has yet to see justice being done, waiting until there is a pattern of TCC failure to hold offenders to account before the UN takes coercive action in terms of countermeasures would seem superfluous.

Resolution 2272, although a significant step of political leadership, has ambiguities that render it insufficient as a solution to the accountability gap. There is no guidance provided to or by the Secretary-General that would help determine what would constitute "credible evidence" or "widespread and systemic" in order to trigger authority for withdrawal.[40] Additionally, the Resolution does not attach withdrawal to a failure to discharge any specific obligation under international law. Instead, the Resolution links these measures to

38 *UN Secretary General* "Note to Correspondents on MINUSCA" United Nations (June 21 2017) <www.un.org>.

39 Reference is made to "widespread and systemic allegations" in [1] yet in [2] also refers to the singular "an allegation" see *Security Council Resolution 2272*, above n 13.

40 For discussion on this point see generally J Whalan *Dealing with Disgrace: Addressing Sexual Exploitation and Abuse in UN Peacekeeping* (International Peace Institute, New York, 2016).

> the primary responsibility of troop-contributing countries to investigate allegations of sexual exploitation and abuse by their personnel and of troop- and police-contributing countries to hold accountable, including through prosecution, where appropriate, their personnel for acts of sexual exploitation and abuse.[41]

It is unclear what steps are required to "hold accountable" personnel who commit sexual exploitation and abuse. If it were referring to the MOU and thus transferring the case to appropriate national authorities, then this would add further support to the argument that the MOU is a treaty and of normative effect. However, the MOU is not mentioned at all, so the standard remains ambiguous. Such uncertainties leave open the opportunities for lengthy delays in responding to allegations and to failures to "hold accountable", which undermines the ability for victims to ultimately see justice being done.

Although withdrawing troops or blacklisting states achieves the removal of perpetrators from the host state community, there is no guarantee that the individual offender will be brought to justice. For example, there has been no move to initiate criminal proceedings against those Congolese peacekeepers withdrawn from CAR in 2017 and alleged of sexual abuse.[42] There is no further process for victims to pursue justice provided by the Resolution, despite the fact it refers to a "victim-centred" rhetoric.[43] Additionally, host states are unlikely to have any ownership in such decisions. Again, the only principle that is fulfilled here is UN leadership. In regard to naming and shaming states, this would again only fulfil the third principle of UN leadership. However, if the naming and shaming led to future improvement in investigation and prosecution of offenders by TCCs, then eventually justice will be seen to be done. However, for individual victims, again, such a waiting game may seem superfluous and perhaps be psychologically and emotionally harmful.

Conclusion

In light of the three guiding principles, sanctions against TCCs are not a solution, particularly in the direction the Security Council has taken with the introduction of Resolution 2272. Although withdrawing troops and blacklisting states achieves the immediate removal of perpetrators from the host state community, there is no assurance that the offender will be brought to justice. Such top-down strategies only serve as a partial response to the problem. They do little to centre the interests of victims, and the host state is totally absent from this framework. The centrality of TCCs remains unchallenged and the accountability gap is unlikely to be addressed.

41 *Security Council Resolution 2272*, above n 13.
42 "Country Report 2018 - Central African Republic" *Human Rights Watch* (2018) <www.hrw.org>.
43 *Security Council Resolution 2272*, above n 13, at [4] and [12].

The removal of troops, blacklisting of states, and naming and shaming of TCCs that fail to exercise criminal jurisdiction are a show of UN leadership in responding to sexual exploitation and abuse. However, this is not meaningful leadership if criminal accountability is not enforced or followed up. Other avenues of responding to sexual exploitation by military contingent members must then be explored. Chapters four and five continue with this exploration by examining other avenues for prosecuting offenders, namely host state jurisdiction and the International Criminal Court.

References

D Akande "International Organizations" in MD Evans (ed) *International Law* (4th ed, Oxford University Press, Oxford, 2014)

Articles on the Responsibility of International Organizations GA Res, A/66/10 (2011)

Convention against Torture and Other Cruel, Inhuman or Degrading Treatment or Punishment 1465 UNTS 85 (opened for signature 10 December 1984, entered into force 26 June 1987)

Convention on the Elimination of All Forms of Discrimination against Women 1249 UNTS 13 (opened for signature 18 December 1979, entered into force 3 September 1981)

Convention on the Rights of the Child 1577 UNTS 3 (opened for signature 20 November 1989, entered into force 2 September 1990)

"Country Report 2018 - Central African Republic" *Human Rights Watch* (2018) <www.hrw.org>

J Crawford and S Olleson "The Character and Forms of International Responsibility" in MD Evans (ed) *International Law* (4th ed, Oxford University Press, Oxford, 2014)

Z Deen-Racsmany "The Amended UN Model Memorandum of Understanding: A New Incentive for States to Discipline and Prosecute Military Members of National Peacekeeping Contingents?" (2011) 16 *Journal of Conflict and Security Law* 32

EF Defeis "UN Peacekeepers and Sexual Abuse and Exploitation: An End to Impunity" (2008) 7 *Washington University Global Studies Law Review* 186

General Assembly Resolution Responsibility of International Organizations GA Res, A/Res/69/126 (2014)

General Assembly Summary Record of the 18th Meeting A/C.6/69/SR.18 (2015)

A Harrington "Victims of Peace: Current Abuse Allegations against UN Peacekeepers and the Role of the Law in Preventing Them in the Future" (2005) 12 *ILSA Journal of International & Comparative Law* 125

International Covenant on Civil and Political Rights 999 UNTS 171 (opened for signature 16 December 1966, entered into force 23 March 1976)

V Kent "Peacekeepers as Perpetrators of Abuse" (2005) 14 *African Security Review* 85

J Klabbers *International Law* (Cambridge University Press, Cambridge, 2013)

C Leck "International Responsibility in United Nations Peacekeeping Operations: Command and Control Arrangements and the Attribution of Conduct" (2009) *Melbourne Journal of International Law* 346

Manual on Policies and Procedures Concerning the Reimbursement and Control of Contingent-Owned Equipment of Troop/Police Contributors Participating in Peacekeeping Missions (COE Manual) GA, A/c.5/69/18 (2014)

R Murphy *UN Peacekeeping in Lebanon, Somalia and Kosovo: Operational and Legal Issues in Practice* (Cambridge University Press, Cambridge, 2007)

M Odello "Tackling Criminal Acts in Peacekeeping Operations: The Accountability of Peacekeepers" (2010) 15 *Journal of Conflict & Security Law* 347

Report of the Group of Legal Experts on Making the Standards Contained in the Secretary-General's Bulletin Binding on Contingent Members and Standardising the Norms of Conduct so That They Are Applicable to All Categories of Peacekeeping Personnel GA, A/61/645 (2006)

Responsibility of States for Internationally Wrongful Acts GA Res, A/Res/56/83 (2001)

Secretary-General *A Comprehensive Strategy to Eliminate Future Sexual Exploitation and Abuse in United Nations Peacekeeping Operations* A/59/710 (2005)

Secretary-General *Special Measures for Protection from Sexual Exploitation and Abuse* GA, A/70/729 (2016)

Security Council Resolution 2272 SC Res, S/Res/2272 (2016)

UN Secretary-General "Note to Correspondents on MINUSCA" United Nations (June 21 2017) <www.un.org>

J Whalan *Dealing with Disgrace: Addressing Sexual Exploitation and Abuse in UN Peacekeeping* (International Peace Institute, New York, 2016)

N White and A Abass "Countermeasures and Sanctions" in MD Evans (ed) *International Law* (4th ed, Oxford University Press, Oxford, 2010)

4 Host State Jurisdiction

In light of the principles underlying this book, host state jurisdiction clearly fulfils two of them. If trials are held within the victim's community, justice is seen to be done, and the host state has total ownership over that process. If host state jurisdiction is achieved through measures that foster cooperation between the relevant international actors (host states, troop-contributing countries [TCCs], and the United Nations [UN]), then the UN will have some leadership in responding to sexual exploitation and abuse as well. Thus, host state jurisdiction seems desirable. However, this chapter will argue that although host state jurisdiction and cooperation between the UN, host states, and TCCs may be achieved through international agreements, it may be more beneficial to explore alternative structural measures, such as judicial institutions.

This chapter will open with a brief overview of the status quo of jurisdiction in peacekeeping operations, followed by the conceptual and practical benefits of host state jurisdiction over peacekeeping crimes. The various methods of incorporating host state jurisdiction will then be discussed. This will include an exploration of the Group of Legal Experts' proposed convention and the North-Atlantic Treaty Organisation (NATO) Status-of-Forces Agreements (SOFAs), which are an example of concurrent jurisdiction. These methods will be analysed further against the particular challenges presented by host state jurisdiction. Although seemingly appropriate, host state jurisdiction will be argued as ultimately unsatisfactory.

Jurisdiction – status quo

Under the UN Model SOFA, the TCC has exclusive criminal jurisdiction over its national military personnel.[1] Therefore, although members of national contingents are expected to respect local laws and customs, the host state waives its territorial jurisdiction under the SOFA.[2] In regard to other categories of personnel, such as

1 The agreement between the UN and the host state *Model Status-of-Forces Agreement between the United Nations and Host Countries* GA, A/45/594 (1990) [Model SOFA] art 47(b).

2 Model SOFA, art 6. A more detailed discussion of the Model SOFA and exclusive criminal jurisdiction is included in Chapter 1.

UN officials and experts on mission, functional immunity is granted under various international instruments.[3] Such immunities are limited to acts committed during official duties; acts of sexual exploitation and abuse are committed outside official capacity and would potentially be subject to host state jurisdiction.[4] However, if the host state judicial system is unstable (for example, due to ongoing conflict, physical destruction, or corruption), it may not be appropriate for the host state to exercise such jurisdiction, and therefore it will likely still be waived under the SOFA.[5]

There are certain practical and conceptual benefits to the host state having jurisdiction over sexual exploitation and abuse. Trials that take place within the community of the victim ensure that justice is seen to be done. As a result, there would also be greater ease of access to victims and witnesses. Having total ownership over the process, the host state will have its specific context reflected within the accountability framework. This includes knowledge of local customs and language, which can be a barrier for foreign investigators. However, as will be seen below, host state jurisdiction may not always be possible or appropriate.

Group of Legal Experts – Draft Convention

In light of the mass reports of sexual exploitation and abuse allegations during the early 2000s, the UN-commissioned Group of Legal Experts explored options for increased accountability of its staff and experts on mission (as well as other personnel).[6] The Group argued that host state jurisdiction should be prioritised when responding to crimes committed by peacekeeping personnel within host state territory.[7] To prioritise host state jurisdiction was to acknowledge the principle of territorial jurisdiction,[8] to follow through with the obligation on peacekeeping personnel to respect local laws and customs, and to make sure victims would see justice being done.[9]

In 2006, the Group of Legal Experts drafted a convention (Draft Convention) as a starting point for discussion among member states (and it is still being considered by member states).[10] The Draft Convention does not consider the

3 Charter of the United Nations, art 105; *Convention on the Privileges and Immunities of the United Nations 1 UNTS 15* (opened for signature 13 February 1946, entered into force 17 September 1946) art VI (22)(b).

4 *Report of the Group of Legal Experts on Ensuring the Accountability of United Nations Staff and Experts on Mission with Respect to Criminal Acts Committed in Peacekeeping Operations* GA, A/60/980 (2006) [Group of Legal Experts Report] at [21].

5 At [22].

6 Group of Legal Experts Report, above n 4; See also, Secretary-General *A Comprehensive Strategy to Eliminate Future Sexual Exploitation and Abuse in United Nations Peacekeeping Operations* GA, A/59/710 (2005).

7 Group of Legal Experts Report, above n 4, at [27].

8 Where the crime takes place within the territory, then that state has jurisdiction over that criminal act.

9 Group of Legal Experts Report, above n 4, at [27(a)]-[27(d)].

10 At [47]; *Criminal Accountability of United Nations Officials and Experts on Mission* GA Res, A/Res/69/114 (2014).

accountability of military contingent members.[11] However, it is useful to examine in regard to jurisdictional issues and how the Group of Legal Experts envisioned a combined effort between host states and TCCs to hold offenders to account. Article four establishes mandatory jurisdiction based on territory (crime committed within state territory) and nationality (offender as a national of that state). Article 4(2) provides that states may also establish jurisdiction based on passive personality (victim is a national) or over a stateless person within their territory. Article four would make concurrent jurisdiction possible: two states having jurisdiction and operating at the same time over a particular offence. The Draft Convention does not attempt to resolve concurrent jurisdiction by prescribing primary or secondary jurisdiction; however, it does include an "extradite or prosecute" provision.

Article 4(4) of the Draft Convention provides the following:

> Each State party shall likewise take such measures as may be necessary to establish its jurisdiction over the crimes set out in article 3 in cases where the alleged offender is present in its territory and it does not extradite such person pursuant to article 8 to any of the States parties which have established their jurisdiction in accordance with paragraphs 1 or 2 of the present article.

Together with article seven, this provision requires states parties to either exercise criminal jurisdiction over the accused or extradite that person to a state that also has jurisdiction to do so. It also provides universal jurisdiction if states parties choose to establish such jurisdiction over crimes included in the Draft Convention.[12] Articles ten and sixteen envision mutual legal assistance between states parties during the exercise of criminal jurisdiction. There is no obligation to prosecute unless double criminality exists (where the conduct is deemed a crime in both the host state and TCC domestic criminal law).[13]

The Draft Convention seems to encourage states to modify their criminal law to incorporate extraterritorial jurisdiction over the prescribed crimes.[14] Moreover, the Draft Convention supports the mutual cooperation between states to hold perpetrators to account in terms of whichever state exercises its criminal jurisdiction.

11 "Draft Convention on the Criminal Accountability of United Nations Officials and Experts on Mission" *Report of the Group of Legal Experts on Ensuring the Accountability of United Nations Staff and Experts on Mission with Respect to Criminal Acts Committed in Peacekeeping Operations* GA, A/60/980 (2006) Annex III [Draft Convention].

12 Such crimes include conduct related to sexual exploitation and abuse. See Draft Convention, above n 11, art 3; see also M O'Brien "Issues of the Draft Convention on the Criminal Accountability of United Nations Officials and Experts on Mission" in N Quenivet and S Shah-Davis (eds) *International Law and Armed Conflict: Challenges in the 21st Century* (YMC Asser Press, The Hague, 2010) 57 at 72.

13 Draft Convention, above n 11, art 9; RS Clark "Peacekeeping Forces, Jurisdiction and Immunity: A Tribute to George Barton" (2012) 43 *Victoria University of Wellington Law Review* 77 at 95.

14 Clark, above n 13, at 96.

This mutual cooperation between states has been highlighted many times by state representatives during General Assembly discussions on the Draft itself.[15]

Overall, the Draft Convention is the Group of Legal Experts' attempt at prioritising host state jurisdiction and promoting cooperation among states parties. If it is adopted at some point in the future, it could prove a useful alternative to TCC exclusive criminal jurisdiction (if military contingent members were also included within its scope, which has not been suggested so far). However, arguably the Draft Convention does not provide an adequate structure to incorporate host state jurisdiction, since much of its application is dependant on whether sexual exploitation and abuse are crimes in either or both the host state and the TCC, and whether extradition treaties exist between such states. Therefore, there will likely be a gap where sexual exploitation is concerned. Moreover, where concurrent jurisdiction exists, the Draft Convention does not address whether the host state will have primary or secondary jurisdiction. Such concurrent jurisdictional agreements have been embraced by NATO.

Concurrent jurisdiction

Outside the context of UN peacekeeping, concurrent jurisdiction agreements (where jurisdiction is shared between the sending and receiving states) are common for foreign military forces operating abroad.[16] Although something to be negotiated between parties, the default in such agreements is to prioritise the primary jurisdiction of the host state (where offences are committed outside the performance of official duties).[17] Such offences would include crimes of a sexual nature. Concurrent jurisdiction agreements are used to reconcile the two principles of jurisdiction that operate at the same time; the receiving state has territorial jurisdiction (as the crime is committed within their territory), and the sending state has the right to exercise jurisdiction over their own national personnel.[18] Such concurrent jurisdiction agreements have been suggested[19] as an alternative arrangement for including the host state in responding to crimes committed by military contingent members in the context of UN peacekeeping operations.

15 See for example General Assembly *Summary Record of the 6th Meeting* GA, A/C.6/62/SR.6 (2007); General Assembly *Summary Record of the 5th Meeting* GA A/C.6/63/SR.5 (2008); General Assembly *Summary Record of the 7th Meeting* GA, A/C.6/64/SR.7 (2009).

16 PJ Conderman "Jurisdiction" in D Fleck (ed) *The Handbook of the Law of Visiting Forces* (Oxford University Press, New York, 2001) 99; APV Rogers "Operational Context" in D Fleck (ed) *The Handbook of the Law of Visiting Forces* (Oxford University Press, New York, 2001) 533.

17 Rogers, above n 16, at 550.

18 Conderman, above n 16, at 103.

19 See for example M Du Plessis and S Pete "Who Guards the Guards?" (2010) 13 *African Security Review* 4 at 6.

The NATO-SOFA recognises the primary jurisdiction of the host state in certain circumstances and incorporates concurrent jurisdiction.[20] Article seven of the NATO-SOFA provides that where an offence is committed outside the performance of official duties, and/or is committed against a national, and is covered by the laws of both sending and receiving states, the receiving state has primary jurisdiction.[21] The sending state has secondary jurisdiction, which will operate where the receiving state has waived its jurisdiction or has been unwilling or unable to exercise it.[22] Members of both parties are expected to cooperate with each other on the arrest and investigation of military personnel.[23] Moreover, if trial can be brought by the receiving state, then the rights of the accused to a fair trial must be substantively guaranteed.[24]

Despite the NATO-SOFA, supplementary agreements are often sought by NATO members to waive the primary jurisdiction of the receiving state and establish exclusive jurisdiction of the sending state.[25] The United States is an example of a NATO member which regularly seeks such agreements.[26] Moreover, in modern practice, NATO has opted for exclusive criminal jurisdiction for sending states in SOFAs, but maintains mutual investigatory assistance clauses.[27] Therefore, the NATO agreements do not often follow through on the receiving state jurisdiction provisions.

The NATO-SOFA and its concurrent jurisdiction arrangements can also be distinguished from UN peacekeeping operations. NATO-SOFAs are reciprocal agreements, governing the permanent stationing of allied forces; thus, the receiving state will often be granted similar immunities.[28] This is quite different to UN peacekeeping military contingent members, who operate independently from host

20 North Atlantic Treaty Organization *Agreement between the Parties to the North Atlantic Treaty Regarding the Status of Their Forces* (entered into force 19 June 1951) [NATO-SOFA]. See also EG Schuck "Concurrent Jurisdiction under the NATO Status of Forces Agreement" 57 *Columbia Law Review* 355; JH Rouse and GB Baldwin "The Exercise of Criminal Jurisdiction under the NATO Status of Forces Agreement" (1957) *The American Journal of International Law* 29.

21 NATO-SOFA, art VII (3)(b).

22 At art VII (3)(c).

23 At art VII (6).

24 At art VII (9).

25 The United States' policy is to require such agreements before military forces are sent, see Conderman, above n 16, at 112.

26 See International Security Advisory Board *Report on Status of Forces Agreements* (United States Department of State, 2015) at 16–19.

27 Particularly where governance on the receiving state is in question. See for example North Atlantic Treaty Organization *Agreement between the North Atlantic Treaty Organisations and the Islamic Republic of Afghanistan on the Status of NATO-Led Activities in Afghanistan* (entered into force 30 September 2014) art 11. Such arrangements are often criticised by human rights NGOs. See for example Amnesty International "Afghanistan: No Justice for Thousands of Civilians Killed in US/NATO Operations" (news release, 11 August 2014).

28 R Burke "Status of Forces Deployed on UN Peacekeeping Operations: Jurisdictional Immunity" (2011) 16 *Journal of Conflict & Security Law* 63 at 77.

state forces on a temporary basis and often on rotation.[29] Therefore, it may not be appropriate to directly compare the two status-of-forces agreements, as they serve slightly different purposes. However, the NATO-SOFA does illustrate that prioritising host state jurisdiction in regard to responding to criminal activity can be achieved via international agreements.

Host state jurisdiction as an alternative to the status quo

After the Group of Legal Experts' Report, academics discussed whether the host state should have primary or secondary jurisdiction over foreign military troops in the context of UN peacekeeping.[30] Some academics consider host state jurisdiction advantageous for practical reasons, such as the proximity to any victims and witnesses, proximity to any evidence, and the principled reason that victims will see justice being done.[31] However, there are certain challenges associated with host state jurisdiction.

A particular challenge is securing custody of peacekeeping personnel who may have been redeployed or otherwise may be outside the host state territory.[32] There may also be difficulties concerning the age of consent where there is disparity between legal age of consent and social practice. Although legal age of consent is 18 years old in CAR, the DRC, Liberia, and South Sudan, customary age of consent is less than 16 years old.[33]

A further challenge to host state jurisdiction might be host states not being in a position to exercise criminal jurisdiction due to ongoing conflict or recent conflict; for example, the legal infrastructure may be weakened by political corruption or may be physically destroyed.[34] This is true for CAR, for example, with a seriously compromised legal system due to ongoing conflict and the continued widespread

29 At 77–78.

30 See for example KJ Allred "Peacekeepers and Prostitutes: How Deployed Forces Fuel the Demand for Trafficked Women and New Hope for Stopping It" (2006) 33 *Armed Forces & Society* 5; Clark, above n 13; AJ Miller "Legal Aspects of Stopping Sexual Exploitation and Abuse in UN Peacekeeping Operations" (2006) 39 *Cornell International Law Journal* 71; M Ndulo "The United Nations Response to the Sexual Abuse and Exploitation of Women and Girls by Peacekeepers during Peacekeeping Missions" (2009) 27 *Berkeley Journal of International Law* 127; and M Odello "Tackling Criminal Acts in Peacekeeping Operations: The Accountability of Peacekeepers" (2010) 15 *Journal of Conflict & Security Law* 347.

31 Ndulo, above n 30, at 153; Odello, above n 30, at 374.

32 Ndulo, above n 30, at 153.

33 Committee on the Rights of the Child *Concluding Observations on the second periodic report of the Central African Republic* CRC/C/CAF/CO/2 (2017) at [22]; Committee on the Rights of the Child *Concluding Observations on the combined third and fifth periodic reports of the Democratic Republic of the Congo* CRC/C/COD/CO/3–5 (2017) at [27]; Committee on the Elimination of Discrimination against Women *Concluding Observations on the combined seventh and eighth periodic reports of Liberia* CEDAW/C/LBR/CO/7–8 (2015) at [43]; and Human Rights Watch *Child Marriage: South Sudan* (2013) available online: <www.hrw.org>.

34 Ndulo, above n 30, at 155.

abuses against civilians by armed groups, both of which contributing to the erosion of the rule of law.[35] Moreover, any legal system still functioning may well not have the human rights guarantees and procedures in place to deliver due process.[36] Haiti and Liberia, for instance, have been highly criticised by human rights treaty bodies for lacking the appropriate human rights standards and protections in their respective criminal justice systems.[37] Finally, where there are local elite groups competing for power (such as in CAR), host state jurisdiction may be impossible, because such groups might politically benefit from ongoing conflict and disruption to legal processes generally.[38]

The Group of Legal Experts noted that "jurisdiction is not an indivisible concept".[39] To exercise criminal jurisdiction involves different components, such as arrest, investigation, prosecution, and sentencing.[40] Therefore, the host state may well be able to carry out some of these steps notwithstanding some of the challenges outlined above, such as weakened judicial infrastructure. The importance of mutual legal assistance and cooperation between the host state, UN, and TCC investigatory teams was highlighted as a way to bridge the gap caused by a compromised criminal justice system.[41]

Additionally, a 2009 Stimson Center Report argued that host state (secondary) jurisdiction should be supported by the UN.[42] In response to criminal conduct committed by UN peacekeepers, the Stimson Center Report made recommendations aimed at improving accountability. Similar to the Group of Legal Experts, the Stimson Center Report limited its research to nonmilitary personnel.[43] Additionally, the Report recommended that primary jurisdiction should remain with TCCs and that the host state should have secondary jurisdiction in circumstances

35 See Human Rights Council *Report of the Independent Expert on the Situation of Human Rights in the Central African Republic* GA, A/HRC/36/64 (2017).
36 Allred, above n 30, at 18; Miller, above n 30, at 92; Ndulo, above n 30, at 155.
37 This is particularly an issue for women's access to justice. See for example, *Concluding Observations on the combined seventh and eighth periodic reports of Liberia*, above n 33, at [15]; Committee on the Elimination of Discrimination against Women *Concluding Observations on the combined eighth and ninth periodic reports of Haiti* CEDAW/C/HTI/CO/8–9 (2016) at [13], [21(e)] and [45]; Human Rights Council *Report of the Independent Expert on the Situation of Human Rights in Haiti* GA, A/HRC/31/77 (2016) at [33], [36], and [77]; Human Rights Committee *Concluding Observations on the initial report of Haiti* CCPR/C/HTI/CO-1 (2014) at [15], and [16]-[17];
38 AK Jarstad and L Olsson "Hybrid Peace Ownership in Afghanistan: International Perspectives of Who Owns What and When" (2012) 18 *Global Governance* 105 at 109.
39 Group of Legal Experts, above n 4, at [40].
40 At [41]-[42] see also Clark, above n 13, at 93–96.
41 Group of Legal Experts Report, above n 4, at [40].
42 WJ Durch, KN Andrews, ML England and MC Weed *Improving Criminal Accountability in United Nations Peace Operations* (STIMSON Center Report, Washington, 2009) [Stimson Center Report]. The Stimson Center is a nonprofit organisation based in the United States that periodically publishes reports aimed at improving international peace and security.
43 At xi.

where the TCC does not have extraterritorial jurisdiction over the crime in question (unable to investigate or prosecute) or does not agree to prosecute (unwilling).[44] However, unlike the Group of Legal Experts, the Stimson Center Report recommended that host state jurisdiction should be assisted by a UN organ specifically created to support host state judicial systems.[45] Such logistical support would be in addition to a roster of international expertise available to fill any gaps in the host state system.[46] A support mechanism centralised in the UN would help in circumstances where the host state's domestic judicial infrastructure is weakened due to ongoing conflict or recent conflict, and would provide clear UN leadership. Nevertheless, the Stimson Center Report's proposals are dependant on whether sexual exploitation and abuse are crimes in the domestic law of either the TCC or the host state. Moreover, unlike the Draft Convention, it is yet to be tabled or discussed at the UN.

The Group of Legal Experts' Draft Convention suggests a system of cooperation between the UN, host state, and TCC whilst prioritising host state jurisdiction, but it does not offer a formal structure.[47] Instead, ad hoc arrangements are recommended.[48] The Stimson Center Report goes a step further and suggests host state jurisdiction supported by a centralised UN organ especially created for the purpose of filling gaps in expertise and providing logistical assistance to the host state's juridical system.[49] However, I argue that a formal judicial structure may be more advantageous if the goal is to achieve accountability while also incorporating the jurisdiction of the host state and TCC (thus, chapter six argues for a series of hybrid courts for peacekeepers). Moreover, host state jurisdiction relies on the host state's criminal laws to cover sexual exploitation and abuse. It is unlikely that aspects of sexual exploitation, particularly survival sex, would be covered adequately in domestic criminal law of host states.

Conclusion

Although host state jurisdiction is desirable, as it places trials within the physical context of the abuse and in view of the victim, it is not satisfactory without structural measures in place to facilitate it. Purely relying on host state jurisdiction may not be possible in practice; the host state's legal infrastructure may be weakened or compromised due to conflict. The Group of Legal Experts' Draft Convention, the NATO-SOFA, and the Stimson Center Report illustrate ways in which host state jurisdiction can be incorporated into international agreements or

44 At xiii.
45 At xvi.
46 At xvi.
47 Although hybrid courts are mentioned and recommended to be "considered" without further developing this idea, see Group of Legal Experts Report, above n 4, at [33]-[37] and [44c].
48 At [44b]. See also *Criminal Accountability of United Nations Officials and Experts on Mission* (2014), above n 10.
49 Stimson Center Report, above n 42, at xvi-xv.

supported, and as such may be achieved in the UN Peacekeeping context through amending both the UN Model-SOFA and the Memorandum of Understanding or simply adopting a version of the Draft Convention. These are possible alternative ways to exercise criminal jurisdiction over military contingent members who commit sexual exploitation and abuse. However, I argue that these options do not go far enough in offering a structural system in which to support cooperation between the UN, host states, and TCCs while also incorporating host state ownership and, in some circumstances, host state jurisdiction. It can be argued that a judicial tribunal of some kind should provide such a structure; for example, the International Criminal Court (discussed in chapter five) or a new court for peacekeepers (discussed in chapter six).

References

KJ Allred "Peacekeepers and Prostitutes: How Deployed Forces Fuel the Demand for Trafficked Women and New Hope for Stopping It" (2006) 33 *Armed Forces & Society* 5

Amnesty International "Afghanistan: No Justice for Thousands of Civilians Killed in US/NATO Operations" (news release, 11 August 2014)

R Burke "Status of Forces Deployed on UN Peacekeeping Operations: Jurisdictional Immunity" (2011) 16 *Journal of Conflict & Security Law* 63

RS Clark "Peacekeeping Forces, Jurisdiction and Immunity: A Tribute to George Barton" (2012) 43 *Victoria University of Wellington Law Review* 77

Committee on the Elimination of Discrimination against Women *Concluding Observations on the combined eighth and ninth periodic reports of Haiti* CEDAW/C/HTI/CO/8–9 (2016)

Committee on the Elimination of Discrimination against Women *Concluding Observations on the combined seventh and eighth periodic reports of Liberia* CEDAW/C/LBR/CO/7–8 (2015)

Committee on the Rights of the Child *Concluding Observations on the combined third and fifth periodic reports of the Democratic Republic of the Congo* CRC/C/COD/CO/3–5 (2017)

Committee on the Rights of the Child *Concluding Observations on the second periodic report of the Central African Republic* CRC/C/CAF/CO/2 (2017)

PJ Conderman "Jurisdiction" in D Fleck (ed) *The Handbook of the Law of Visiting Forces* (Oxford University Press, New York, 2001)

Convention on the Privileges and Immunities of the United Nations 1 UNTS 15 (opened for signature13 February 1946, entered into force 17 September 1946)

Criminal Accountability of United Nations Officials and Experts on Mission GA Res, A/Res/69/114 (2014)

M Du Plessis and S Pete "Who Guards the Guards?" (2010) 13 *African Security Review* 4

WJ Durch, KN Andrews, ML England and MC Weed *Improving Criminal Accountability in United Nations Peace Operations* (STIMSON Center Report, Washington, 2009)

General Assembly *Summary Record of the 5th Meeting* GA, A/C.6/63/SR.5 (2008)

General Assembly *Summary Record of the 6th Meeting* GA, A/C.6/62/SR.6 (2007)

General Assembly, *Summary Record of the 7th Meeting* GA, A/C.6/64/SR.7 (2009)

Human Rights Committee *Concluding Observations on the initial report of Haiti* CCPR/C/HTI/CO-1 (2014)

Human Rights Council *Report of the Independent Expert on the Situation of Human Rights in the Central African Republic* GA, A/HRC/36/64 (2017)

Human Rights Council *Report of the Independent Expert on the Situation of Human Rights in Haiti* GA, A/HRC/31/77 (2016)

Human Rights Watch "Child Marriage: South Sudan" (2013) <www.hrw.org>

International Security Advisory Board *Report on Status of Forces Agreements* (United States Department of State 2015)

AK Jarstad and L Olsson "Hybrid Peace Ownership in Afghanistan: International Perspectives of Who Owns What and When" (2012) 18 *Global Governance* 105

AJ Miller "Legal Aspects of Stopping Sexual Exploitation and Abuse in UN Peacekeeping Operations" (2006) 39 *Cornell International Law Journal* 71

Model Status of Forces Agreement between the United Nations and Host Countries GA, A/*45/594* (1990)

M Ndulo "The United Nations Response to the Sexual Abuse and Exploitation of Women and Girls by Peacekeepers during Peacekeeping Missions" (2009) 27 *Berkeley Journal of International Law* 127

North Atlantic Treaty Organization *Agreement between the North Atlantic Treaty Organisations and the Islamic Republic of Afghanistan on the Status of NATO-Led Activities in Afghanistan* (entered into force 30 September 2014)

North Atlantic Treaty Organization *Agreement between the Parties to the North Atlantic Treaty Regarding the Status of Their Forces* (entered into force 19 June 1951)

M O'Brien "Issues of the Draft Convention on the Criminal Accountability of United Nations Officials and Experts on Mission" in N Quenivet and S Shah-Davis (eds) *International Law and Armed Conflict: Challenges in the 21st Century* (YMC Asser Press, The Hague, 2010)

M Odello "Tackling Criminal Acts in Peacekeeping Operations: The Accountability of Peacekeepers" (2010) 15 *Journal of Conflict & Security Law* 347

Report of the Group of Legal Experts on Ensuring the Accountability of United Nations Staff and Experts on Mission with Respect to Criminal Acts Committed in Peacekeeping Operations GA, A/60/980 (2006)

APV Rogers "Operational Context" in D Fleck (ed) *The Handbook of the Law of Visiting Forces* (Oxford University Press, New York, 2001)

JH Rouse and GB Baldwin "The Exercise of Criminal Jurisdiction under the NATO Status of Forces Agreement" (1957) *The American Journal of International Law* 29

EG Schuck "Concurrent Jurisdiction under the NATO Status of Forces Agreement" 57 *Columbia Law Review* 355

Secretary-General *A Comprehensive Strategy to Eliminate Future Sexual Exploitation and Abuse in United Nations Peacekeeping Operations* GA, A/59/710 (2005)

5 The International Criminal Court

The International Criminal Court (ICC) has been discussed by many commentators as a legitimate option for improving accountability of peacekeepers, particularly for crimes of a sexual nature.[1] It has been argued that where the troop-contributing country (TCC) is unwilling or unable to prosecute its nationals for sexual exploitation and abuse, the ICC should be considered.[2] It has been equally argued that extending the jurisdiction of crimes currently listed is unlikely and that perhaps it is better to amend the treaty that established the ICC, the Rome Statute, in order to incorporate the prosecution of sexual exploitation and abuse by peacekeepers.[3] Such a considerable call within the academic literature therefore requires consideration.

It is necessary to note here that, like the options discussed in chapter three, this option for improving accountability does little to challenge the primary role of TCCs, because ICC jurisdiction relies on the non-action of TCCs. The ICC does not give the UN an opportunity to show leadership. The UN has very little control over the work of the Court itself, save for Security Council referrals and

1 R Burke "UN Military Peacekeeper Complicity in Sexual Abuse: The ICC or a Tri-hybrid Court" in M Bergsmo (ed) *Thematic Prosecution of International Sex Crimes* (Torkel Opsahl, Beijing, 2012) 317; M Du Plessis and S Pete "Who Guards the Guards? The ICC and Serious Crimes Committed by United Nations Peacekeepers in Africa" (2004) 12 *African Security Review* 5; M O'Brien "Sexual Exploitation and Beyond: Using the Rome Statute of the International Criminal Court to Prosecute UN Peacekeepers for Gender-Based Crimes" (2011)11 *International Criminal Law Review* 803; N Quenivet "The Role of the International Criminal Court in the Prosecution on Peacekeepers for Sexual Offences" in R Arnold (ed) *Law Enforcement within the Framework of Peace Support Operations* (Koninklijke Brill NV, Leiden, 2008) 399; and RA Vezina "Combating Impunity in Haiti: Why the ICC Should Prosecute Sexual Abuse by UN Peacekeepers" (2012) 1 *Ave Maria International Law Journal* 431.

2 O'Brien "Sexual Exploitation and Beyond", above n 1, at 808; Burke, above n 1, at 320; Vezina, above n 1, at 447.

3 On the problems with ICC jurisdiction, see A Harrington "Victims of Peace: Current Abuse Allegations against UN Peacekeepers and the Role of Law in Preventing Them in the Future" (2005) 12 *ILSA Journal of International & Comparative Law* 125, 140–143. See also O'Brien "Sexual Exploitation and Beyond", above n 1, at 826; Quenivet, above n 1, at 411.

deferrals (discussed below). Moreover, the host state is unlikely to have ownership over the process as the ICC is physically located in The Hague. As a result, unless an effective outreach programme is employed, victims may not hear about cases or see justice being done. However, ICC jurisdiction is worth exploring because the potential investigation and prosecution of sexual exploitation and abuse on the international stage would centre the seriousness of the conduct and the gravity of the harm caused to victims.

Although there are pragmatic advantages to the ICC having jurisdiction, such as the existence of a judicial infrastructure and agreed standards of investigation and trial, this chapter will examine three major barriers complicit with ICC current jurisdiction and procedure that indicate the unlikelihood that the Court would prosecute peacekeepers for sexual exploitation and abuse. The first possible limitation is that ICC jurisdiction is currently restricted to a narrow set of international crimes. Although some authors have argued that the Rome Statute should be amended to include sexual exploitation and abuse by peacekeepers,[4] this is unlikely given the drafting history of the Rome Statute itself. A second hurdle to prosecution by the ICC is the complementarity principle, which portends that the Court shall only intervene in cases where member states are unable or unwilling to prosecute. Thirdly, the discretion of the ICC Prosecutor, which potentially operates to limit admissibility based on the ranking of personnel involved and the gravity of the crime(s) committed, will also be a major limitation to the application of the Court in cases of sexual exploitation and abuse by peacekeepers.

Lastly, this chapter will consider the possible impact of Security Council referrals in the peacekeeping context. This may be an advantage because it avoids many of the pitfalls associated with other ICC triggering mechanisms. However, overall, although a desirable option to improve accountability of military contingent members who commit sexual exploitation and abuse, the ICC is unlikely to actually improve accountability at all.

The crimes within ICC jurisdiction

The jurisdiction of the ICC is set out under Part II of the Rome Statute.[5] The listed crimes are limited to genocide, crimes against humanity, war crimes, and aggression.[6] Additionally, gender-based crimes have been included under genocide, crimes against humanity, and war crimes, and these are described in articles six to eight under the Statute.[7] The inclusion of gender-based crimes is an important aspect of the ICC, as stated by the UN Secretary-General in 2005: "Sexual-based violence which may have occurred before, during and

4 O'Brien "Sexual Exploitation and Beyond", above n 1, at 808; Burke, above n 1, at 320; Vezina, above n 1, at 447.

5 *Rome Statute of the International Criminal Court* 2187 UNTS 3 (opened for signature 17 July 1998, entered into Force 1 July 2002) [Rome Statute].

6 Rome Statute, art 6 (genocide), art 7 (crimes against humanity), art 8 (war crimes), art 8 *bis* (definition of crime of aggression adopted in 2010).

7 Rome Statute, arts 6(b) and (c),7(1)(g), 8(2)(b)(xxii) and 8(2)(c)(vi).

after conflict can seriously jeopardise peacebuilding efforts during this early phase".[8] Sexual exploitation and abuse by peacekeepers can fall under this general concern. However, the ICC has been constructed with a narrowly defined jurisdiction that will exclude sexual exploitation by peacekeeping personnel.

Many forms of sexual exploitation and abuse are committed in the context of opportunistic situations. Although it is possible, it is nevertheless unlikely that sexual exploitation and abuse by peacekeepers would fulfil the requirements of rape or sexual violence for the purposes of genocide, war crimes, and crimes against humanity.[9] These requirements include that the sexual exploitation committed be "directed towards a civilian population as a whole" and be a "widespread and systematic attack". There also must be evidence that the abuse was part of an overall policy.[10] However, some authors[11] have argued that sexual abuse and sexual exploitation should be included in the Rome Statute as separate crimes.

A new crime of sexual exploitation and abuse by peacekeepers?

The drafting history of the Rome Statute reveals that tightly defined crimes were preferred in order to gain widespread agreement across many states. Although at the negotiation stage some states preferred a broad range of crimes, it became apparent that in order to reach consensus, the listed crimes would need to be clearly and narrowly defined.[12] Additionally, the agreed list represented the most serious international crimes of universal concern, or so-called core crimes.[13] Such a narrow window in which to introduce new crimes will hinder the adoption of sexual exploitation and abuse by peacekeepers into the Rome Statute. Nevertheless, it is possible for the Rome Statute to be amended in order to extend its jurisdiction or add new crimes.

The mechanism on hand to make such changes is agreement of the Assembly of State Parties (ASP) at a Review Conference on the Rome Statute, the first of which was held in 2010.[14] The ASP acts as the legislative body to the Rome Statute. Therefore, any new crime would need the support of these states. Proposals for new crimes are considered by the Working Group on

8 *United Nations World Summit Outcome* GA Res, A/Res/60/1 (2005).

9 But see Burke, above n 1; Du Plessis and Pete, above n 1; and O'Brien "Sexual Exploitation and Beyond", above n 1.

10 Rome Statute, art 7.

11 O'Brien, "Sexual Exploitation and Beyond", above n 1, at 826; Quenivet, above n 1, at 411.

12 B Broomhall *International Justice and the International Criminal Court: Between Sovereignty and the Rule of Law* (Oxford University Press, Oxford, 2003) at 76; Rome Statute, art 5.

13 T Otto "The Object of Review Mechanisms: Statutes' Provisions, Elements of Crimes and Rules of Procedure and Evidence" in R Bellelli (ed) *International Criminal Justice: Law and Practice from the Rome Statute to Its Review* (Ashgate, Surrey, 2010) 355 at 370.

14 Rome Statute, art 121.

Amendments (WGA).[15] There have been several such proposals, including for terrorism and drug trafficking, but to date, none have been successful.[16]

The Working Group considers new crimes with certain principles in mind in order to appropriately justify their inclusion in the Rome Statute alongside genocide and crimes against humanity. Additional crimes proposed by states should attract universal condemnation.[17] For example, the drug trafficking proposal has been described by some states as traditionally a domestic law issue.[18] Although its transnational nature means that trafficking of narcotic drugs affects more than one state, it is not generally considered to have universal impact.[19] This may have implications for sexual exploitation by peacekeepers as defined by the UN; the current definition includes survival sex and may be considered a purely domestic issue.[20]

The "universal" aspect of sexual exploitation and abuse by peacekeepers could be supported by the very fact that UN peacekeepers represent the international community. The context in which sexual abuse occurs may also have an impact on the truly international character of such conduct. The position of trust and differential of power present in the peacekeeper–beneficiary-of-assistance dynamic adds to a potentially coercive situation in post-conflict territories.[21] However, the context still does not align with the unique characteristic associated with the current crimes listed: that the conduct be committed as part of a wider policy or is widespread and systematic.[22] As Harrington argues, the primary focus of the ICC when it was created was to prosecute persons for political or military atrocities committed as part of a widespread and/or systematic attack on civilians or towards a particular group of civilians.[23] Generally, it was not envisioned that prosecutions of crimes committed outside this context would be tried by the ICC.[24] The current critique of the proposals for terrorism and drug trafficking supports this conclusion.[25]

A new provision in the Rome Statute may be justified by pointing to the increased international attention paid to the protection of human rights during

15 *Official Record of the Assembly of State Parties to the Rome Statute of the International Criminal Court* ICC-ASP/8/Res.6 (2011).
16 *Proposal for the Inclusion of the Crime of Terrorism in the Rome Statute* ICC-ASP/10/32 Annex III (2011); *Trinidad and Tobago and Belize* ICC-ASP/10/32 Annex IV (2011) (on drug trafficking).
17 *Resolutions and Recommendations Adopted by the Assembly of State Parties* ICC-ASP/11/20 Annex II (2012) at [9].
18 *Report on the Working Group on Amendments* ICC-ASP/10/32 (2011) at [19].
19 At [19].
20 UN Secretary-General's Bulletin *Special Measures for Protection from Sexual Exploitation and Sexual Abuse* SG B, ST/SGB/2003/13 (9 October 2003) [S-G Bulletin (2003)] at 1.
21 O'Brien "Sexual Exploitation and Beyond", above n 1, at 826.
22 Harrington, above n 3, at 143.
23 At 143.
24 At 143.
25 *Report on the Working Group on Amendments,* above n 18, at [16] and [21].

and after conflict. The importance of human rights is pointed out in the Rome Statute itself and in all resolutions adopted by the ASP.[26] At the time of state negotiations, the inclusion of gender-based crimes was evidence of progressive drafting.[27] However, the definitions themselves had already been thoroughly discussed in both ad hoc international tribunals: International Criminal Tribunal for the Former Yugoslavia (ICTY)[28] and the International Criminal Tribunal for Rwanda (ICTR).[29] Therefore, there was sufficient legal support for their inclusion. The same cannot be said for sexual exploitation and abuse by peacekeepers.

As discussed previously, not all forms of sexual exploitation and abuse are reflected in human rights treaties. There is no universally agreed definition. In the case of the terrorism proposal to the Working Group on Amendments, it was an important factor that there was no universally agreed definition of "terrorism".[30] It has been argued by O'Brien and Quenivet that a criminal definition of sexual exploitation and abuse could be developed from the UN Secretary-General's *Special Measures for Protection from Sexual Exploitation and Sexual Abuse* (S-G Bulletin).[31] However, the definition of sexual exploitation in particular under the Bulletin is ambiguous and highly criticised in feminist scholarship. Survival sex as a discrete notion is not found anywhere else in international law. This would have a dramatic impact on any proposed universal definition. Additionally, the S-G Bulletin is not drafted with the intention of being a basis for criminal prosecution, but is instead a creature of policy. Again, there is no universally agreed definition on which to draw an international crime. If in the unlikely circumstance a new provision governing sexual exploitation by peacekeepers was accepted into the Rome Statute, ICC prosecution would nevertheless be hindered.

Complementarity principle

The principle of complementarity is considered fundamental to the ICC.[32] This principle deals with the ICC's relationship with national courts. Essentially, the Court cannot investigate or prosecute a case unless a state that has jurisdiction over the case is unable or unwilling to do so.[33] Even then, the ICC Prosecutor

26 *Strengthening the International Criminal Court and the Assembly of State Parties* ICC-ASP/11/Res.8 (2012) at 45; Rome Statute, arts 21(3), 36(3)(b)(ii) and 69(7).
27 S Ratner, J Abrams and J Bischoff *Accountability for Human Rights Atrocities in International Law: Beyond the Nuremberg Legacy* (3rd ed, Oxford University Press, New York, 2009) at 234.
28 *Prosecutor v Furundzija (Judgment)* ICTY Trial Chamber IT-95–17/1-T, 10 December 1998.
29 *The Prosecutor v Jean-Paul Akayesu (Judgment)* ICTR Trial Chamber ICTR-96–4-T, 2 September 1998.
30 *Report on the Working Group on Amendments*, above n 18, at [14].
31 O'Brien "Sexual Exploitation and Beyond", above n 1, at 826; Quenivet, above n 1, at 411.
32 *Report of the Bureau on Stocktaking: Complementarity* "Taking Stock of the Principle of Complementarity: Bridging the Gap" ICC-ASP/8/20/Add.1 (2010) at [3].
33 Rome Statute, art 17(1)(a).

must notify states that have jurisdiction of the ICC's intention to prosecute.[34] Additionally, an offender cannot be tried in the ICC if the case has already been heard in a national court.[35] The complementarity principle is specified in article 17 of the Rome Statute, which also details in what circumstances a state is considered "unwilling" or "unable" to investigate and prosecute. A state is deemed unwilling to investigate or prosecute if the alleged offender is being shielded by that state, if there is unjustified delay in bringing an investigation or prosecution, or if proceedings are not impartial.[36] A total collapse of legal or administrative institutions would render a state unable to investigate and prosecute under the Rome Statute.[37] Overall, the ICC is meant to be a Court of last resort.[38]

Applying the complementarity principle to sexual exploitation and abuse by peacekeepers would be beneficial, because TCC inaction would be remedied with the ICC's secondary jurisdiction. A TCC would also need to ensure the new crime is considered a crime under its domestic criminal law in order to avoid being deemed unable to prosecute and thereby possibly triggering ICC jurisdiction.[39] Moreover, it is important to note that the ICC also has the advantage of an established judicial system with agreed standards of investigation, evidence, and procedure.[40] Judges, registrars, and other personnel are already sourced and a budget is already in place.

In order to ascertain whether a state is unwilling or unable to investigate or prosecute, there would need to be evidence or monitoring in place.[41] Evidence could be attained through TCC reports to the UN, as required by the Memorandum of Understanding (MOU).[42] Therefore, some commentators argue that the knowledge that the ICC may investigate an allegation may at least encourage TCCs to comply with reporting obligations under the MOU.[43] Moreover, the Rome Statute goes further than the MOU in relation to where such information can be obtained. The ICC Prosecutor, for example, may gather information from states themselves, nongovernmental organisations (NGOs), intergovernmental organisations, and "other reliable sources".[44] Additionally, it can be presumed that

34 Rome Statute, art 18(1).
35 Rome Statute, arts 17(1)(c) and 17(1)(d).
36 Rome Statute, art 17(2)(a)-(c).
37 TH McCormack and S Robertson "Jurisdictional Aspects of the Rome Statute for the New International Criminal Court" (1999) *Melbourne University Law Review* 635 at 645.
38 *Report of the Bureau on Stocktaking: Complementarity*, above n 32, at [3].
39 McCormack and Robertson, above n 37, at 645.
40 The Rules of Procedure and Evidence *Official Records of the Assembly of States Parties to the Rome Statute of the International Criminal Court* ICC-ASP/1/3 and Corr. 1 Part II.A (New York, 2002).
41 Du Plessis and Pete, above n 1, at 13; Rome Statute, art 14(2).
42 *Manual on Policies and Procedures concerning the Reimbursement and Control of Contingent-Owned Equipment of Troop/Police Contributors Participating in Peacekeeping Missions (COE Manual)* GA, A/c.5/69/18 (2014) Ch 9 Memorandum of Understanding at art *sexiens* [7.24].
43 Burke, above n 1, at 363; Du Plessis and Pete, above n 1, at 13.
44 Rome Statute, art 15; see also McCormack and Robertson, above n 37, at 642.

if TCCs continued to be unwilling to prosecute, then the ICC would have jurisdiction. Such jurisdiction of the Court is unlikely to be welcomed by many TCCs and so may encourage such states to genuinely investigate and prosecute cases of sexual exploitation and abuse.

However, the evidence and monitoring required in order to prove that a TCC is unwilling or unable to investigate or prosecute is a disadvantage flowing from the complementarity principle. TCCs have been lax in their reporting duties, and the level of detail provided may vary state to state. As a result, reporting may not be a wholly reliable source of information. There may have to be further investigation into the reasons behind non-accountability. Such intrusive steps are likely to be rejected by TCCs, particularly when concerning the conduct of military contingent members. Moreover, the delay that will inevitably occur between the case being transferred to the TCC and the determination that the state has failed to investigate or prosecute in order to trigger ICC jurisdiction can lead to a number of issues. Such issues include the likelihood that the alleged offender, witnesses, and even the victim have relocated or are otherwise difficult to locate in order to properly investigate the case. As a result, justice may never be seen to be done. For these reasons, the complementarity principle may mean that ICC jurisdiction does not in fact fill the accountability gap.

Prosecutorial discretion

As O'Brien rightly points out, prosecutorial discretion may be the most limiting factor on ICC prosecution of sexual exploitation and abuse by peacekeepers.[45] In order to safeguard the independence of the ICC Prosecutor, considerable discretion has been granted under the Rome Statute.[46] The Prosecutor may choose which cases or situations to investigate.[47] The crime must be of sufficient gravity to warrant the exercise of ICC jurisdiction.[48] As part of prosecutorial discretion, the Prosecutor may consider a number of factors in order to assess the gravity of the crime alleged.[49]

The gravity threshold described by the preamble of the Rome Statute dictates that the Court shall prosecute "the most serious crimes of concern to the international community as a whole" and such "grave" crimes that threaten international peace and security.[50] According to the ICC Prosecutor, the gravity of the crime is central for admissibility.[51] The importance of gravity is reiterated several

45 M O'Brien "Prosecutorial Discretion as an Obstacle to Prosecution of United Nations Peacekeepers by the International Criminal Court: The Big Fish/Small Fish Debate and the Gravity Threshold" (2012) *Journal of International Criminal Justice* 525.
46 At 527.
47 Rome Statute, art 15.
48 Rome Statute, arts 17(1)(d), 53(1)(b) and 53(2)(b).
49 O'Brien "Prosecutorial Discretion as an Obstacle to Prosecution of United Nations Peacekeepers by the International Criminal Court", above n 45, at 534–536.
50 Rome Statute, Preamble.
51 *Paper on Some Policy Issues before the Office of the Prosecutor* ICC-OPT (2003) at 7.

times throughout the Rome Statute.[52] Overall, the policy favoured by the ICC Prosecutor is to focus on "representative rather than comprehensive" cases.[53] This means that not all cases that come within the jurisdiction of the Court will be investigated or prosecuted.

The ICC Prosecutor will favour prosecution of the most senior leaders rather than lower-ranking officials or soldiers. The general policy of the Prosecutor is to focus on individuals who "bear the most responsibility".[54] This generally equates to higher-ranking officials.[55] Additionally, this recognises the reality that the "Court will never be able to prosecute all those responsible for crimes under its jurisdiction in a given situation".[56] This limitation also acknowledges the restricted resources and budget allocated to the Court itself.[57] Although it is unclear from statistics provided by the UN Secretary-General in his annual reports on sexual exploitation and abuse in peacekeeping, it can be assumed that not all allegations are directed towards high-ranking personnel.[58] A single act of rape by a low-ranking peacekeeper may not reach the required threshold. This general restriction in the assessment of gravity may severely limit ICC jurisdiction over peacekeepers.

The practice of the ICC Prosecutor indicates that the number of victims is a highly valued factor when assessing gravity.[59] As noted by both Burke and O'Brien, this may considerably limit the admissibility of sexual exploitation and abuse by peacekeepers.[60] Although the number of victims in the Central African Republic in 2016 overall pushed over 200, the usual number of victims per allegation is unlikely to be as high.[61] Moreover, in dismissing a potential case, the Prosecutor has pointed out the number of victims of current cases before the Court to be in the hundreds or thousands. Waiting for such a "magic number" of victims is particularly unsatisfactory, because it is not the number of victims of sexual exploitation and abuse that is concerning, it is the fact that these abuses happen at all. In circumstances where the local population is meant to be protected by peacekeepers, that acts of sexual exploitation and abuse are committed by these "protectors" is the most alarming aspect of such violations. One victim

52 Rome Statute, Preamble, arts 17, 53, 59, 77, 78, 84, 85, 90 and 93.
53 B Schiff *Building the International Criminal Court* (Cambridge University Press, New York, 2008) at 118.
54 *Paper on Some Policy Issues*, above n 51, at 3 and 7.
55 O'Brien "Prosecutorial Discretion as an Obstacle to Prosecution of United Nations Peacekeepers by the International Criminal Court", above n 45, at 528.
56 *Report of the Bureau on Stocktaking: Complementarity*, above n 32, at [12].
57 At [15].
58 O'Brien, "Prosecutorial Discretion as an Obstacle to Prosecution of United Nations Peacekeepers by the International Criminal Court", above n 45, at 531.
59 At 531.
60 Burke, above n 1, at 348–350.
61 M Deschamps, HB Jallow and Y Sooka *Taking Action on Sexual Exploitation and Abuse by Peacekeepers: Report of an Independent Review on Sexual Exploitation and Abuse by International Peacekeeping Forces in the Central African Republic* (December, 2015).

should be enough to be a valued factor when assessing gravity. For sexual exploitation and abuse to be considered, a different approach would need to be taken by the Prosecutor in assessment of gravity, such as the nature of the crimes themselves, or the impact on the victims and their communities, or the violation of trust in the peacekeeping mandate.[62]

Burke's and O'Brien's counterargument to the barrier prosecutorial discretion presents is an interesting one and deserves discussion.[63] Peacekeepers are potentially given special status under the Rome Statute via article 8(2)(e)(iii) when they are victims of intentional attacks. This provision has been used once in connection to a case against two rebel leaders of a movement in Sudan, who allegedly carried out an attack that killed 12 peacekeepers.[64] The number of victims in this case was small. However, as the victims in this case were peacekeepers, they were viewed as having a special status, which had an impact on the Prosecutor's assessment of gravity. O'Brien argues that because peacekeepers have special status as victims, thereby having a bearing on the assessment of gravity, then the same should apply to peacekeepers as offenders.[65] However, this provision does not apply to all peacekeepers. Where the mandate of the mission requires peacekeepers to take the role of combatants or allows for self-defence, they will be considered part of the conflict and will not be afforded special protection.[66] Consequently, Burke's and O'Brien's counterargument would result in unequal distribution of justice, as this special status may apply to one group of peacekeepers but not to others. This is unsatisfactory. This special status would need to apply to peacekeepers as a group, regardless of whether they are party to armed conflict or not.

Security Council referral

An additional triggering mechanism for the ICC that might be an advantage in the context of peacekeeping is a Security Council referral. Because the Security Council has indicated its commitment to responding to sexual exploitation and abuse already through Resolution 2272,[67] it might be possible for the Council to refer situations to the ICC through article 13(b) of the Rome Statute. Referring a situation that covers a peacekeeping operation is advantageous, because it may mean that sexual exploitation and abuse committed by contingent members from

62 O'Brien, "Prosecutorial Discretion as an Obstacle to Prosecution of United Nations Peacekeepers by the International Criminal Court", above n 45, at 535.

63 Burke, above n 1, at 357; O'Brien "Prosecutorial Discretion as an Obstacle to Prosecution of United Nations Peacekeepers by the International Criminal Court", above n 45, at 532–533.

64 M Bangura "Prosecuting the Crime of Attack on Peacekeepers: A Prosecutor's Challenge" (2010) 23 *Leiden Journal of International Law* 165 at 174.

65 O'Brien "Prosecutorial Discretion as an Obstacle to Prosecution of United Nations Peacekeepers by the International Criminal Court", above n 45, at 533.

66 Bangura, above n 64, at 168.

67 *Security Council Resolution 2272* SC Res, S/Res/2272 (2016).

TCCs not currently party to the Rome Statute could be caught within the scope of ICC jurisdiction. This would include India and Pakistan, major contributing states not party to the Rome Statute. However, situations are often tied to territories rather than particular individuals; thus, it would be the host state and alleged crimes therein that would be referred.[68] Presumably, more than just peacekeeping crimes could come within the ambit of the Court's jurisdiction as a result. This might not be particularly wise or reasonable, given that many host states are on the African continent.[69] Because the ICC has come under scrutiny from the African Union for allegedly targeting African states in their current situations, with some states parties threatening to leave the Rome Statute, it might be considered problematic for the ICC to then be referred further African states.[70] Additionally, in the end, the ICC Prosecutor still maintains the discretion to ultimately open a formal investigation into cases.[71]

Conclusion

Having discussed the relevant theories on the potential for the ICC to deal with sexual exploitation and abuse by peacekeepers, it is unlikely the ICC can provide a legitimate avenue for filling the accountability gap. It is doubtful that sexual exploitation and abuse by peacekeepers will fit within the narrowly defined crimes currently listed in the Rome Statute. Furthermore, to attempt to introduce a new provision into the Statute would be challenging, given the lack of universality attached to the crimes and lack of agreed definition. The complementarity principle means that the ICC may have secondary jurisdiction; however, the required evidence to prove that a TCC is unable or unwilling to prosecute its nationals would mean long delays and possibly intrusive monitoring. Finally, prosecutorial discretion favours high-ranking officials and a higher number of victims in the assessment of gravity. For these reasons, ICC jurisdiction is unlikely to be the solution for holding peacekeepers to account for sexual exploitation and abuse. As it is unlikely that national (host state) or international courts alone can provide an adequate solution to the accountability gap, it is perhaps time to consider a hybrid court instead.

68 WA Schabas *An Introduction to the International Criminal Court* (5th ed, Cambridge University Press, Cambridge, 2017) at 143.

69 The Central African Republic, Darfur, and the Democratic Republic of the Congo are already situation states, but to refer peacekeeping states would mean the further inclusion of Liberia, Mali, and Western Sahara.

70 See for example "South Africa to Quit International Criminal Court" *Al Jazeera* (22 October 2016) <www.aljazeera.com>.

71 Although the ICC Prosecutor must undertake a preliminary examination and decide whether there is a reasonable basis to continue with formal investigation. See Schabas, above n 68, at 142.

References

M Bangura "Prosecuting the Crime of Attack on Peacekeepers: A Prosecutor's Challenge" (2010) 23 *Leiden Journal of International Law* 165

B Broomhall *International Justice and the International Criminal Court: Between Sovereignty and the Rule of Law* (Oxford University Press, Oxford, 2003)

R Burke "UN Military Peacekeeper Complicity in Sexual Abuse: The ICC or a Tri-hybrid Court" in M Bergsmo (ed) *Thematic Prosecution of International Sex Crimes* (Torkel Opsahl, Beijing, 2012)

M Deschamps, HB Jallow and Y Sooka *Taking Action on Sexual Exploitation and Abuse by Peacekeepers: Report of an Independent Review on Sexual Exploitation and Abuse by International Peacekeeping Forces in the Central African Republic* (December, 2015)

M Du Plessis and S Pete "Who Guards the Guards? The ICC and Serious Crimes Committed by United Nations Peacekeepers in Africa" (2004) 12 *African Security Review* 5

A Harrington "Victims of Peace: Current Abuse Allegations against UN Peacekeepers and the Role of Law in Preventing Them in the Future" (2005) 12 *ILSA Journal of International & Comparative Law* 125

Manual on Policies and Procedures concerning the Reimbursement and Control of Contingent-Owned Equipment of Troop/Police Contributors Participating in Peacekeeping Missions (COE Manual) GA, A/c.5/69/18 (2014)

TH McCormack and S Robertson "Jurisdictional Aspects of the Rome Statute for the New International Criminal Court" (1999) *Melbourne University Law Review* 635

M O'Brien "Prosecutorial Discretion as an Obstacle to Prosecution of United Nations Peacekeepers by the International Criminal Court: The Big Fish/Small Fish Debate and the Gravity Threshold" (2012) *Journal of International Criminal Justice* 525

M O'Brien "Sexual Exploitation and Beyond: Using the Rome Statute of the International Criminal Court to Prosecute UN Peacekeepers for Gender-Based Crimes" (2011) 11 *International Criminal Law Review* 803

Official Record of the Assembly of State Parties to the Rome Statute of the International Criminal Court ICC-ASP/8/Res.6 (2011)

T Otto "The Object of Review Mechanisms: Statutes' Provisions, Elements of Crimes and Rules of Procedure and Evidence" in R Bellelli (ed) *International Criminal Justice: Law and Practice from the Rome Statute to Its Review* (Ashgate, Surrey, 2010)

Paper on Some Policy Issues before the Office of the Prosecutor ICC-OPT (2003)

Proposal for the Inclusion of the Crime of Terrorism in the Rome Statute ICC-ASP/10/32 Annex III (2011)

Prosecutor v Furundzija (Judgment) ICTY Trial Chamber IT-95–17/1-T, 10 December 1998

N Quenivet "The Role of the International Criminal Court in the Prosecution on Peacekeepers for Sexual Offences" in R Arnold (ed) *Law Enforcement within the Framework of Peace Support Operations* (Koninklijke Brill NV, Leiden, 2008)

S Ratner, J Abrams and J Bischoff *Accountability for Human Rights Atrocities in International Law: Beyond the Nuremberg Legacy* (3rd ed, Oxford University Press, New York, 2009)

Report of the Bureau on Stocktaking: Complementarity "Taking Stock of the Principle of Complementarity: Bridging the Gap" ICC-ASP/8/20/Add.1 (2010)

Report on the Working Group on Amendments ICC-ASP/10/32 (2011)

Resolutions and Recommendations Adopted by the Assembly of State Parties ICC-ASP/11/20 Annex II (2012)

Rome Statute of the International Criminal Court 2187 UNTS 3 (opened for signature 17 July 1998, entered into force 1 July 2002)

WA Schabas *An Introduction to the International Criminal Court* (5th ed, Cambridge University Press, Cambridge, 2017)

B Schiff *Building the International Criminal Court* (Cambridge University Press, New York, 2008)

Security Council Resolution 2272 SC Res, S/Res/2272 (2016)

"South Africa to Quit International Criminal Court" *Al Jazeera* (22 October 2016) <www.aljazeera.com>

Strengthening the International Criminal Court and the Assembly of State Parties ICC-ASP/11/Res.8 (2012)

The Prosecutor v Jean-Paul Akayesu (Judgment) ICTR Trial Chamber ICTR-96–94-T, 2 September 1998

The Rules of Procedure and Evidence *Official Records of the Assembly of States Parties to the Rome Statute of the International Criminal Court* ICC-ASP/1/3 and Corr. 1 Part II.A (New York, 2002)

Trinidad and Tobago and Belize ICC-ASP/10/32 Annex IV (2011)

United Nations World Summit Outcome GA Res, A/Res/60/1 (2005)

UN Secretary-General's Bulletin *Special Measures for Protection from Sexual Exploitation and Sexual Abuse* SG B, ST/SGB/2003/13 (9 October 2003)

RA Vezina "Combating Impunity in Haiti: Why the ICC Should Prosecute Sexual Abuse by UN Peacekeepers" (2012) 1 *Ave Maria International Law Journal* 431

6 A Series of Hybrid Courts

In order to centralise the interests of victims and decentralise the role of troop-contributing countries (TCCs), this chapter will argue for the establishment of a series of hybrid courts. The hybrid model will be put forward as the option that best serves the underlying principles of this book: namely, that justice will be seen to be done by having the trial within the community where the crime has taken place, that an appropriate form of host state ownership can be structurally facilitated, and that the United Nations (UN) should show leadership by creating a centralised administrative system for the series of courts. Furthermore, having sexual exploitation and abuse prosecuted on the international stage would recognise the seriousness of such conduct and the gravity of harm caused to victims. Additionally, this chapter will also argue that sexual exploitation and abuse committed by peacekeepers is an international crime.

For structure, this chapter will start with a brief examination of the hybrid model. Such courts have been utilised in Kosovo, Sierra Leone, East Timor, and Cambodia. These courts will be compared and common attributes will be drawn in order to determine whether they are applicable to the peacekeeping context. This chapter will then consider the arguments previously made for a special court for peacekeepers, which will include the tri-hybrid model put forward by academic Roisin Burke. This model will be significantly developed further.

A proposed new framework will be submitted, and possible options for both the legal basis of multiple courts and their structure will be explored. This will include a discussion of three potential barriers to a series of new courts: firstly, the material jurisdiction and possible offences within sexual exploitation and abuse; secondly, the political will of states (i.e., how states will sign up to such courts); and thirdly, resourcing such courts.

Hybrid courts – common and defining features

So-called hybrid tribunals are internationalised national courts.[1] These courts have been utilised as a response to mass atrocities and typically have jurisdiction over

1 R Burke *Sexual Exploitation and Abuse by UN Military Contingents: Moving Beyond the Current Status Quo and Responsibility under International Law* (Leiden, Brill, 2014) at 385.

both international and domestic crimes.[2] They also tend to have mixed international and national personnel acting as registrars, judges, and lawyers. Hybrid tribunals have been established in Kosovo, Sierra Leone, East Timor, and Cambodia with varying degrees of success.

The Regulation 64 Panels were implemented as a response to the Serbian-directed ethnic cleansing of local Albanians in Kosovo.[3] In 1999 the UN Interim Administration Mission in Kosovo (UNMIK) was confronted with the mass investigation, detention, and prosecution of alleged offenders.[4] The physical infrastructure of Kosovo's legal system was destroyed.[5] Only few local Albanians were legally trained.[6] Applying local law and international human rights standards, the Panels held trials against accused war criminals using mixed international and national personnel to fill the gaps in expertise.[7]

Arguably one of the more successful examples of hybrid tribunals, in terms of creation and overall number of prosecutions completed, is the Special Court of Sierra Leone (SCSL).[8] After a civil war that spanned a decade, Sierra Leone's fractured legal system faced the investigation and prosecution of mass atrocities, including the recruitment of child soldiers.[9] The government of Sierra Leone negotiated an agreement with the UN establishing a hybrid tribunal to put war criminals on trial using a mix of international and national personnel.[10]

In the wake of the vote for independence from Indonesian rule, the Timorese were subjected to targeted killings by the Indonesian army and local militia groups in 1999.[11] The Special Panels of the Dili District Court was created to prosecute

2 S Williams *Hybrid and International Criminal Tribunals* (Hart Publishing, Oxford, 2012) at 385.

3 *Security Council Resolution 1244* SC Res, S/Res/1244 (1999).

4 LA Dickinson "Notes and Comments: The Promise of Hybrid Courts" (2003) *The American Journal of International Law* 295 at 297.

5 At 297.

6 At 297.

7 *Regulation 1999/1 on the Authority of the Interim Administration in Kosovo* UNMIK/REG/1999/1 (1999), *Regulation 1999/24 on the Law Applicable in Kosovo* UNMIK/REG/1999/24 (1999). International criminal law was applied through pre-existing domestic legislation. See J Cerone and C Baldwin "Explaining and Evaluating the UNMIK Court System" in CR Romano, A Nollkaemper and JK Kleffner (eds) *Internationalized Criminal Courts: Sierra Leone, East Timor, Kosovo and Cambodia* (Oxford University Press, Oxford, 2004) 41 at 44–47.

8 Argued by D Cohen "Hybrid Justice in East Timor, Sierra Leone and Cambodia: Lessons Learned and Prospects for the Future" (2007) 43 *Stanford Journal of International Law* 1, at 23.

9 Cohen, above n 8, at 11; E Nielsen "Hybrid International Criminal Tribunals: Political Interference and Judicial Independence" (2010) 15 *UCLA Journal of International Law & Foreign Affairs* 289 at 317.

10 *Agreement between the United Nations and the Government of Sierra Leone on the Establishment of a Special Court for Sierra Leone*, Letter dated March 6 2002 from the Secretary-General addressed to the President of the Security Council S/2002/246 (2002).

11 Cohen, above n 8, at 7; S Linton "Rising from the Ashes: The Creation of a Viable Criminal Justice System in East Timor" (2001) 25 *Melbourne University Law Review*

those associated with these mass atrocities.[12] The Special Panels were established as part of the UN peacekeeping operation.[13] In terms of structure, the Special Panels operated within the domestic legal system, with appeals taken up by the national East Timorese Appeals Court (also with mixed international and domestic personnel).[14]

The process of forming the Extraordinary Chambers in the Courts of Cambodia (ECCC) was initiated by the Cambodian government in order to investigate and prosecute those involved in the Khmer Rouge regime, which resulted in the deaths of 1.5 million people from 1975 to 1979.[15] An eight-year delay between the request for a tribunal and the establishment of the ECCC was partially due to many disagreements between the government and the UN and concern about possible corruption on the part of the Cambodian government.[16] The ECCC itself comprises three Trial Chambers with mixed international and domestic personnel.[17]

These four examples illustrate the diversity of the hybrid model, each with different legal foundations and structures. However, there are a number of common features that can be pulled out and used as a basic blueprint for future hybrid courts. Based on examination of practice, Sarah Williams contends that there are six defining features of the hybrid model:[18] first, that the court should have a

122. Additionally, the *Statue of the Special Court for Sierra Leone* has been the only constituent instrument of the hybrid tribunals to explicitly address criminal conduct by peacekeepers (article 1(3)). This provision has never been utilised. See *Statute of the Special Court for Sierra Leone (2001) as Established by Security Council Resolution 1315* SC Res, S/Res/1315 (2000), arts 2–5.

12 Cohen, above n 8, at 7; Linton, above n 11, at 123-125; *Report of the International Commission of Inquiry on East Timor* S/2000/59 (2000).

13 *Situation of Human Rights in East Timor* GA, A/54/660 (1999) at [6]; *Security Council Resolution 1272* SC Res, S/Res/1272 (1999).

14 *Regulation 2000/15 On the Establishment of Panels with Exclusive Jurisdiction over Serious Criminal Offences* UNTAET/REG/2000/15 (2000) at Section 1.

15 See generally C Etcheson "The Politics of Genocide Justice in Cambodia" in CR Romano, A Nollkaemper and JK Kleffner (eds) *Internationalized Criminal Courts: Sierra Leone, East Timor, Kosovo, and Cambodia* (Oxford University Press, Oxford, 2004) 181; H Horsington "The Cambodian Khmer Rouge Tribunal: The Promise of a Hybrid Tribunal" (2004) 5 *Melbourne Journal of International Law* 462; B Kiernan "Historical and Political Background to the Conflict in Cambodia" in K Ambos and M Othman (eds) *New Approaches in International Criminal Justice: Kosovo, East Timor, Sierra Leone and Cambodia* (Freiburg I Br, Berlin, 2003) 173.

16 *Agreement between the United Nations and the Royal Government of Cambodia concerning the Prosecution under Cambodian Law of Crimes Committed during the Period of Democratic Kampuchea* GA Res, A/Res/57/228 B (2003). See also S Scully "Judging the Success and Failures of the Extraordinary Chambers of the Courts of Cambodia" (2011) 13 *Asian-Pacific Law & Policy Journal* 301 at 322–334.

17 *Agreement between the United Nations and the Royal Government of Cambodia concerning the Prosecution under Cambodian Law of Crimes Committed during the Period of Democratic Kampuchea*, above n 16, art 2 (2)(a)-(b).

18 The following discussion is based off of Williams' "defining features", above n 2, at 249.

criminal function, and secondly, that they are temporary or transitional in nature. Williams's third defining feature is that courts should have a mix of international and domestic personnel. Fourthly, hybrid courts should have international assistance with resources. The fifth feature is the inclusion of both international and domestic crimes. The sixth and final purported attribute is that hybrid tribunals should involve the participation of more than just the affected state.

Hybrid courts – benefits and limitations

The hybrid model has particular conceptual and practical benefits. These can be described broadly as perceived legitimacy, local capacity building, and norm penetration.[19] The domestic location and host state ownership of the court support legitimacy from the point of view of the local population.[20] The inclusion of international personnel can also negate local perceptions of partiality.[21] Mixed international and national personnel can fill gaps in local expertise, and ongoing training and professional development of local personnel promote sustainable accountability once international experts leave, contributing to local capacity building.[22] Moreover, the promotion of local and international networks may lead to adoption and development of broad human rights standards and accountability for serious violations of human rights.

However, it is important to note that the past and present examples of hybrid courts have in practice fallen short of such ideals. The purported success of the hybrid courts has been limited to the number of completed prosecutions of high-ranking officials complicit in international crimes.[23] While these courts "should be commended for establishing accountability as a standard of law and public policy where the alternative was systematic impunity", they struggled with realising the more holistic goals.[24] For example, many hybrid courts were unsuccessful at securing sufficient local ownership to foster legitimacy from the perspective of the community.[25] Conversely, the ECCC has been criticised for allowing too much local ownership, resulting in significant delay and political interference, negatively impacting the perception of

19 Dickinson, above n 4.

20 JD Ciorcian and A Heindel *Law, Meaning and Violence: Hybrid Justice: The Extraordinary Chambers in the Courts of Cambodia* (University of Michigan Press, Michigan, 2014) at 70.

21 P McAuliffe "Hybrid Courts in Retrospect: Of Lost Legacies and Modest Futures" in Y McDermott, W Schabas and N Hayes (eds) *The Ashgate Research Companion to International Criminal Law: Critical Perspectives* (Taylor and Francis, London, 2013) at 455.

22 At 455; see also PK Mendez "The New Wave of Hybrid Tribunals: A Sophisticated Approach to Enforcing International Humanitarian Law or an Idealistic Solution with Empty Promises?" (2009) 20 *Criminal Law Forum* 53.

23 See for example A Cassese *Report on the Special Court for Sierra Leone* (Submitted by the Independent Expert, 2006); *Summary of the Report to the Secretary-General of the Commission of Experts to Review the Prosecution of Serious Violations of Human Rights in Timor-Leste (then East Timor) in 1999* S/2005/458 (2005).

24 McAuliffe, above n 21, at 458.

25 For these criticisms see T Perriello and M Wierda *Lessons from the Deployment of International Judges and Prosecutors in Kosovo* (International Center for Transitional Justice, March 2006); C Reiger and M Wierda *The Serious Crimes Process in Timor-*

impartiality.[26] A focus on prosecution and conviction meant transferring a significant role to international judges and prosecutors and weakening the participation of domestic personnel.[27] Additionally, some hybrid courts lacked the required funding for adequately staffed witness protection units or competent defence counsel.[28] Some scholars[29] argue that the above issues with hybrid courts are related to implementation rather than their underlying ideals. Collectively, the hybrid courts lacked the essential resources and training for community outreach and local inclusivity.[30]

A hybrid model for peacekeeping crimes

The hybrid model is the best option for the investigation and prosecution of sexual exploitation and abuse committed by peacekeepers. The concept of hybridity generally envisions more than one actor or entity in operation together or being mixed in some way. Certainly, previous examples of hybrid courts have involved both domestic and international actors in their structure or day-to-day operation. Adoption of this concept would directly challenge the primary role of TCCs. A hybrid model would instead encourage active cooperation between the three relevant international actors in the peacekeeping context: TCCs, the host state, and the UN.

To date, hybrid courts have been established in the aftermath of mass atrocities, such as genocide or crimes against humanity, and sexual exploitation and abuse by peacekeepers has not yet been accepted as reaching the same level of seriousness as these international crimes. However, although a common feature of hybrid courts is their criminal function, it is not a requirement that they should prosecute solely international crimes as defined by the Rome Statute.[31] As argued further below, sexual exploitation and abuse committed in the peacekeeping context is of international concern, which warrants prosecution at the international level. The use of a hybrid-style court to respond to such conduct would recognise the seriousness of the conduct itself and the gravity of harm caused to victims – a far cry from the status quo.

The broad benefits of the hybrid model align with the goals of this book. Justice is seen to be done because the trial takes place within the affected community. The domestic location overcomes practical limitations currently experienced with offences investigated abroad, such as having greater access to evidence and witnesses.

Leste: In Retrospect (International Center for Transitional Justice, March 2006); P Rapoza "Hybrid Criminal Tribunals and Concept of Ownership: Who Owns the Process?" (2006) 21 *American University International Law Review* 525.

26 Ciorcian and Heindel, above n 20, at 71.

27 McAuliffe, above n 21, at 460.

28 Cohen, above n 8, at 15–17.

29 For example, Dickinson, above n 4, at 307; N Jain "Conceptualising Internationalisation in Hybrid Courts" (2009) 12 *Singapore Yearbook of International Law* 81 at 85.

30 Cohen, above n 8, at 14; McAuliffe, above n 21, at 463.

31 *Report of the Group of Legal Experts on Making the Standards Contained in the Secretary-General's Bulletin Binding on Contingent Members and Standardising the Norms of Conduct so That They Are Applicable to All Categories of Peacekeeping Personnel* GA, A/61/645 (2006) [Group of Legal Experts Report] at [34].

Victims and their communities also have access to information about their complaint, case, or trial. Host state ownership and inclusivity are supported by the notion of hybridity, by having mixed personnel and the ability to build local capacity through the process of a hybrid court. A hybrid model also necessitates incorporating or acknowledging the particular historical, legal, and cultural context of host states; the element of mixing is different depending on each host state, avoiding a one-size-fits-all approach to criminal justice. With a more cooperative function, a hybrid court could also facilitate transparency more easily by reporting the outcome of complaints or cases to the international community quickly, rather than waiting for TCCs to issue reports. Additionally, norm penetration could be central to UN leadership in responding to sexual exploitation and abuse through a hybrid court, as the investigation and prosecution of such behaviour could significantly improve the enforcement of the zero-tolerance policy across peacekeeping operations. Overall, the hybrid model helps centralise the interests of victims and decentralise the role of TCCs.

Hybrid courts have been previously suggested by commentators, including the UN-appointed Group of Legal Experts (in 2006),[32] academic Roisin Burke (in 2014),[33] and Radhika Coomaraswamy, lead author of the global study on the implementation of Security Council Resolution 1325 (in 2015).[34] The Group of Legal Experts argued that "a new international judiciary with jurisdiction to deal with serious crimes by peacekeepers" could fill the accountability gap.[35] Coomaraswamy included among her recommendations related to Resolution 1325 the "establishment of a UN tribunal for sexual exploitation and abuse" for peacekeepers.[36] Coomaraswamy did not include any more information about her recommendation. So far, Burke has been one of the few academics to seriously tackle alternative trial mechanisms in the context of peacekeeping, specifically military contingent members.[37] Although only briefly mentioned by a few other scholars,[38] Burke has broadly explored the possibility of a hybrid tribunal to govern crimes committed by peacekeepers.

32 Group of Legal Experts Report, above n 31.
33 Burke *Sexual Exploitation and Abuse by UN Military Contingents,* above n 1.
34 *Security Council Resolution 1325* SC Res, S/Res/1325 (2000).
35 The Group of Legal Experts Report ultimately dismissed the option due to the perceived limitations that will be discussed below. See Group of Legal Experts Report, above n 31, at [76].
36 R Coomaraswamy *Open Letter to Permanent Representatives of the Security Council Dated 23 June 2015* (2015) at 4; R Coomaraswamy *Preventing Conflict, Transforming Justice, Securing the Peace: A Global Study on the Implementation of United Nations Security Council Resolution 1325* (2015) at 149 and 156–157.
37 R Burke *Sexual Exploitation and Abuse by UN Military Contingents*, above n 1; R Burke "UN Military Peacekeeper Complicity in Sexual Abuse: The ICC or a Tri-hybrid Court" in M Bergsmo (ed) *Thematic Prosecution of International Sex Crimes* (Torkel Opsahl Academic EPublisher, Beijing, 2012) 317.
38 A Cahillane "International Law, Sexual Violence and Peacekeepers" 17 *Irish Student Law Review* 1 at 14; T Innes "The Accountability of Peacekeeping Operations: A Focus on Allegations of Sexual Abuse" (2011) 1 *Warwick Student Law Review* 19 at 31; M Odello "Tackling Criminal Acts in Peacekeeping Operations: The Accountability of Peacekeepers" (2010) 15 *Journal of Conflict & Security Law* 347 at 375; Office of the United Nations High Commissioner for Human Rights *Rule-of-Law*

Under general jurisdictional principles in international law, the criminal conduct of peacekeepers can give rise to both territorial jurisdiction (host state) and jurisdiction based on active personality (TCC). According to Burke, this "dual jurisdiction" should be expressly acknowledged in the creation of a new tribunal.[39] Therefore, jurisdiction should be apportioned between the host state and the TCC, with the UN having a significant role.[40] A "tri-hybrid" model may be a way to reconcile or balance the two perspectives (between host state jurisdiction and TCC exclusive jurisdiction) and the UN itself. However, it should be noted that at the heart of Burke's alternative court is the retention of the primary role of TCCs.[41] Burke's tri-hybrid court would exercise secondary jurisdiction in the event that the TCC is unable or unwilling to take action (similar to the situation of complementarity under the International Criminal Court).[42] Based on purely doctrinal analysis, Burke's model does not challenge the primary role of TCCs, nor does it seek to centralise the interests of victims and their communities. Nevertheless, the emphasis on increased cooperation between TCCs, host states, and the UN in responding to sexual exploitation and abuse by peacekeepers facilitated through a hybrid court underlined by Burke's model is generally supported by the principles of this book. The next section will develop this model further.

A hybrid solution – a series of courts for peacekeepers

In order to improve accountability for sexual exploitation and abuse by peacekeepers in a way that centralises the interests of victims, challenges the primary role of TCCs, and realises the conceptual ideals underlining this book, it is necessary to propose a series of hybrid courts rather than just one. A truly hybrid solution would need to incorporate the ownership of several host states, each with its own unique historic, legal, and cultural contexts. One hybrid court would not be able to achieve this goal. Moreover, for justice to be seen to be done, trials would need to take place where the crime has been committed. Allegations of sexual exploitation and abuse occur in different mission areas simultaneously and so require a series of courts to adequately respond to each allegation in a timely manner, simultaneously.

Tinkering of the current framework of the zero-tolerance policy has not provided a solution; a significantly different approach is required. The creation of a series of hybrid courts for peacekeepers calls for an entirely new structure, tailored to the legal and political landscape of each peacekeeping mission. The remainder of this chapter will examine the possible structure of this model, including the

Tools for Post-Conflict States: Maximising the Legacy of Hybrid Courts (United Nations, New York and Geneva, 2008) at 4.

39 Burke "UN Military Peacekeeper Complicity in Sexual Abuse", above n 37, at 394.

40 At 394.

41 Burke *Sexual Exploitation and Abuse by UN Military Contingents,* above n 1, at 232.

42 At 232; *Rome Statute of the International Criminal Court* 2187 UNTS 3 (opened for signature 17 July 1998, entered into force 1 July 2002) [Rome Statute] art 17.

legal basis, administration, arrest and investigation, temporal jurisdiction, sentencing, and appeals. The chapter will then explore the three potential hurdles to this model: firstly, material jurisdiction; secondly, political will; and thirdly, resources. For consistency, Williams's six defining features of hybrid courts will provide the basis of the structure for the proposed series of hybrid courts for peacekeepers. This chapter will note also that previous examples of hybrid courts have not been fully successful in implementing their holistic goals, and that these limitations must be overcome.

A court of first instance

As discussed above, under Burke's tri-hybrid model the TCC would have primary jurisdiction. Justification for the retention of exclusive or primary criminal jurisdiction by TCCs has been sovereign prerogative.[43] This is the notion that the criminal investigation and prosecution of military members are a special part of a state's exercise of sovereignty and an integral feature of the command and control structures of their forces.[44] The fear associated with removing the exclusive jurisdiction of TCCs is the decline of contributed troops from states.[45] The UN may fail to draw enough personnel from states if there is a possibility that another state or institution would investigate and prosecute their military members. This fear has never been tested. Moreover, member states who contribute troops receive funding from the UN; for the top contributing states (many of which are developing states), peacekeeping can generate a substantial amount of funding for their local economies.[46] The question is whether such states would likely forgo monetary benefits if the exclusive jurisdiction were removed. Furthermore, sexual exploitation and abuse are human rights abuses and, when committed by peacekeepers, this is of grave international concern. The international community should be able to expect that states will continue to contribute troops even if personnel are held accountable by an independent judicial institution.

For a series of hybrid courts to be a solution, the response to allegations of sexual exploitation and abuse would need to be fast, transparent, and effective. The new framework would need to be the first response, and so the courts should be of first instance. Creating courts around the idea of first instance, rather than of secondary jurisdiction or a court of last resort, would decentralise the role of TCCs. The new framework would instead represent the collective enforcement of the zero-tolerance policy. Being of first instance would mean that relevant information would be collected by and received from one entity, rather than from

43 Burke *Sexual Exploitation and Abuse by UN Military Contingents,* above n 1, at 245.
44 At 245; see also Secretary-General *A Comprehensive Strategy to Eliminate Future Sexual Exploitation and Abuse in United Nations Peacekeeping Operations* GA, A/59/710 (2005) prepared by Prince Zeid Ra'ad Zeid Al-Hussein [Zeid Report] at [33].
45 Burke *Sexual Exploitation and Abuse by UN Military Contingents,* above n 1, at 245; Zeid Report, above n 44, at [33].
46 See for example, K Krishnasamy "Pakistan's Peacekeeping Experiences" (2002) 9 *International Peacekeeping* 103 at 111–113; see also United Nations Peacekeeping "Financing Peacekeeping" (August 2015) <www.un.org>.

the TCC and the UN separately. This would enable victims to gain greater access to information related to their own complaints and cases.

If the new hybrid court followed models such as Burke's, then TCCs would need to be deemed as unwilling or unable to exercise jurisdiction themselves in order for the alternative court to have jurisdiction. This is similar to the requirements under the Rome Statute for the exercise of jurisdiction by the International Criminal Court (ICC).[47] Chapter five noted that this was a negative attribute of the ICC. Although it could be argued that the possibility of another court having jurisdiction over their personnel may encourage more states to take steps in investigating and prosecuting sexual exploitation and abuse cases, the time delay between the decision or failure to exercise jurisdiction and the conclusion that the state is indeed unable or unwilling may drastically hinder subsequent efforts to ensure accountability.[48] In criminal cases involving sexual conduct, the timeliness of investigation is essential to proving an offence in prosecution, particularly in regard to collecting medical or forensic evidence.[49] Issues relating to undue delay have been recognised in the Memorandum of Understanding (MOU), which provides that where a TCC has not notified the UN of its intention to investigate within ten working days, then the UN will initiate its own administrative investigation in order to preserve evidence.[50] Furthermore, leaving TCCs with the primary role would not ensure transparency to victims or their communities. There have already been numerous attempts made by the UN to encourage such reporting, and these changes have not been sufficient.[51] Thus, for a court to have secondary jurisdiction or be of last resort would not solve the accountability problem. A court of first instance would likely be a faster avenue for justice.

In order to facilitate courts of first instance, absolute immunity, currently granted to military contingent members, should be replaced with functional immunity. This would allow military contingent members to be immune from host state legal action (or the jurisdiction of another judicial institution) involving conduct performed within their official capacity and would align with immunity granted to other categories of peacekeeping personnel.[52] Acts within official capacity could

47 Rome Statute, art 17.

48 For the point that exercise of jurisdiction by another court may encourage domestic prosecution, see generally Y Shany "How Can International Criminal Courts Have a Greater Impact on National Criminal Proceedings? Lessons from the First Decades of International Criminal Justice in Operation" (2013) 46 *Israel Law Review* 431.

49 See generally J Morse "Documenting Mass Rape: Medical Evidence Collection Techniques as Humanitarian Technology" (2014) 8 *Genocide Studies and Prevention: An International Journal* 63.

50 *Manual on Policies and Procedures concerning the Reimbursement and Control of Contingent-Owned Equipment of Troop/Police Contributors Participating in Peacekeeping Missions (COE Manual)* GA, A/c.5/69/18 (2014) Ch 9 Memorandum of Understanding [2007 MOU], art 7 *quater* 3(a).

51 See Office of Internal Oversight Services *Evaluation Report: Evaluation of the Enforcement and Remedial Assistance Efforts for Sexual Exploitation and Abuse by the United Nations and Related Personnel in Peacekeeping Operations* (May 2015) at 22 and 24.

52 See *Model Status of Forces Agreement between the United Nations and Host Countries* GA, A/45/594 (1990) art 47(b) [Model SOFA] art 46.

never include serious misconduct, such as sexual exploitation and abuse. Status-of-Forces Agreements (SOFAs) and MOUs would need to be redrafted to reflect this change.

Legal basis

One of Williams's defining features for hybrid courts generally is that they should require the participation of more than one state. A series of hybrid courts for peacekeepers necessitates the involvement of many states, notably the TCCs and host states. To achieve effective cooperation and build the required framework for hybrid courts, there needs to be a clear agreement between relevant parties. The choice of legal basis for this framework is therefore important. A particular lesson learned from previous practice of hybrid courts was that an agreement between the affected state and the UN was a major advantage to the courts' overall success.[53] In the example of the hybrid court in Kosovo, the local Albanian Kosovars viewed the Panels with scepticism. The lack of confidence in the domestic legal system is likely to have stemmed from the lack of consultation with the affected communities.[54] This can be compared with the process in Sierra Leone, where the government initiated negotiation for the Special Court with the UN. There was also the advantage of having an outreach program so that the local communities had a stronger connection to the Special Court itself.[55] An outreach program to raise awareness of a court and connect its work with the affected communities will be necessary to achieve an adequate level of host state ownership and justice being seen to be done for the victims and their communities.

The difficulty with peacekeeping missions is that each one is different in terms of its mandate and the context of the community in which it is deployed. Each host state may have different needs in terms of justice mechanisms and thus may have different levels of involvement in a court for peacekeepers. The precise split of jurisdiction may depend on each mission and the particular host state. For example, while one host state may have the infrastructure in place to have jurisdiction over the investigation, prosecution, and sentencing, another host state may not. To incorporate the relevant host state's context successfully, an agreement as to the split of jurisdiction would need to be negotiated between the parties. The UN, as the entity undertaking peacekeeping operations, is in the best position to facilitate such negotiations.

Other potential barriers to agreement could involve the host state itself. Depending on the state, there may be a lack of identifiable government with which to consult or negotiate. However, the concept of ownership is not limited to state institutions and can also include local community groups or civil society. Therefore, there may be other groups to negotiate with. However, even where

53 Cohen, above n 8, at 23.
54 Mendez, above n 22, at 76–77.
55 At 79–80; Perriello and Wierda, above n 25, at 35–37.

there are identifiable nation states, they may be weakened by diverse local elites competing for political power.[56] Ongoing conflict and competition for ownership in a hybrid court for peacekeepers might then complicate negotiations.[57] Moreover, the host state itself might be reluctant to engage in dialogue with any international actor for a hybrid court. The overarching goal of the new framework is to hold peacekeepers to account for sexual exploitation and abuse. It may be the case that in such circumstances the principle of UN leadership should prevail, and a hybrid court should be established without formal inclusivity of the host state. This would enable victims to see justice being done notwithstanding a reluctance or failure to secure partial jurisdiction with the host state.

Overall, a necessary first step would be consultation with local communities, especially victims or victim representative organisations, and this could be undertaken by the UN. Specifically, the newly established Victims' Rights Advocate (or similar) would be an ideal position within the UN to engage with victims and local organisations.[58]

(i) Bilateral treaty

Due to its binding nature, a bilateral treaty would be an applicable instrument in which to have an agreement regarding the split of jurisdiction between the UN, TCCs, and host states, perhaps through the pre-existing SOFAs and MOUs.[59] Each host state having its own agreement with the UN would have the greatest chance of reflecting each state's unique context and relevant ownership details. However, this process would be long and tedious if there are fundamental disagreements between the host states and the UN. Also, in separate agreements it may be difficult to reconcile the demands of the host state versus those of the TCC. The structure agreed between the host state and the UN must then be reflected in the corresponding agreements between the UN and TCCs involved.

(ii) Multilateral treaty

Alternatively, there could be a general multilateral treaty determining major structural components of the hybrid courts as well as material jurisdiction, leaving details relating to host state ownership to be negotiated within bilateral agreements. An overarching multilateral treaty could provide a starting point for a framework for a series of hybrid courts, which could be openly debated by member states through the UN General Assembly. This could be less time consuming than solely relying on bilateral agreements while encouraging active cooperation

56 AK Jarstad and L Olsson "Hybrid Peace Ownership in Afghanistan: International Perspectives of Who Owns What and When" (2012) 18 *Global Governance* 105, at 109.

57 At 109.

58 See Secretary-General *Special Measures for Protection from Sexual Exploitation and Sexual Abuse* GA, A/71/818 (2017) at [27]-[35].

59 2007 MOU, above n 50; Model SOFA, art 47(b).

between relevant states. However, a multilateral treaty may mean states can make reservations, perhaps limiting criminalised conduct (to exclude survival sex, for example). Although, states cannot make specific reservations that target the object and purpose of the treaty; as improving accountability for sexual exploitation and abuse committed by peacekeepers would be within the object and purpose of a treaty, then reservations seeking to limit its scope may not be valid.

(iii) Security Council Resolution

A series of hybrid courts may be established through a Security Council resolution. This would avoid the need for state consent and possible issues with host state reluctance or a lack of identifiable local government. Resolution 2272 signalled that sexual exploitation and abuse by peacekeepers is a matter of great concern for the Security Council and that robust action should be taken to hold perpetrators to account.[60] It is therefore reasonable to consider that the Security Council could pass an additional resolution providing a framework for hybrid courts. However, there are certain permanent members of the Council, such as the United States (US), that might veto a resolution. The US has historically been vocal in its opposition of internationalised courts having jurisdiction over its military personnel operating abroad.[61] Although the US initially proposed Resolution 2272 and is not among the top TCCs for UN peacekeeping operations, a veto might still be likely. Nevertheless, a Security Council resolution does not offer a legal basis that would engage with the particular context of each host state, and so host state ownership might be altogether lacking.

Centralised administration and mixed personnel

Taking the example of the more successful hybrid tribunals, such as the Special Court of Sierra Leone, the UN should have a significant role in administration through a centralised registrar. This would ensure direct UN leadership in response to sexual exploitation and abuse. A new UN organ should be established specifically to oversee a series of hybrid courts and to facilitate the centralised registrar. This new UN organ, perhaps called the *UN Commission for Hybrid Courts in Peacekeeping Operations*, could be responsible to the Secretary-General. In addition to providing central administration for the hybrid courts, such a body could assess the host state's judicial system and available expertise and provide logistical support and assistance accordingly.

A defining feature of previous examples of hybrid courts is that they are staffed by mixed domestic and international personnel. The element of mixed personnel aligns with a policy of inclusivity and supports legitimacy within the principle of host state ownership. Mixed personnel would need to have a certain level of

60 *Security Council Resolution 2272* SC Res, S/Res/2272 (2016).

61 Bureau of Political-Military Affairs *Fact Sheet: The International Criminal Court* (Washington DC, 2002).

expertise and sensitivity, particularly in cases involving sexual offences. Some TCCs may lack such expertise or sensitivity, and this gap may be filled by experts from other TCCs or by additional training, perhaps provided by the new *UN Commission for Hybrid Courts in Peacekeeping Operations.* Mixed personnel could cover host state gaps in arrest and investigation, judges, clerks, and other associated expert positions. The current Rapid Response Teams[62] could be further developed to incorporate such a team of international experts, which could be promptly deployed if required.

Arrest and investigation

Jurisdiction should be appropriately apportioned between the host state, the TCC, and the UN. The precise split of components of arresting officers and investigating teams may be something to be worked out through negotiations and consultations between states and the UN. However, it may be possible for the current system regarding investigation and prosecution to be further refined to accommodate mixed personnel. Currently, where necessary, the UN, through the Office of Internal Oversight Services (OIOS), will cooperate with national investigation officers sent by the TCC on any investigations into serious misconduct (this includes acts of sexual exploitation and abuse).[63]

Cooperation is currently in the form of gathering administrative evidence, sharing information, obtaining consent from the host state's authorities where appropriate, and other logistical assistance.[64] This method of joint investigation is a reflection of the Zeid Report's recommendation:

> the participation of the troop-contributing country at an expert level [in the United Nations investigation] would help to ensure that evidence was gathered in conformity with the laws of the troop-contributing country so it could be subsequently used by the country to take action against the contingent member.[65]

However, the procedure of cooperative investigation of serious misconduct committed by military contingents has come under some scrutiny.

Under the Model MOU there is a required procedure for the conduct of investigations of serious misconduct by military contingent members. This procedure includes a time limit on the TCCs to initiate an investigation of allegations (ten days), and the ability of the UN (through the OIOS and mission Conduct and Discipline Teams) to conduct administrative fact-finding investigations if the time limit expires

62 See for example, "Strengthening the UN Response to Sexual Exploitation and Abuse" *UN News Centre* (6 April 2017) <www.un.org>.

63 2007 MOU, art 7 *quater* 4(a)-(g).

64 At art 7 *quater* 4(d).

65 *Revised Draft Model Memorandum of Understanding between the United Nations and [Participating State] Contributing Resources to [the United Nations Peacekeeping Operation]* GA, A/61/494 (2006) at 9; Zeid Report, above n 44, at [33].

or the TCC is otherwise unresponsive.[66] Nevertheless, UN investigations must also attempt to include a representative from the national contingent investigation team (if available).[67] Although a seemingly delineated process, examining OIOS reports reveals that this process is not always followed.[68]

The OIOS has noted that in the majority of cases (of sexual exploitation and abuse) involving military contingents, TCCs have not complied with the ten-day deadline for responding to an allegation.[69] In fact, some TCCs were scrutinised in the OIOS 2015 report for causing long delays.[70] Moreover, the OIOS has noted the varied standards of investigation between TCCs, leading to disagreements about factual information regarding cases.[71] However, the OIOS and mission Conduct and Discipline Teams do not currently have the capacity to undertake criminal investigations and so are open for criticism about standards of investigation (for example, administrative investigations do not involve obtaining medical evidence, whereas criminal investigations do).[72] Leaked internal UN documents reveal that the UN's own investigations are not always comprehensive, with cases being closed without interviewing the alleged victim.[73] Therefore, standards are different across TCCs and the UN investigative organs. In 2015, the OIOS noted a call to redraft the procedures in the MOU.[74]

Although the procedure in the MOU for cooperative investigation has been criticised, in some cases cooperation has been successful. In 2012, an allegation of sexual abuse was made against the Pakistani Formed Police Unit in Haiti.[75] In response, the OIOS investigative team cooperated with the Department of Peacekeeping Operations (Police Division) and the Haitian National Police to conduct an investigation.[76] The cooperative element of the investigation saved

66 2007 MOU, art 7 *quater* 12.
67 At art 7 *quater* 12–13.
68 See for example *Evaluation Report*, above n 51, at 16–17.
69 At [22].
70 At [30]-[31].
71 See Report of the Office of Internal Oversight Services *Activities of the Office of Internal Oversight Services on Peacekeeping Operations for the Period 1 January to 31 December 2012* GA, A/67/297 (Part II) (2013) at [58]-[59]: Case 0405/11 involved the alleged sexual abuse of a casual UN employee by a national contingent member in the Democratic Republic of the Congo. The TCC informed the UN that the complainant withdrew her allegation, whereas the OIOS disagreed with this factual information, requesting an investigation regardless. No further response was received from the TCC. See also Report of the Office of Internal Oversight Services *Administrative and Budgetary Aspects of the Financing of the United Nations Peacekeeping Operations* GA, A/65/271 (Part II) (2011) at [47].
72 TA Shockley "The Investigation Procedures of the United Nations Office of Internal Oversight Services and the Rights of the United Nations Staff Member: An Analysis of the United Nations Judicial Tribunals' Judgments on Disciplinary Cases in the United Nations" (2015) 27 *Pace International Law Review* 468 at 482.
73 "Leaked Files Reveal Hidden Scope of UN Sex Abuse" (13 September 2017) *Code Blue: A Campaign by Aids-Free World*<www.codebluecampaign.com>.
74 *Evaluation Report*, above n 51, at 16–17.
75 At 18.
76 At 18.

time and a preliminary report was made to the contributing country within two weeks.[77]

A similar cooperative element could be used to incorporate mixed international and national personnel for the purposes of investigation for a series of hybrid courts. Such personnel may also be drawn from a team of rapidly deployable experts, so as to avoid delay in initiating investigations. However, taking into consideration the above issues with the current procedure of cooperation in investigation, it would be necessary for the UN to fill the gap in investigation standards and streamline the cooperative aspect more clearly under the MOU. Nevertheless, as the series of courts are of first instance and centrally administered by the UN, it would be necessary for the UN to negotiate an agreed standard of investigation and prosecution with its member states. Any agreed standards would need to be adopted through international agreements, such as the SOFAs and MOUs, or perhaps imposed by a Security Council resolution.

Temporal jurisdiction

A defining feature of previous examples of hybrid courts is that they are temporary, and so a series of hybrid courts for peacekeepers would remain only for the duration of any particular mission. However, this would mean that allegations of sexual exploitation and abuse that are reported after the mission ends may not be investigated or adjudicated. This could potentially be a significant limitation of temporary jurisdiction; for example, with the UN's mission in Haiti officially ended, there could be many unidentified victims of sexual exploitation and abuse who would be left without justice.[78]

On other matters of jurisdiction; because the purpose of a series of hybrid courts is to prosecute international personnel, it may be appropriate that the tribunal operates separately from the host state's national courts.[79] This may be even more appropriate where domestic legal institutions have suffered from conflict or natural disaster (for example, where physical infrastructure is destroyed).[80]

Trial, sentencing, and appeals

As with arrest and investigation, international personnel would need to be appointed to staff the judiciary alongside domestic judges (if applicable). International support might also be required for an adequately staffed defence team in

77 At 19.

78 *Security Council Resolution 2350* SC Res, S/Res/2350 (2017).

79 For example, the Special Court of Sierra Leone operated outside the domestic court system. S Nouwen "'Hybrid Courts': The Hybrid Category of a New Type of International Crimes Court" *Utrecht Law Review* (research paper, University of Cambridge Faculty of Law, 2011) 190, at 202.

80 As was the case in East Timor, where there was widespread destruction of legal and political infrastructure. See Mendez, above n 22, at 84.

order to safeguard the rights of the accused. Moreover, to ensure international fair trial rights, there must also be a mechanism for appeal or review of trial decisions. Upon conviction, any sentence could be served in the perpetrator's home state (similar to the procedure under the Rome Statute).[81]

Three potential hurdles

Having explored what a series of hybrid courts for peacekeepers might look like and what the jurisdiction of such a court might be, this chapter will now turn to three particular issues: material jurisdiction (sexual exploitation and abuse as criminalised conduct), political will (how states may sign up to a court), and court resources.

Material jurisdiction – criminalised conduct

Two defining features of existing hybrid courts are firstly, that they have a criminal function, and secondly, that they prosecute both international and domestic crimes. In 2006, the Group of Legal Experts noted that sexual exploitation and abuse by peacekeepers falls "between an ordinary criminal offence and an international crime".[82] In a later report, the Group reemphasised this point, adding that peacekeepers are in a position of trust and that they represent the international community; how they interact with locals contributes to the reputation of the UN.[83] By default, any serious misconduct committed by peacekeeping personnel against local populations is of international concern. As such, sexual exploitation and abuse, as defined by this book, should be included in the crimes within the jurisdiction of hybrid courts for peacekeepers.

Forms of sexual exploitation and abuse are included in the *Draft Convention on the Criminal Accountability of the United Nations Officials and Experts on Mission* (still under consideration by member states a decade after it was first introduced).[84] The Draft Convention was suggested by the Group of Legal Experts as a long-term solution to the accountability gap, but is aimed purely at categories of peacekeeping personnel falling outside military contingents.[85] However, the crimes listed in the Draft Convention are useful for determining the forms of sexual exploitation and abuse that UN officials have deemed to be worthy of criminalising in a proposed multilateral treaty.

There are currently two options proposed for the material jurisdiction of the Draft Convention. The first option is article 3(2), which provides the following:

81 Rome Statute, art 103.
82 Group of Legal Experts Report, above n 31, at [58].
83 *Report of the Group of Legal Experts on Criminal Accountability of United Nations Officials and Experts on Mission* GA, A/62/329 (2007) [Criminal Accountability Report] at [32].
84 *Draft Convention on the Criminal Accountability of the United Nations Officials and Experts on Mission* GA, A/60/980 Annex III (2007): [Draft Convention].
85 Criminal Accountability Report, above n 83, at [70].

> The serious crimes referred to in paragraph 1 of the present article are, for each State party establishing and exercising jurisdiction pursuant to this Convention, those which, under the national law of that State party, correspond to:
>
> ...
>
> (c) Rape and acts of sexual violence;
> (d) Sexual offences involving children;

It would seem that forms of sexual abuse have been included in the list of crimes, but not those relating to sexual exploitation. "Sexual abuse" covers the following conduct: rape, sexual violence, and sex with minors. The forms relating to survival sex are missing.

The alternative article 3(2) of the Draft Convention is potentially broader:

> The serious crimes referred to in paragraph 1 of the present article, for each State party establishing or exercising jurisdiction pursuant to this Convention, are:
>
> (a) Crimes of intentional violence against the person and sexual offences punishable under the national law of that State party by imprisonment or other deprivation of liberty for a maximum period of at least [one/two] year(s), or by a more severe penalty.

The reference to sexual offences in this alternate article has the potential to encompass many forms of sexual exploitation and abuse.[86] However, it is entirely reliant on the national laws of member states and does not seek to proscribe offences to be criminalised under domestic criminal law. It is less likely that forms of sexual exploitation would be included among member states' criminal law, particularly survival sex.

Both proposed articles of the Draft Convention seem to indicate that forms of sexual abuse committed by peacekeeping personnel are important enough to be described as crimes in a multilateral treaty. During the ongoing discussions between member states, it seems that the inclusion of crimes of a serious nature has been generally supported.[87] For the most part, though, state representatives have not endeavoured to differentiate "serious" crimes from "non-serious" crimes when talking about sexual exploitation and abuse.[88] Additionally, Roisin Burke has argued, in relation to her tri-hybrid model, such a tribunal should only have

86 For critique see M O'Brien "Issues of the Draft Convention on the Criminal Accountability of United Nations Officials and Experts on Mission" in N Quenivet and S Shah-Davis (eds) *International Law and Armed Conflict: Challenges in the 21st Century* (YMC Asser Press, The Hague, 2010).

87 General Assembly *Summary Record of the 5th Meeting* GA, A/C.6/63/SR.6 (2008) examples at [19], [35], and [36]; General Assembly *Summary Record of the 9th Meeting* GA, A/C.6/66/SR.9 (2011) examples at [10], [18], [24] and [43];

88 *Summary Record of the 5th Meeting,* above n 87, examples at [12] and [38]; *Summary Record of the 9th Meeting,* above n 87, examples at [34], [44], and [50].

jurisdiction over "serious incidents of [sexual exploitation and abuse]".[89] However, Burke does not elaborate on what forms of sexual exploitation and abuse she would consider "serious incidents".

Sexual exploitation (as survival sex) and sexual abuse committed by peacekeepers are international crimes. International crimes are more than just the narrowly defined "core crimes" included in the Rome Statute. Using Bassiouni's criteria for international criminalisation supports interpreting sexual exploitation and abuse by peacekeepers as international crimes.[90] These criteria include the following:[91]

a The prohibited conduct affects a significant international interest;
b The prohibited conduct constitutes egregious conduct deemed offensive to the commonly shared values of the world community, including what has historically been referred to as conduct shocking to the conscience of humanity;
c The prohibited conduct has transnational implications, in that it involves or affects more than one state in its planning, preparation, or commission, either through the diversity of nationality of its perpetrators or victims, or because the means employed transcend national boundaries;
d The conduct is harmful to an internationally protected person or interest; and
e The conduct violates internationally protected interests, but it does not rise to the level required by (a) or (b); however, because of its nature, it can best be prevented and suppressed by international criminalization.

The relevant criteria are (c), (d), and (e). In relation to (e), I argue that forms of sexual abuse (rape, sexual violence, and sexual activity with children) must be included in a list of applicable crimes within material jurisdiction of any alternative series of courts for peacekeepers, as that conduct has been accepted by member states and treaty bodies as serious in nature.[92] In regard to survival sex, the relationship is based on dependency and focuses on the peacekeeper's position of power in relation to the beneficiary of assistance. Survival sex often occurs within a broader context of social and cultural inequalities (including extreme poverty) that marginalise women in post-conflict states. The presence of a (overwhelmingly masculine and militarised) peacekeeping force may exacerbate the inequalities that already exist. Peacekeepers will also have access to food, money, medicine, and other kinds of assistance that the local population does not, and this creates the situation of differential power. Peacekeepers represent the international community as well as their contributing state, and they are in a position of trust within the

89 Burke *Sexual Exploitation and Abuse by UN Military Contingents,* above n 1, at 243.
90 M Bassiouni *International Criminal Law Series: Introduction to International Criminal Law* (2nd ed, Brill Nijhoff, Leiden, 2012) at 142.
91 At 142.
92 These particular acts are considered "crimes" in the Draft Convention, art 3(2).

community in which they are deployed. To abuse the unequal power dynamic by exchanging assistance for sex is exploitation and is of international concern.

Additionally, sexual exploitation and abuse committed by peacekeepers has transnational implications. UN Peacekeeping Operations are made up of multinational forces, and sexual abuse is committed in a foreign state. Because personnel represent the international community under the umbrella of the UN, it is argued that the criteria for (c) is met in these circumstances. Furthermore, sexual exploitation and abuse are human rights abuses, and the UN, as a human rights promoter, should be a place where victims are protected from such harm. As a result, I argue that peacekeepers committing sexual exploitation and abuse should meet the criteria for (d).

Overall, sexual abuse (defined in this book as rape, sexual violence, and sexual activity with children) and sexual exploitation (defined in this book as survival sex, where sex is exchanged for aid or assistance to which peacekeepers have access or which is already owed by the UN to the local population) should be included within the material jurisdiction of a series of hybrid courts for peacekeepers as international crimes.

Political will

The second potential hurdle for a series of hybrid courts for peacekeepers is political will. As previously noted, TCC exclusive criminal jurisdiction (for peacekeeping operations) exists as the default due to states' continuing fears surrounding the jurisdiction of another judicial institution over their military forces.[93] These fears include being subject to trials without appropriate human rights standards and the subversion of the sovereign prerogative to discipline or prosecute their own military forces.[94] Therefore, the point of this section is to discuss various options of signing up to a series of hybrid courts for peacekeepers that may be offered in a situation of compromise to placate such fears. It also serves as an acknowledgement that hybrid courts, as an option for improving accountability, are ultimately subject to the political will of states.

(i) Opt-in

The first option that may be available is a so-called opt-in measure, whereby a multilateral agreement could be used to set up the major aspects of the court, but it would only be applicable to and applied by those states who have signed up. An advantage to such a mechanism is that it does not need consensus across all member states and may avoid delay caused by negotiations. An opt-in measure may also allow states that

93 Zeid Report, above n 44, at [80]; see also Dag Hammarskjold *Summary Study of the Experience Derived from the Establishment and Operation of the Force: Report of the Secretary-General* GA, A/3943 XIII (1958) at [136]; D Fleck "Introduction" in D Fleck (ed) *The Handbook of the Law of Visiting States* (Oxford University Press, Oxford, 2001) at 5.

94 See generally D Fleck "Securing Status and Protection of Peacekeepers" in R Arnold and GA Knoops (eds) *Practice and Policies of Modern Peace Support Operations under International Law* (Transnational Publishers, New York, 2006) 141.

do not have the resources necessary to conduct investigations in a foreign state to share in the resources of a UN-administrated hybrid court.[95] However, peacekeeping personnel may be treated differently depending on whether their state has chosen to opt in, and therefore an uneven application of justice may occur.

Another advantage of an opt-in measure may be that it could represent best practice – the idea that enough state interest and application would develop a model of behaviour and encourage improvement of accountability among states that are not a party. An example of best practice can be seen in the international criminal courts and their effect on non-affected states' prosecution of international crimes. It has been suggested by academics that the presence of international courts can increase the consciousness of the international community in relation to the seriousness of the conduct being prosecuted.[96] Moreover, such tribunals may encourage prosecution by domestic courts; for example, local prosecutions in the Democratic Republic of the Congo against military groups for international crimes have increased since the ICC began its trials over such crimes in the territory.[97] Therefore, states that do not opt in to a tribunal for peacekeepers may still be encouraged to exercise jurisdiction over their personnel by the practice of those states that do choose to opt in.

(ii) Opt-out

A second option is an opt-out measure, where peacekeeping personnel would be subject to the jurisdiction of a hybrid court outright, unless the TCC could establish that it is both willing and able to investigate and prosecute offenders. This is essentially the opposite of the ICCs complementarity principle. An opt-out measure would encourage states to make the necessary changes to their domestic arrangements to investigate and prosecute their military contingent members if they wish to avoid the jurisdiction of an independent tribunal. In the interim, the jurisdiction of a hybrid court would ensure that sexual exploitation and abuse does not continue to be committed with impunity. In the early negotiations of the Rome Statute, there was some support for a similar opt-out measure, with support for the ICC having primary jurisdiction, particularly over genocide.[98] The opt-out measure was rejected in favour of complementarity in order to support state sovereignty, achieve consensus, and increase public confidence in national criminal institutions.[99] Although these negotiations took place many decades ago, there is

95 Shany, above n 48, at 437 and 439.
96 At 436.
97 At 436.
98 International Commission of Jurists *The International Criminal Court: Third ICJ Position Paper* (presented at the 1st Preparatory Committee of the ICC, August 1995) at 30–35.
99 United Nations Information Centre in Sydney for Australia, New Zealand and the South Pacific *Preparatory Committee on International Criminal Court Discusses Complementarity between National, International Jurisdictions* (1st Session of the Preparatory Committee, 11th Meeting, April 1996); United Nations Information Centre in Sydney for Australia, New Zealand and the South Pacific *Preparatory Committee on International Criminal Court Continues Considering Complementarity*

no indication that the positions of states have changed in regard to complementarity. An opt-out measure would be best delivered through a binding Security Council resolution. As argued above, this would also solve issues related to host state reluctance, but would suffer the possibility of a permanent member veto, particularly from the US.

Resources

Adequate resources are crucial for achieving the conceptual goals of the hybrid model. In order to be truly inclusive of the host state and centre the interests of victims, there must be funding allocated for community outreach, training, victim support (see chapter seven), and witness protection and security. Significant costs also relate to salaries of international personnel, travel, rental of courtroom facilities (if applicable), defence services, and overall administration. In order to avoid or mitigate limitations of existing hybrid courts, hybrid courts for peacekeepers would need to be sufficiently resourced.

It has long been recognised that hybrid court models are resource intensive.[100] A hybrid court for peacekeepers would likely be similarly expensive. The SCSL annual budget averaged USD 20.1 million, and in the early years of its operation, expenditure was consistently over budget, so the SCSL required further funds from donating states.[101] The ECCC annual budget averages USD 31.8 million.[102] The majority of costs in both courts are related to salaries of international personnel, particularly of permanent staff.

The ECCC and SCSL might be distinguishable from the proposed series of hybrid courts for peacekeepers. Whereas the ECCC and SCSL operate full time, it would be unlikely that peacekeeping courts would be required all the time in every mission, as the number of allegations may simply not require it. For compromise on a resource-intensive enterprise, it might be possible to create a series of hybrid travelling courts. Instead of a hybrid court being physically established on-site in each mission area, the structure and jurisdiction could be pre-agreed between relevant parties but only operational when required. The relevant personnel (of investigators, lawyers, judges, etc.) would then be drawn from a small team of

between National, International Jurisdictions (1st Session of the Preparatory Committee, 13th Meeting, April 1996); and United Nations Information Centre in Sydney for Australia, New Zealand and the South Pacific *International Criminal Court Should Not Have Inherent Jurisdiction, Preparatory Committee Told* (1st Session of the Preparatory Committee, 15th Meeting, April 1996).

100 Cohen, above n 8, at 13; Group of Legal Experts Report, above n 31, at [37]; Williams, above n 2, at 210.

101 Average taken across annual budgets from 2008 to 2013. See Annual Reports of the President for Sierra Leone available online: <www.rscsl.org>. See also *First Annual Report of the President of the Special Court for Sierra Leone* (for the period December 2002-December 2003) Annex III; *Second Annual Report of the President of the Special Court for Sierra Leone* (for the period 1 January 2004–17 January 2005) Annex III.

102 Average taken across annual budgets from 2012 to 2017, available online: <www.eccc.gov.kh/en>.

rapidly deployable experts. An advantage of a model that is mobile in nature is the possible connection with remote areas. For example, the court could be set up in the victim's community directly. However, some peacekeeping operations are more complex than others. Where mission mandates are long term, such as they are in the DRC or CAR, these may still require full-time hybrid courts.

Although it is acknowledged that a hybrid court is an expensive option and that the cost may be a barrier for states, it is not accepted that courts cannot be budgeted for. UN gender- or victim-related projects are often under-financed, as evidenced by the failure to adequately fund the *United Nations Comprehensive Strategy on Assistance and Support to Victims of Sexual Exploitation and Abuse by UN Staff and Related Personnel* (discussed below in chapter seven).[103] To sufficiently resource a series of hybrid courts for peacekeepers would require a change in approach to funding priorities.

International assistance with funding is a defining feature of existing hybrid courts. Past practice indicates that the best method (so far) for resourcing is to set up a specific fund into which member states, and other interested parties, pay on a regular basis.[104] In his 2015 report, the Secretary-General stated the desire to set up a voluntary fund for victim assistance (related to sexual exploitation and abuse).[105] As a voluntary fund has already been established to respond to sexual exploitation and abuse, the financing of a series of hybrid courts for peacekeepers could also be attached to such a fund.

Overall, the question of resourcing will inevitably be an issue when proposing any new mechanism at the international level. Currently, there appears to be enough money available to finance peacekeeping operations. A recent report regarding the UN mission in CAR revealed a surplus of unspent money (approximately USD 34 million).[106] In this report the Secretary-General recommended this surplus be credited to member states.[107] Perhaps such money could be redirected into other projects related to peacekeeping, such as hybrid courts. If there is enough money to send peacekeeping personnel to missions abroad, then there

103 See for example H Charlesworth "Not Waving but Drowning: Gender Mainstreaming and Human Rights in the United Nations" (2005) 18 *Harvard Human Rights Journal* 1 at 11–13; H Charlesworth "Transforming the United Men's Club: Feminist Futures for the United Nations" (1994) 4 *Transnational Law & Contemporary Problems* 421 at 432 and 447. See also Secretary-General *Special Measures for Protection from Sexual Exploitation and Sexual Abuse* GA A/69/779 (2015) at [68].

104 This was the case with the Special Court of Sierra Leone. Although still underfunded, the Special Court was far better resourced than the Special Panels in East Timor where funding was located within the UN mission budget: see Cohen, above n 8, at 13 and 25; Williams, above n 2, at 211.

105 *Special Measures for Protection from Sexual Exploitation and Sexual Abuse* (2015), above n 103, at [65]-[66].

106 Report of the Secretary-General *Final Performance Report of the United Nations Mission in the Central African Republic and Chad* GA, A/70/559 (2015). Also noted by G Mathurin "Put Victims First: Time for UK Leadership at the UN" (media release by AIDS-Free World, 25 November 2015).

107 *Final Performance Report of the United Nations Mission in the Central African Republic and Chad,* above n 106, at [7].

should be enough money available to ensure accountability for crimes committed by such personnel. Sexual exploitation and abuse is a human rights issue, and ultimately, if the international community (particularly the UN) is serious about human rights protection and accountability for violations, adequate resources will be found and allocated accordingly.

Conclusion – the first of a twofold solution

This chapter has argued for the establishment of an entirely new framework. A series of hybrid courts was put forward as the best option to improve accountability of military contingent members for sexual exploitation and abuse. Despite some limitations, the hybrid model has the greatest potential to encourage international cooperation, decentralise the primary role of TCCs, and enable victims to see justice being done. The proposal is for the creation of a series of courts of first instance, with centralised administration and mixed international and domestic (host state) personnel. A new UN organ, the *UN Commission for Hybrid Courts in Peacekeeping Operations*, responsible to the Secretary-General, should be established to oversee such courts.

A necessary first step is consultation with states, particularly host states, as their consent is generally required for genuine inclusivity. Most importantly, whichever legal basis is utilised (international agreement or Security Council resolution), there must be an agreed scope as to host state ownership and precise split of jurisdiction between relevant states. International funding for the courts must also be secured.

If the goal is to improve accountability, then the option must be visible and legitimate in the eyes of the victims and the international community. A series of hybrid courts for peacekeepers will ensure host state inclusivity and transparency, and will ensure that the UN takes leadership in a collective response to sexual exploitation and abuse.

However, in order to truly centre the interests of victims and achieve justice more broadly, the establishment of a series of hybrid courts is only one part of the solution. The next chapter discusses restorative measures and the role of victims in this proposed hybrid framework.

References

Agreement between the United Nations and the Government of Sierra Leone on the Establishment of a Special Court for Sierra Leone, Letter dated March 6 2002 from the Secretary-General addressed to the President of the Security Council S/2002/246 (2002)

Agreement between the United Nations and the Royal Government of Cambodia concerning the Prosecution under Cambodian Law of Crimes Committed during the Period of Democratic Kampuchea GA Res, A/Res/57/228 B (2003)

M Bassiouni *International Criminal Law Series: Introduction to International Criminal Law* (2nd ed, Brill Nijhoff, Leiden, 2012)

Bureau of Political-Military Affairs *Fact Sheet: The International Criminal Court* (Washington DC, 2002)

R Burke *Sexual Exploitation and Abuse by UN Military Contingents: Moving Beyond the Current Status Quo and Responsibility under International Law* (Brill, Leiden, 2014)

R Burke "UN Military Peacekeeper Complicity in Sexual Abuse: The ICC or a Tri-Hybrid Court" in M Bergsmo (ed) *Thematic Prosecution of International Sex Crimes* (Torkel Opsahl Academic EPublisher, Beijing, 2012)

A Cahillane "International Law, Sexual Violence and Peacekeepers" 17 *Irish Student Law Review* 1

A Cassese *Report on the Special Court for Sierra Leone* (Submitted by the Independent Expert, 2006)

J Cerone and C Baldwin "Explaining and Evaluating the UNMIK Court System" in CR Romano, A Nollkaemper and JK Kleffner (eds) *Internationalized Criminal Courts: Sierra Leone, East Timor, Kosovo and Cambodia* (Oxford University Press, Oxford, 2004)

H Charlesworth "Not Waving but Drowning: Gender Mainstreaming and Human Rights in the United Nations" (2005) 18 *Harvard Human Rights Journal* 1

H Charlesworth "Transforming the United Men's Club: Feminist Futures for the United Nations" (1994) 4 *Transnational Law & Contemporary Problems* 421

JD Ciorcian and A Heindel *Law, Meaning and Violence: Hybrid Justice: The Extraordinary Chambers in the Courts of Cambodia* (University of Michigan Press, Michigan, 2014)

D Cohen "Hybrid Justice in East Timor, Sierra Leone and Cambodia: Lessons Learned and Prospects for the Future" (2007) 43 *Stanford Journal of International Law* 1

R Coomaraswamy Open Letter to Permanent Representatives of the Security Council Dated 23 June 2015 (2015)

R Coomaraswamy Preventing Conflict, Transforming Justice, Securing the Peace: A Global Study on the Implementation of United Nations Security Council Resolution 1325 (2015)

LA Dickinson "Notes and Comments: The Promise of Hybrid Courts" (2003) *The American Journal of International Law* 295

Draft Convention on the Criminal Accountability of the United Nations Officials and Experts on Mission GA, A/60/980

C Etcheson "The Politics of Genocide Justice in Cambodia" in CR Romano, A Nollkaemper and JK Kleffner (eds) *Internationalized Criminal Courts: Sierra Leone, East Timor, Kosovo, and Cambodia* (Oxford University Press, Oxford, 2004)

D Fleck "Introduction" in D Fleck (ed) *The Handbook of the Law of Visiting States* (Oxford University Press, Oxford, 2001)

D Fleck "Securing Status and Protection of Peacekeepers" in R Arnold and GA Knoops (eds) *Practice and Policies of Modern Peace Support Operations under International Law* (Transnational Publishers, New York, 2006)

First Annual Report of the President of the Special Court for Sierra Leone (for the period December 2002-December 2003)

General Assembly *Summary record of the 5th Meeting* GA, A/C.6/63/SR.6 (2008)

General Assembly *Summary record of the 9th Meeting* GA, A/C.6/66/SR.9 (2011)

D Hammarskjold *Summary Study of the Experience Derived from the Establishment and Operation of the Force: Report of the Secretary-General* GA, A/3943 XIII (1958)

H Horsington "The Cambodian Khmer Rouge Tribunal: The Promise of a Hybrid Tribunal" (2004) 5 *Melbourne Journal of International Law* 462

T Innes "The Accountability of Peacekeeping Operations: A Focus on Allegations of Sexual Abuse" (2011) 1 *Warwick Student Law Review* 19

International Commission of Jurists *The International Criminal Court: Third ICJ Position Paper* (presented at the 1st Preparatory Committee of the ICC, August 1995)

N Jain "Conceptualising Internationalisation in Hybrid Courts" (2009) 12 *Singapore Yearbook of International Law* 81

AK Jarstad and L Olsson "Hybrid Peace Ownership in Afghanistan: International Perspectives of Who Owns What and When" (2012) 18 *Global Governance* 105

B Kiernan "Historical and Political Background to the Conflict in Cambodia" in K Ambos and M Othman (eds) *New Approaches in International Criminal Justice: Kosovo, East Timor, Sierra Leone and Cambodia* (Freiburg I Br, Berlin, 2003)

K Krishnasamy "Pakistan's Peacekeeping Experiences" (2002) 9 *International Peacekeeping* 103

"Leaked Files Reveal Hidden Scope of UN Sex Abuse" (13 September 2017) *Code Blue: A Campaign by Aids-Free World* <www.codebluecampaign.com>

S Linton "Rising from the Ashes: The Creation of a Viable Criminal Justice System in East Timor" (2001) 25 *Melbourne University Law Review* 122

Manual on Policies and Procedures concerning the Reimbursement and Control of Contingent-Owned Equipment of Troop/Police Contributors Participating in Peacekeeping Missions (COE Manual) GA, A/c.5/69/18 (2014)

P McAuliffe "Hybrid Courts in Retrospect: Of Lost Legacies and Modest Futures" in Y McDermott, W Schabas and N Hayes (eds) *The Ashgate Research Companion to International Criminal Law: Critical Perspectives* (Taylor and Francis, London, 2013)

PK Mendez "The New Wave of Hybrid Tribunals: A Sophisticated Approach to Enforcing International Humanitarian Law or an Idealistic Solution with Empty Promises?" (2009) 20 *Criminal Law Forum* 53

Model Status of Forces Agreement between the United Nations and Host Countries GA, A/45/594 (1990)

J Morse "Documenting Mass Rape: Medical Evidence Collection Techniques as Humanitarian Technology" (2014) 8 *Genocide Studies and Prevention: An International Journal* 63

E Nielsen "Hybrid International Criminal Tribunals: Political Interference and Judicial Independence" (2010) 15 *UCLA Journal of International Law & Foreign Affairs* 289

S Nouwen "'Hybrid Courts': The Hybrid Category of a New Type of International Crimes Court" *Utrecht Law Review* (research paper, University of Cambridge Faculty of Law, 2011)

M O'Brien "Issues of the Draft Convention on the Criminal Accountability of United Nations Officials and Experts on Mission" in N Quenivet and S Shah-Davis (eds) *International Law and Armed Conflict: Challenges in the 21st Century* (YMC Asser Press, The Hague, 2010)

M Odello "Tackling Criminal Acts in Peacekeeping Operations: The Accountability of Peacekeepers" (2010) 15 *Journal of Conflict & Security Law* 347

Office of Internal Oversight Services *Evaluation Report: Evaluation of the Enforcement and Remedial Assistance Efforts for Sexual Exploitation and Abuse by the United Nations and Related Personnel in Peacekeeping Operations* (May 2015)

Office of the United Nations High Commissioner for Human Rights *Rule-of-Law Tools for Post-Conflict States: Maximising the Legacy of Hybrid Courts* (United Nations, New York and Geneva, 2008)

T Perriello and M Wierda *Lessons from the Deployment of International Judges and Prosecutors in Kosovo* (International Center for Transitional Justice, March 2006)

P Rapoza "Hybrid Criminal Tribunals and Concept of Ownership: Who Owns the Process?" (2006) 21 *American University International Law Review* 525

Regulation 1999/1 On the Authority of the Interim Administration in Kosovo UNMIK/REG/1999/1 (1999)

Regulation 1999/24 On the Law Applicable in Kosovo UNMIK/REG/1999/24 (1999)

Regulation 2000/15 On the Establishment of Panels with Exclusive Jurisdiction over Serious Criminal Offences UNTAET/REG/2000/15 (2000)

C Reiger and M Wierda *The Serious Crimes Process in Timor-Leste: In Retrospect* (International Center for Transitional Justice, March 2006)

Report of the Group of Legal Experts on Criminal Accountability of United Nations Officials and Experts on Mission GA, A/62/329 (2007)

Report of the Group of Legal Experts on Making the Standards Contained in the Secretary-General's Bulletin Binding on Contingent Members and Standardising the Norms of Conduct so That They Are Applicable to All Categories of Peacekeeping Personnel GA, A/61/645 (2006)

Report of the Office of Internal Oversight Services *Administrative and Budgetary Aspects of the Financing of the United Nations Peacekeeping Operations* GA, A/65/271 (Part II) (2011)

Report of the Office of Internal Oversight Services *Activities of the Office of Internal Oversight Services on Peacekeeping Operations for the Period 1 January to 31 December 2012* GA, A/67/297 (Part II) (2013)

Report of the International Commission of Inquiry on East Timor S/2000/59 (2000)

Report of the Secretary-General *Final Performance Report of the United Nations Mission in the Central African Republic and Chad* GA, A/70/559 (2015)

Revised Draft Model Memorandum of Understanding between the United Nations and [Participating State] Contributing Resources to [the United Nations Peacekeeping Operation] GA, A/61/494 (2006)

Rome Statute of the International Criminal Court 2187 UNTS 3 (opened for signature 17 July 1998, entered into force 1 July 2002)

S Scully "Judging the Success and Failures of the Extraordinary Chambers of the Courts of Cambodia" (2011) 13 *Asian-Pacific Law & Policy Journal* 301

Secretary-General *A Comprehensive Strategy to Eliminate Future Sexual Exploitation and Abuse in United Nations Peacekeeping Operations* GA, A/59/710 (2005) prepared by Prince Zeid Ra'ad Zeid Al-Hussein

Second Annual Report of the President of the Special Court for Sierra Leone (for the period 1 January 2004–17 January 2005)

Secretary-General *Special Measures for Protection from Sexual Exploitation and Sexual Abuse* GA, A/69/779 (2015)

Secretary-General *Special Measures for Protection from Sexual Exploitation and Sexual Abuse* GA, A/71/818 (2017)*Security Council Resolution 1244* SC Res, S/Res/1244 (1999)

Security Council Resolution 1272 SC Res, S/Res/1272 (1999)

Security Council Resolution 1325 SC Res, S/Res/1325 (2000)

Security Council Resolution 2272 SC Res, S/Res/2272 (2016)

Security Council Resolution 2350 SC Res, S/Res/2350 (2017)

Y Shany "How Can International Criminal Courts Have a Greater Impact on National Criminal Proceedings? Lessons from the First Decades of International Criminal Justice in Operation" (2013) 46 *Israel Law Review* 431

TA Shockley "The Investigation Procedures of the United Nations Office of Internal Oversight Services and the Rights of the United Nations Staff Member: An Analysis of the United Nations Judicial Tribunals' Judgments on Disciplinary Cases in the United Nations" (2015) 27 *Pace International Law Review* 468

Situation of Human Rights in East Timor GA, A/54/660 (1999)

Statute of the Special Court for Sierra Leone (2001) as established by Security Council Resolution 1315 SC Res, S/Res/1315 (2000)

"Strengthening the UN Response to Sexual Exploitation and Abuse" *UN News Centre* (6 April 2017) <www.un.org>

Summary of the Report to the Secretary-General of the Commission of Experts to Review the Prosecution of Serious Violations of Human Rights in Timor-Leste (then East Timor) in 1999 S/2005/458 (2005)

United Nations Information Centre in Sydney for Australia, New Zealand and the South Pacific *International Criminal Court Should Not Have Inherent Jurisdiction, Preparatory Committee Told* (1st Session of the Preparatory Committee, 15th Meeting, April 1996)

United Nations Information Centre in Sydney for Australia, New Zealand and the South Pacific *Preparatory Committee on International Criminal Court Continues Considering Complementarity between National, International Jurisdictions* (1st Session of the Preparatory Committee, 13th Meeting, April 1996)

United Nations Information Centre in Sydney for Australia, New Zealand and the South Pacific *Preparatory Committee on International Criminal Court Discusses Complementarity between National, International Jurisdictions* (1st Session of the Preparatory Committee, 11th Meeting, April 1996)United Nations Peacekeeping "Financing Peacekeeping" (August 2015) <www.un.org>

S Williams *Hybrid and International Criminal Tribunals* (Hart Publishing, Oxford, 2012)

7 Victim Participation and Reparations

Victims must be at the centre of a new framework for accountability but have been largely ignored for the past two decades. A series of hybrid courts for peacekeepers must centralise the interests of victims in a material and genuine way. This chapter argues for a mixed retributive-restorative justice model that incorporates direct victim participation during proceedings. Moreover, for victims of sexual exploitation and abuse to receive effective remedies for the harm committed by the very people sent to protect them, appropriate reparations must also be provided. Only with the realisation of effective remedies will justice be seen to be done.

This chapter will start with an overview of victims' right to participate throughout the criminal justice process. This will explore international instruments that highlight victims' rights to receive information, to be heard, and to be protected. As restorative justice theory aims to give effect to victim participatory rights, this chapter will then examine current examples of internationalised criminal courts that have adopted a mixed retributive-restorative model. A similar model will be argued as an appropriate approach for a series of hybrid courts for peacekeepers.

As prosecution is only part of the right to an effective remedy and restorative justice, the possibility of reparations must also be addressed. Thus, this chapter will explore the current UN strategy for victim support and compare the status quo to remedial trends in international human rights law. It will be argued that although recent UN reforms are seemingly positive, significant improvement in assistance and support to victims is required to provide adequate reparations. The International Criminal Court (ICC) Trust Fund for Victims will then be examined as an example of a reparations scheme that is attached to an internationalised court. The Trust Fund offers a blueprint for future developments of a reparations mechanism for victims of sexual exploitation and abuse, but it is not without its challenges. The establishment of a separate mechanism for victim reparations that provide full rehabilitation and have transformative goals will be proposed as the second arm of accountability to sit alongside hybrid courts.

The role of victims in international criminal justice

Traditionally, international and domestic criminal justice theory has marginalised the role of victims. Until relatively recently, the punishment of offenders was considered the sole purpose of criminal institutions. Under the criminal justice theory of retribution, the role of victims is understood as less integral to the criminal process.[1] Victim participation under purely retributive models is restricted to victim-as-witness, to provide information about the wrongdoing that took place.[2] Not only are victim participatory rights largely ignored under retribution theory, but so are other victims' rights generally, including the right to effective remedies.

During the victims' rights movement of the 1960s there was a push for more participatory rights and remedies for victims in the criminal justice process. This push primarily came from victims' groups and nongovernmental organisations (NGOs), and paralleled the development of victim reparations in international human rights law. Early victimology research from the United States (US) illustrated mass underreporting of victimisation due to distrust of law enforcement and the criminal justice system.[3] This corresponded with the women's rights movement in the US, which highlighted the issue of underreporting of violence against women (particularly domestic violence and rape), where victims felt unsafe and isolated from the criminal justice system itself.[4] Criminal institutions that include greater victim participation and long-term remedies generally take on a restorative justice model. Under restorative justice, greater emphasis is placed on victim participation and on repairing the harm caused to the victim and their community, whilst often including the offender in that process.[5]

There are various modalities in which restorative justice is practiced; these include victim-offender mediation, rehabilitation services, victim compensation schemes, and community service.[6] At the international level, restorative justice is practiced through alternative dispute resolution mechanisms, such as Truth Commissions, rehabilitative services and support for victims, and greater participatory rights in international tribunals. Although there remains tension in international criminal tribunals between traditional retributive models and restorative models,

1 B Leyh *Procedural Justice? Victim Participation in International Criminal Proceedings* (Intersentia, Cambridge, 2011) at 37.
2 Leyh, above n 1, at 41; R Henham and M Findlay *Exploring the Boundaries of International Criminal Justice* (Ashgate, Furnham, 2011) at 86.
3 This was also due to racial tensions surrounding the US civil rights movement. See LW Sherman *Trust and Confidence in Criminal Justice* (2001) available online: <www.ncjrs.org> at 4–5; AM Cellini "The Proposed Victims' Rights Amendment to the Constitution of the United States: Opening the Door of the Criminal Justice System to the Victim" (1997) 14 *Arizona Journal of International and Comparative Law* 839 at 848–856. See also JT Davis "The Grassroots Beginnings of the Victims' Rights Movement" (2005) *National Crime Victim Law Institute News.*
4 Cellini, above n 3, at 853; Davis, above n 3.
5 H Strange "Exploring the Effects of Restorative Justice on Crime Victims for Victims of Conflict in Transitional Societies" in SG Sholham, P Knepper and M Kett (eds) *International Handbook of Victimology* (Taylor and Francis, Hoboken, 2010) 537 at 538.
6 See generally JP Vevan, G Hall, I Froyland, B Steels and D Goulding "Restoration or Renovation? Evaluating Restorative Justice Outcomes" (2005) 12 *Psychiatry, Psychology and Law* 194.

some tribunals have been embracing restorative aspects of criminal justice and a wider concept of victim participation.

Because the aim of the series of hybrid courts for peacekeepers is to centralise the interests of victims of sexual exploitation and abuse, it would be counterproductive to adopt a purely retributive model of criminal justice. Although retributive justice is important, as it focuses on the criminal accountability of the individual perpetrator, victims must have a role in the process in order to reflect a truly victim-centred framework. Participation is a fundamental aspect to restorative justice models and thus important to explore. In order to determine what roles are appropriate for victims of sexual exploitation and abuse, it is necessary to, firstly, consider what participatory rights victims have (as recognised under international law) and, secondly, to investigate the restorative justice models that have been utilised by international institutions.

Victim participatory rights

Victim participatory rights during criminal trials have developed relatively recently. The victims' rights campaign during the 1960s, noted above, advocated for greater participatory rights before and during criminal proceedings.[7] Additionally, campaigners argued for improved services-related support for victims participating in the criminal justice system.[8] These goals are supported by the few examples of empirical research available that investigate victims' experience of the criminal process.[9] Research on what victims perceive as fairness during criminal trials shows that victims greatly appreciate receiving information about their rights, the procedure, and the outcome of their case.[10] Moreover, victims who actively participate during trials value being heard, appreciate being able to tell their version of events, and appreciate being protected in order to do that.[11]

7 Leyh *Procedural Justice? Victim Participation in International Criminal Proceedings*, above n 1, at 45; MC Bassiouni "International Recognition of Victims' Rights" (2006) 6 *Human Rights Law Review* 203 at 210; C Hoyle and L Ullrich "New Court, New Justice? The Evolution of 'Justice for Victims' at Domestic Courts and at the International Criminal Court" (2014) *International Criminal Justice* 1 at 2–3; and CP Trumbull "The Victims of Victim Participation in International Criminal Proceedings" (2008) 29 *Michigan Journal of International Law* 777 at 781.

8 Leyh *Procedural Justice? Victim Participation in International Criminal Proceedings*, above n 1, at 45.

9 Leyh *Procedural Justice? Victim Participation in International Criminal Proceedings*, above n 1, uses the following source (which ties together the few examples of empirical research in this area and looks at victims participating in domestic criminal and civil courts) J Thibaut and L Walker *Procedural Justice: A Psychological Analysis* (Lawrence Erlbaim, New Jersey, 1975).

10 Leyh *Procedural Justice? Victim Participation in International Criminal Proceedings*, above n 1, at 49; J Wemmers "The Meaning of Justice for Victims" in SG Sholham, P Knepper and M Kett (eds) *International Handbook of Victimology* (Taylor and Fancis, Hoboken, 2010) 27, at 34 and 38.

11 Leyh *Procedural Justice? Victim Participation in International Criminal Proceedings*, above n 1, at 49–50.

A key international legal instrument dealing with participatory rights of victims is *The Declaration of Basic Principles of Justice for Victims of Crime and Abuse of Power 1985* (Basic Principles 1985).[12] Based on article eight (the right to an effective remedy) of the Universal Declaration of Human Rights, the Basic Principles 1985 provide guidance to states on implementing such a right to remedies, with a particular focus on participation during criminal proceedings.[13]

Concerning victims of crime, the Basic Principles 1985 encourage judicial and administrative procedures to respond to the particular needs of victims.[14] The Basic Principles 1985 reiterate the importance of providing information to victims regarding their rights, the criminal procedure, and outcomes.[15] Allowing the victim to express their views at "appropriate stages" of the proceedings is also encouraged.[16] Victims should be provided assistance during the criminal justice process and their privacy and safety should be protected.[17] The protection of victims and witnesses who participate during the criminal justice process has been considered an "emerging right" and has been highlighted under several international legal documents (and picked up by the ICC).[18]

Participation can offer victims the ability to take ownership over part of the process, which can have an empowering and rehabilitative effect.[19] Such ownership may be especially beneficial to vulnerable or marginalised groups, such as victims of sexual violence, where traditionally these victims have been silenced, stigmatised, or otherwise rendered invisible. However, this might depend on implementation, as criminal institutions and courts have been criticised for re-traumatising victims of rape, particularly through the approach of adversarial trials.[20] Moreover, victims of sexual crimes are likely to experience various obstacles to full participation in the criminal process. Such obstacles could include the need for immediate or emergency care in the case of sex crimes, gender discrimination, the lack of financial aid or information, social stigma, and issues

12 *The Declaration of Basic Principles of Justice for Victims of Crime and Abuse of Power* GA Res, A/Res/40/43 (1985) [Basic Principles 1985].

13 Bassiouni, above n 7, at 216.

14 Basic Principles 1985, art 6.

15 At art 6(a).

16 At art 6(b).

17 At art 6(c)-(d).

18 Bassiouni, above n 7, at 258. See for example Committee on the Elimination of Discrimination against Women *Concluding Observations on the combined sixth and seventh periodic reports of the Democratic Republic of the Congo* CEDAW/C/COD/CO/6–7 (2013) at [10(d)]; Committee on the Rights of the Child *Concluding Observations on the combined third, fourth and fifth periodic reports of Hungary* CRC/C/HUN/CO/3–5 (2014) at [59].

19 S Kelly "The Role of Victims in the International Criminal Court: Challenges & Opportunities" (2012) 18 *New England Journal of International & Comparative Law* 243 at 246.

20 F Marsh and N Wager "Restorative Justice in Cases of Sexual Violence: Exploring the Views of the Public and Survivors" (2015) 62 *Probation Journal* 336 at 338; A Kasparian "Justice Beyond Bars: Exploring the Restorative Justice Alternative for Victims of Rape and Sexual Assault" (2014) 37 *Suffolk Transnational Law Review* 1.

relating to protection.[21] Therefore, for victim participation to be meaningful, these perceived barriers need to be mitigated.

In sum, among the most important participatory rights are the right to information, the right to be heard, and the securement of victim safety. These rights align with the victim-centred approach underlying the proposed series of hybrid courts for peacekeepers as they seek to make visible the harm caused and the person or community harmed by the perpetrator. For example, in order for victims of sexual exploitation and abuse to see justice being done and have legitimate access to justice, it is fundamental that they receive timely information about reporting mechanisms and their cases.

Restorative justice models

To facilitate participatory rights, international criminal institutions have incorporated, in various ways, restorative justice models. There are different modalities of restorative justice that have been used in different contexts; some may be more suitable to responding to victims of sexual exploitation and abuse than others.

There is tension between legal experts who suggest victims should participate during trials[22] and those who argue that victim participation hinders the accused's right to a fair trial.[23] On the one hand, long procedural delays caused by incorporating victim participation interfere with the accused's right to an expeditious trial.[24] Moreover, there is a chance that crimes that emotionally impact and cause further suffering to victims may endanger the court's impartiality.[25] On the other hand, it has also been argued that purely retributive criminal institutions, particularly in post-conflict settings, do not take the wider context of trust and reconciliation into consideration.[26] For instance, the context of structural violence and discrimination against women may not be taken into account where the outcomes of the criminal court are solely driven by retributive justice.[27]

Restorative justice models are still developing, and there are different approaches within restorative criminal justice theory. Some domestic models tend to

21 REDRESS *Participation in Transitional Justice Processes by Survivors of Sexual and Gender-Based Violence* (Submission to the Office of the High Commissioner of Human Rights, 2014) at 6.

22 SM Mitchell "Restorative Justice, RPF Rule, and the Success of Gacaca" in HF Carey and SM Mitchell (eds) *Trials and Tribulations of International Prosecution* (Lexington Books, Lanham, 2013) 255 at 258.

23 Wemmers, above n 10, at 29.

24 B Leyh "Victim-Orientated Measures at International Criminal Institutions: Participation and Its Pitfalls" (2012) 12 *International Criminal Law Review* 375 at 399; REDRESS *The Participation of the Practice and Consideration of Options for the Future* (London, 2012) at 6; and S Zappala "The Rights of Victims v the Rights of the Accused" (2010) 8 *Journal of International Criminal Justice* 137 at 145–146.

25 Leyh "Victim-Orientated Measures at International Criminal Institutions: Participation and Its Pitfalls", above n 24, at 401; Zappala, above n 24, at 147–148.

26 Mitchell, above n 22, at 258.

27 At 258.

focus on victim-offender interaction, where both the victim and the offender participate equally in the proceedings, the harm is acknowledged, and the victim is in an empowered position to express their views directly to the offender.[28] In the context of sexual offences, however, this approach may not be appropriate. Direct victim-offender contact or interaction can be re-traumatising for the victim. Moreover, there may continue to be an uneven power dynamic operating between the UN peacekeeper (perpetrator) and beneficiary of assistance (victim) that may compound the harm already suffered by the victim.

When it comes to responding to crimes committed under post-conflict circumstances, there has generally been a restorative objective to accountability.[29] This has seen the introduction of Truth Commissions, participation in hybrid tribunals, and the notion of collective reparations. Truth Commissions have been utilised alongside hybrid courts, such as in Sierra Leone. Truth Commissions serve a complementary role to the prosecution of offenders and include the active participation of both victims and perpetrators.[30] They have multiple goals: to create a historical record of mass atrocities, to promote community-wide healing and reconciliation, and to help prevent future egregious violations of human rights.[31] Additionally, Truth Commissions fulfil the right to truth and victims' right to have their story heard after mass atrocities have been committed.[32]

Truth Commissions have been implemented in specific contexts, involving mass crimes against humanity or war crimes. Although the ability to be heard in a nonjudicial or quasi-judicial setting may help centralise the interests of victims, the goals relating to transitional justice may not be at all applicable to the context of responding to victims of sexual exploitation and abuse by peacekeepers. Truth Commissions help with recording events of mass atrocities, such as genocide, rather than opportunistic crimes, as sexual exploitation and abuse often are.[33] Moreover, at the end of a peacekeeping operation the peacekeepers leave the country – thus, there is no need for long-term reconciliation between peacekeepers and locals. Therefore, it is unlikely that Truth Commissions would be appropriate for responding to victims of sexual exploitation and abuse.

Other models that have been taken up by certain international criminal institutions, such as the ICC, have more *transformative* goals. Such restorative criminal justice systems aim to incorporate victim participation and also award reparations that address issues beyond those of the victim and offender, including the wider context of social-economic structural inequalities (the Trust Fund for Victims is an

28 At 258.
29 Leyh *Procedural Justice? Victim Participation in International Criminal Proceedings*, above n 1, at 59.
30 At 158–159.
31 WA Schabas "Internationalised Courts and Their Relationship with Alternative Accountability Mechanisms: The Case of Sierra Leone" in CR Romano, A Nollkaemper and JK Kleffner (eds) *International Criminal Courts: Sierra Leone, East Timor, Kosovo, and Cambodia* (Oxford University Press, Oxford, 2004) at 157.
32 Bassiouni, above n 7, at 276.
33 At 276.

example of this and is discussed further below).[34] Another restorative measure is to directly incorporate victim participation in criminal proceedings.

International criminal courts and victim participation in proceedings

Previous examples of hybrid tribunals have had mixed results in putting rights into practice. The Special Panels of East Timor, for example, had extensive measures available for victim participation and reparations. Under its regulations, participation in the Special Panels went beyond victim-as-witness and included the ability to request a specific investigation, the right to be heard at a review hearing, the right to be notified of hearings and progress of cases, and the right to request a review of the prosecutor's decision not to investigate and/or prosecute.[35]Although such provisions reflected rights outlined in the Basic Principles 1985, they were never utilised in practice due to a lack of resources (both financial and human) and political will.[36] Instead, the prosecution and punishment of perpetrators were considered paramount. Contrasted with the failed practice of the Special Panels, the Extraordinary Chambers in the Courts of Cambodia (ECCC) could be considered (mostly) successful in implementing similar provisions.

The ECCC Internal Rules noted three modes of victim participation: as complainant, as civil party, or as witness. Victims participating as a civil party are granted the most rights under the Rules, allowing for participation during criminal procedure and reparation claims.[37] Such rights include the ability to access information, such as the case file itself; to make submissions; to attend hearings and question the accused (through legal representation); and to request reparations.[38] Although praised by commentators for its significant incorporation of victim participatory rights, the ECCC has also been heavily criticised by victims themselves for not meeting expectations and for lengthy delays in proceedings.[39] Moreover, with the sheer number of victims requesting participation, delays are unavoidable and may only be mitigated by simplifying the application process as much as possible.

34 Mitchell, above n 22, at 258.

35 *Regulation 2000/30 on Transitional Rules of Criminal Procedure* UNTAET/REG/2000/30 (2000); *Regulation 2001/25 (amendment) on Transitional Rules of Criminal Procedure* UNTAET/REG/2000/25 (2000) at 12.1–12.8; and Leyh *Procedural Justice? Victim Participation in International Criminal Proceedings*, above n 1, at 153.

36 *Report to the Secretary General of the Commission of Experts to Review the Prosecution of Serious Violations of Human Rights in Timor-Leste (the East Timor) in 1999* S/2005/458 (Annex II) (2005); Leyh *Procedural Justice? Victim Participation in International Criminal Proceedings*, above n 1, at 154; and E Evans *The Right to Reparation in International Law for Victims of Armed Conflict* (Cambridge University Press, Cambridge, 2012) at 112.

37 "Civil parties" are those victims who have suffered physical, mental, or material harm directly from an international crime.

38 See *Extraordinary Chambers in the Courts of Cambodia Internal Rules (Rev. 9)* ECCC (January 2015) at Rules 23, 23 *quinquiens*, 83, 86, 90, 92, 94.

39 Leyh *Procedural Justice? Victim Participation in International Criminal Proceedings*, above n 1, at 179.

Academics have deemed the Rome Statute a significant step forward for victim participatory rights and transformative justice.[40] NGOs and victims' rights groups advocated for greater victim participation during the negotiation of the Rome Statute.[41] Thus, the Rome Statute and Rules of Procedure and Evidence have created a sophisticated approach to victims' rights and remedies.[42] Victims may participate during legal proceedings, they have a right to be protected, and they have the right to reparations.[43] Additionally, the Rome Statute established a Trust Fund for Victims, which facilitates long-term reparations for victims and their communities.[44]

Article 68(3) of the Rome Statute dictates that victims as participants may express their views at all levels of proceedings, if such participation does not impinge on the rights of the accused to a fair trial. This encapsulates a general right of victim participation in ICC proceedings.[45] The ICC's definition of "victims" also recognises that serious human rights crimes (such as torture and genocide) can have an effect beyond the individual, and victims may also be family members, dependants, and the wider community.[46] Applications for victim participation must be considered case by case in order to appropriately balance the rights of the accused against the victim's right to participate (taking into account the needs of all victims, particularly children or victims of sexual violence).[47]

As victim participation is at the discretion of the particular Chamber, jurisprudence is essential to its development, and an important case in this regard is *Lubanga*. The Trial Chamber accepted the right of victims to lead evidence at trial and challenge the admissibility of evidence without being a party to the proceedings.[48] The right of participation is attached to victims' role to assist the ICC in determination of truth.[49] At pre-trial level, victims may also participate by

40 C McCarthy *Reparations and Victim Support in the International Criminal Court* (Cambridge University Press, Cambridge, 2012) at 46; Henham and Findlay, above n 2, at 86; Hoyle and Ullrich above n 7, at 4; and Kelly, above n 19, at 244.

41 Although incorporated last minute due to a prolonged lack of consensus among state representatives. See Leyh *Procedural Justice? Victim Participation in International Criminal Proceedings*, above n 1, at 232–234; McCarthy, above n 40, at 50; and Kelly, above n 19, at 247.

42 *Rome Statute of the International Criminal Court* 2187 UNTS 3 (opened for signature 17 July 1998, entered into force 1 July 2002) [Rome Statute]; The Rules of Procedure and Evidence *Official Records of the Assembly of States Parties to the Rome Statute of the International Criminal Court* ICC-ASP/1/3 and Corr. 1 Part II.A (New York, 2002) [Rules of Procedure and Evidence].

43 Rome Statute, arts 43, 57, 68, 68(3), 79 and 85; Bassiouni, above n 7, at 230.

44 Rome Statute, art 75.

45 Kelly, above n 19, at 251.

46 Rules of Procedure and Evidence, above n 42, at Rule 85; Kelly, above n 19, at 247.

47 Rules of Procedure and Evidence, above n 42, at Rule 86.

48 Victims are framed as "participants" under the ICC rather than parties. See H Friman "The International Criminal Court and Participation of Victims: A Third Party to the Proceedings?" (2009) 22 *Leiden Journal of International Law* 485 at 493; *Prosecutor v Lubanga Dyilo Judgment on the Appeals of the Prosecutor and the Defence against Trial Chamber I's Decision on Victims' Participation of 18 January 2008* ICC Appeals Chamber ICC-01/04–01/06–1432, 11 July 2008 at [94–105].

49 Rome Statute, arts 64(6)(d) and 69(3).

providing their views and concerns regarding the investigation.[50] Victims may also have access to public material relating to cases, and in some circumstances, may request confidential materials.[51] Additionally, victims may attend all public hearings and, in some circumstances, closed hearings.[52]

Article 86 of the Rome Statute (which provides that the ICC shall take into account the needs of all victims and witnesses, particularly children and victims of sexual or gender violence)[53] is partially facilitated through the Victims and Witnesses Unit.[54] The Court may order the protection of witnesses both before and during trial.[55] Such protection includes physical and psychological wellbeing, safety, and privacy.[56] In order for victims to participate (especially as witnesses), safeguards need to be put in place to ensure their security and confidence in the Court.[57] This is particularly true of victims of sexual offences, for which the ICC ensures special protection measures.[58]

The mixed retributive-restorative goals pursued by the ICC have come under criticism by some, claiming that it is unlikely that the Court will receive enough resources (human and financial) to realistically achieve both.[59] Victim participation itself adds many hours and long delays for applications to be processed by the Registry's Victim Participation and Reparations Section.[60] For example, in 2011 there had been over 9,000 applications for participation in the situation in the

50 *Situation in Democratic Republic of Congo Decision on the Applications for Participation on the Proceedings of VPRS 1, VPRS 2, VPRS 3, VPRS 4, VPRS 5 and VPRS 6* ICC Pre-Trial Chamber ICC-01/04–101, 17 January 2006.

51 *Prosecutor v Lubanga Dyilo (Situation in the Democratic Republic of the Congo) Decision on the Arrangements for Participation of Victims a/0001/06, a/0002/06, and a/0003/06 at the Confirmation Hearing ICC Pre-Trial Chamber* ICC-01/04–01/06, 22 September 2006 at 7–8.

52 *Prosecutor v Lubanga Dyilo (Situation in the Democratic Republic of the Congo) Decision on Victims' Participation* ICC Trial Chamber ICC-01/04–01/06–1119, 18 January 2008 at [113].

53 Child witnesses are also entitled to special protection (physical and legal) under the *Convention on the Rights of the Child* 1577 UNTS 3 (opened for signature 20 November 1989, entered into force 2 September 1990) [CRC]. See also Committee on the Rights of the Child *Concluding Observations on the combined third and fifth periodic report of Hungary* CRC/C/HUN/CO/3–5 (2014) at [59].

54 Rome Statute, art 43(6).

55 Rome Statute, arts 57(3)(c), 68; Rules of Procedure and Evidence, above n 42, at Rule 87.

56 Rome Statute, art 68(1).

57 SN Ngane "Witnesses before the International Criminal Court" (2009) 8 *The Law and Practice of International Courts and Tribunals* 431 at 449.

58 See Rome Statute, art 68.

59 Hoyle and Ullrich, above n 7, at 10 and 18; M Damaska "What Is International Criminal Justice?" (2008) 83 *Chicago-Kent Law Review* 329, at 330 and 343; and Kelly, above n 19, at 260.

60 REDRESS "Hundreds of Victims Prevented from Participating in Crucial Court Hearings due to Lack of Resources at the International Criminal Court" (press release, 15 July 2011); M Pena and G Carayon "Is the ICC Making the Most of Victim Participation?" (2013) *The International Journal of Transitional Justice* 1 at 10.

Democratic Republic of Congo with only approximately 3,000 processed.[61] However, the sheer number of applications point to the clear interest victims have in participation.[62] Not only may the extensive participatory rights of victims compromise the rights of the accused, the wider transformative justice aims may undermine the so-called ultimate goal of the ICC – to punish offenders.[63] Moreover, these expansive goals may conflict with the neutral or nonpolitical aspect of criminal institutions.[64] However, the approach taken by the ICC and the Trust Fund for Victims (discussed more below) has arguably broadened the definition of international criminal justice to include a more holistic perspective.[65]

For all of the criticism, it appears the general impression of victim participation is that it plays a valuable part in the workings of the ICC.[66] In fact, only logistical or practical recommendations have been made by victim groups in order to make participation more meaningful for participants and manageable for the Court.[67] Moreover, an outreach programme to get more information into the wider community in which the ICC operates has been a priority.[68]

Victims under the ICC system are seen as having valuable experience and insight regarding their community, which has suffered massive human rights violations (such as genocide).[69] These crimes harm more than individuals, but devastate entire communities.[70] Thus, the ICC needs to consider the historical context of these crimes, from the point of view of the victims. Moreover, these crimes are committed by either members of the same community or their state officials. The context of peacekeeping may be compared, where sexual exploitation is committed by foreign personnel against individual locals living (temporarily) in the same country. Nevertheless, the particular context in which sexual exploitation and abuse occurs may still be important. Victims of sexual exploitation may have insight and views that expose the structural inequalities that exist and shed light on the nature of the exploitation itself. Therefore, although the high level of victim participation that is warranted under the ICC may not be as necessary in a hybrid court, some level of inclusivity of victims and their views would be of value.

61 See C Van der Wyngaert "Victims before International Criminal Courts: Some Views and Concerns of an ICC Trial Judge" (2011) 44 *Case Western Reserve Journal of International Law* 475 at 482.
62 *The Participation of the Practice and Consideration of Options for the Future*, above n 24, at 10.
63 Hoyle and Ullrich, above n 7, at 10; Damaska, above n 59, at 331.
64 Hoyle and Ullrich, above n 7, at 16.
65 At 11.
66 *The Participation of the Practice and Consideration of Options for the Future*, above n 24, at 24. See also Victims' Rights Working Group "Making Victim Participation Effective and Meaningful" (June 2014).
67 Such recommendations include strengthening outreach to victims and simplifying the application process. See *The Participation of the Practice and Consideration of Options for the Future*, above n 24, at 24.
68 See for example, International Criminal Court *Integrated Strategy for External Relations, Public Information and Outreach* available online: <www.icc-cpi.int>.
69 Pena and Carayon, above n 60, at 7.
70 At 7.

Victim participation in a series of hybrid courts for peacekeepers

There appears to be an overall trend in international criminal justice towards giving victims a greater role. Under a series of hybrid courts for peacekeepers, a victim of sexual exploitation and abuse may benefit from participation beyond acting as a witness. A mixed retributive-restorative justice system may best realise a victim-centred approach and serve the principles underlying this book. For example, the mixed model sees the goal of prosecuting the offender, whilst also incorporating the opportunity for victims to have their voices heard, to be included, and to see justice being done. A victim of sexual exploitation and abuse may have their voice heard by being consulted by the court or by submitting their views of the charges. For legitimacy, fairness, and fulfilment of the right to information, victims should be partial to material regarding their cases and should have the ability to attend hearings.

Hybrid courts are proposed because they offer an opportunity for trials to be visible and legitimate for victims and their communities; therefore, direct participation of victims should be a key part of the framework. Consultation with the host state is a necessary first step with hybrid courts, specifically consultation with victims and their communities. To support centralising the role of victims, it is necessary that they are heard at the early stage of development. The precise form victim participation takes may differ between hybrid courts, because they may reflect differing contexts and victim needs, so the following explores general implementation possibilities.

Building a framework with the interests of victims at its core would require the removal of barriers that have prevented and continue to prevent victims of sexual crimes from coming forward. These barriers include stigmatisation, isolation, and lack of financial aid. Therefore, the right to information can be addressed in two ways: first, raising awareness of sexual exploitation and abuse generally in order to sensitise communities to such conduct; and second, to inform victims of their rights, the criminal process, and possible outcomes. Victims should also have access to legal assistance where appropriate.

The right to be heard can be incorporated by allowing for victims' views to be expressed or considered before and during trial. Allowing victims to be heard can have both an empowering and rehabilitative effect, especially for vulnerable or marginalised groups. Prosecutors should therefore have an open dialogue with victims and their communities throughout trial. This might also better reflect the context in which sexual exploitation takes place and lead to a better understanding of survival sex itself. The rights of victims must, however, be balanced with the rights of the accused to a fair trial.

Victims of sexual violence may also need to feel safe to participate fully; therefore, having the necessary security is important. This is particularly true for child victims. A hybrid court for peacekeepers should therefore have a way to facilitate the protection of victims who participate in proceedings. A specific *Victim Support Unit* should be established to facilitate the implementation of these rights. *Victim Support Units* should be utilised in the field to help victims report allegations, to make referrals for legal assistance, and to organise the security of victims and witnesses if and when necessary.

It must be acknowledged that victims of sexual crimes may be especially reluctant to face their perpetrators directly. This can be compounded if these victims are subject to marginalisation or discrimination based on gender or wider structural oppression. Participation should always be voluntary, as some victims might be re-traumatised through engaging with the criminal justice system. The framework must always be guided by the needs of victims.

Victim reparations

Participation is an important aspect of restorative justice, and effective remedies are another. Victims' access to justice has been increasingly seen as forming part of the right to an effective remedy under international human rights law.[71] However, prosecution of the offender is not enough to discharge the obligation to provide a remedy.[72] Therefore, victim participation during trial is not enough. Steps must also be taken to respond to the needs of victims in the form of reparations.[73]

Over the past two decades the UN has failed to implement an adequate remedial response to victims of sexual exploitation and abuse. The next section will compare the current direction of the UN with the expected remedial trends under international human rights law.

Status quo for victims of sexual exploitation and abuse

In 2005, the Zeid Report highlighted the need for the UN to look at providing victim assistance.[74] However, the report also noted that (at that stage) the organisation did not have the mandate to provide full victim support, and instead favoured emergency medical assistance and referrals to local networks to provide

71 R Burke "Shaming the State: Sexual Offences by UN Military Peacekeepers and the Rhetoric of Zero Tolerance" in G Heathcore and D Otto (eds) *Rethinking Peacekeeping, Gender and Equality and Collective Security* (Palgrave Macmillan, Basingstoke, 2014) at 85; Bassiouni, above n 7, at 212, and 263–266.

72 Burke, above n 71. See also R Manjoo *Report of the Special Rapporteur on Violence against Women, Its Causes and Consequences* A/HRC/14/22 (2010); Human Rights Committee *General Comment No 31: The Nature of the General Legal Obligation Imposed on States Parties to the Covenant* CCPR/C/21/Rev.1/Add.13 (2004) [General Comment No 31] at [16]; and Committee on the Elimination of Discrimination against Women *General Recommendation No 28 on the Core Obligations of States Parties under Article 2 of the Convention on the Elimination of All Forms of Discrimination against Women* CEDAW/C/2010/47/GC.2 (2010) at [32].

73 *Resolution Adopted by the General Assembly, Further Actions and Initiatives to Implement the Beijing Declaration and Platform for Action* GA Res, A/RES/S-23/3 (2000) at [68(b)].

74 Secretary-General *A Comprehensive Strategy to Eliminate Future Sexual Exploitation and Abuse in United Nations Peacekeeping Operations* GA, A/59/710 (2005) [Zeid Report] at [52].

comprehensive care.[75] Nevertheless, since 2005 the UN has been proposing a wide-ranging approach to provide victim assistance.

Building on the Zeid Report, the *United Nations Comprehensive Strategy on Assistance and Support to Victims of Sexual Exploitation and Abuse by UN Staff and Related Personnel* (UN Strategy) purports to introduce "bold measures" to respond to victims.[76] When the draft strategy was submitted for discussion in 2006, Kofi Annan asserted that a "truly comprehensive approach will leave no uncertainty for the victims and will restore the reputation of the Organization [UN] as one that acts responsibly towards the communities it serves."[77]

The UN Strategy highlights the importance of working within local (host state) organisations and networks that already provide medical, psychological, and legal support.[78] The response to sexual exploitation and abuse may be different depending on the particular host state and the cultural and social context.[79] Local community ownership over assistance and support of victims also helps with legitimacy.[80] Working with local networks is important not only for host state ownership, but also to avoid alienating or discriminating against victims of gendered violence generally.[81] Therefore, the UN's position under the Strategy is to facilitate victim support through such networks, and to offer help in the creation of assistance mechanisms if gaps exist.[82] It has since been confirmed that this does not mean the UN will fully fund the establishment of new victim support networks, but it will provide proportionate funding whilst working with local organisations.[83] It was envisioned that the UN will facilitate referrals between service providers using "Victim Support Facilitators".[84] These roles have yet to be established.

75 At [53]-[56].
76 K Annan *Comprehensive Review of the Whole Question of Peacekeeping Operations in All Their Aspects* Letter dated 25 May 2006 from the Secretary-General to the President of the General Assembly GA, A/60/877 (2006) at 2.
77 At 2.
78 At [10].
79 Schabas, above n 31, at 541.
80 At 543.
81 K Annan *Comprehensive Review of the Whole Question of Peacekeeping Operations in All Their Aspects* Letter dated 25 May 2006 from the Secretary-General to the President of the General Assembly GA, A/60/877 (2006) Annex: A "Draft United Nations Policy Statement on Assistance and Support to Victims of Sexual Exploitation and Abuse by UN Staff or Related Personnel" [2006 Draft Policy], at [9]; *United Nations Comprehensive Strategy on Assistance and Support to Victims of Sexual Exploitation and Abuse by United Nations Staff and Related Personnel* GA Res, A/RES/62/214 (2008) [2008 UN Strategy] at [9].
82 2008 UN Strategy, above n 81, at [10].
83 ECHA/ECPS UN and NGO Task Force on Protection from Sexual Exploitation and Abuse *Sexual Exploitation and Abuse Victim Assistance Guide: Establishing Country-Based Mechanisms or Assisting Victims of Sexual Exploitation and Abuse by UN/NGO/IGO Staff and Related Personnel* (April, 2009) [Victim Assistance Guide] at 9.
84 2008 UN Strategy, above n 81, at [12].

There are three categories for recipients of assistance under the UN Strategy: complainants, victims, and children born as a result of sexual exploitation and abuse.[85] The different categories reflect different stages of inquiry and corresponding forms of support. Complainants represent individuals who have alleged they have been sexually exploited or abused, and whose complaint has not yet been verified by an administrative process (either UN or TCC).[86] Under the UN Strategy, complainants are entitled to emergency or immediate care, including medical, psychological, social, and legal assistance, along with protection, such as shelter.[87]

"Victims" under the UN Strategy are individuals whose claim has been verified (or the category seems appropriate) by an administrative, civil, or criminal process.[88] Victims are entitled to additional support, depending on individual needs.[89] However, the 2006 draft Strategy had referred to forward-looking support for victims, such as continued education, vocational skills training, and assistance with the goal of reintegration into the community.[90] This reference was excluded in the final version of the UN Strategy adopted in 2008.

In terms of implementation of the UN Strategy, progress has been poor and has been largely stalled in the first phase: mapping local networks in countries in which the UN operates. Information regarding the mapping of services has been sporadic; in 2009, there appeared to be a disparity between implementation progressions across host states. In the Democratic Republic of Congo (DRC), for instance, a number of steps have been taken, including the identification of pre-existing legal, medical, and psychosocial care services; the hiring of an individual with the role of network coordinator; and the designation of focal points for implementation of the UN Strategy.[91] However, in Timor-Leste there was a complete lack of a formal network identified or established for responding to victims of sexual exploitation and abuse (with no explanation as to this absence).[92] Out of only five missions that conducted mapping of basic services for victims, three had some form of assistance described under the UN Strategy for the three categories of complainants, victims, and children born from sexual exploitation and abuse (in Liberia, Haiti, and the DRC).[93]

Currently, there is no system-wide implementation of the UN Strategy as intended. This was made clear in the Secretary-General's 2015 annual report, which noted that the failure of implementation has been due to a lack of resources.[94] Moreover,

85 At [5(c)], [5(d)] and [5(e)].
86 At [5(c)].
87 At [6].
88 At [5(d)].
89 At [7].
90 2006 Draft Policy, above n 81, at [20].
91 At [28].
92 At [44].
93 Report of the Secretary-General *Overview of the Financing of the United Nations Peacekeeping Operations: Budget Performance for the Period from 1 July 2010 to 30 June 2011 and Budget for the Period 1 July 2012 to 30 June 2013* GA, A/66/679 (2010) at [129].
94 Secretary-General *Special Measures for Protection from Sexual Exploitation and Sexual Abuse* GA, A/69/779 (2015) at [68].

where assistance has been administered by UN organs, such as UNICEF, they have been accused of failing to adequately provide such care.[95]

The UN Strategy was given new life in 2016 (and 2017) with the introduction of a flurry of reforms. These included the establishment of a Trust Fund in Support of Victims of Sexual Exploitation and Abuse and the appointment of a Victims' Rights Advocate.[96] Member states have been asked to voluntarily contribute to the Fund, which would go towards general support services for victims. The Secretary-General has recently signalled his intention to modify the terms of reference to include individual payments assisting victims' access to justice – for example, to attend trials.[97]

The Victims' Rights Advocate, acting within the Assistant Secretary-General level, has been established to "monitor, oversee, and coordinate" the implementation of the UN Strategy.[98] Importantly, the Advocate is to liaise with local NGOs and civil society in an effort to map current services and assess specific gaps in victim support and assistance.[99] This is a positive development from the UN that demonstrates a move towards centring victims; however, progress of implementation remains in phase one for now (as it has since 2009). The question is whether the current direction of the UN Strategy is the best avenue for victim reparations. The answer requires examination of trends in international human rights law.

Reparations in international human rights law

It has been generally accepted that victims of crime have a right to reparations, particularly for those crimes connected to gross human rights violations.[100] Sexual exploitation and abuse are violations of international human rights law.[101] Relevant human rights instruments to examine include the *International Covenant on Civil and Political Rights* (ICCPR), the *Convention against Torture and Other Cruel, Inhuman or Degrading Treatment or Punishment* (CAT),[102] the *Convention on the*

95 See for example M Deschamps, HB Jallow and Y Sooka *Taking Action on Sexual Exploitation and Abuse by Peacekeepers: Report of an Independent Review on Sexual Exploitation and Abuse by International Peacekeeping Forces in the Central African Republic* (December, 2015) at iv.

96 See generally Secretary-General Special *Measures for Protection from Sexual Exploitation and Sexual Abuse* GA, A/71/818 (2017).

97 At [34].

98 At [27]-[35]. See also *Terms of Reference Victims' Rights Advocate* (2017) available online: <www.un.org>.

99 *Terms of Reference Victims' Rights Advocate*, above n 98, at 2.

100 *Nairobi Declaration on Women's and Girls' Rights to a Remedy and Reparation* (2007) available online: <www.redress.org> [Nairobi Declaration] at [3(E)].

101 See discussion in chapter two.

102 *International Covenant on Civil and Political Rights* 999 UNTS 171 (opened for signature 16 December 1966, entered into force 23 March 1976) [ICCPR]; *Convention against Torture and Other Cruel, Inhuman or Degrading Treatment or Punishment* 1465 UNTS 85 (opened for signature 10 December 1984, entered into force 26 June 1987) [CAT].

Rights of the Child (CRC),[103] the *Convention on the Elimination of All Forms of Discrimination against Women* (CEDAW), and *General Recommendation 19*.[104] It was acknowledged by the Special Rapporteur on Violence against Women in 2010 that "coherent theory and practice for remedies does not exist under international law".[105] Nevertheless, international human rights instruments and associated monitoring bodies have confirmed a right to effective remedies for victims of serious violations of human rights.[106] These remedies include reparations.

For information about what reparations mean in the context of human rights law, the *Basic Principles and Guidelines on the Right to a Remedy and Reparation for Victims of Gross Violations of International Human Rights Law and Serious Violations of International Humanitarian Law* (Basic Principles 2006) offer detailed insight.[107] This instrument is intended to reflect international norms regarding the implementation of the right to an effective remedy.[108] Whereas the Basic Principles 1985 focus on victim participation (primarily) during criminal proceedings, the Basic Principles 2006 focus on the right to an effective remedy and reparations, specifically within the context of human rights and humanitarian norms. Although the document itself is not legally binding, the Basic Principles 2006 are still relevant to legal obligations arising from international human rights and humanitarian norms.[109] Overall, the Basic Principles 2006 aim to "identify mechanisms, modalities, procedures, and methods" of the right to a remedy, including reparations.[110]

There are five accepted forms of reparations under the provisions of the Basic Principles 2006: restitution (where the victim is restored to the position they were in before the violation or crime took place);[111] financial compensation (for the economically measurable harm);[112] rehabilitation (assistance such as medical or psychological care and legal and social services);[113] satisfaction (a form of moral reparations, such as official declarations as to the victim's or victims' dignity, memorials, and public apologies);[114] and guarantees of non-

103 Above n 53.
104 Committee on the Elimination of Discrimination against Women *General Recommendation 19* CEDAW/C/GC/19 (1992).
105 Manjoo (2010), above n 72, at [13].
106 At [13]. See also ICCPR, art 2; CAT, art 14; CRC, art 14.
107 *Basic Principles and Guidelines on the Right to a Remedy and Reparation for Victims of Gross Violations of International Human Rights Law and Serious Violations of International Humanitarian Law* GA Res, A/RES/60/147 (Annex) (2006) [Basic Principles 2006].
108 Leyh *Procedural Justice? Victim Participation in International Criminal Proceedings*, above n 1, at 100.
109 Basic Principles 2006, above n 107, at 2; Manjoo (2010), above n 72, at [15].
110 Basic Principles 2006, above n 107, at Preamble.
111 At [19].
112 At [20].
113 At [21].
114 At [22(b), (d), (e)].

repetition (which includes endorsing the observance of codes and standards of conduct).[115]

Overall, when responding to human rights violations of a sexual nature, treaty bodies note that compensation is not enough for an effective remedy, and that states parties should aim for full rehabilitation.[116] Full rehabilitation has been specifically mentioned in the jurisprudence of the Committee against Torture, the Human Rights Committee, the Committee on the Rights of the Child, and the Committee on the Elimination of Discrimination against Women (CEDAW Committee).[117] Rehabilitation includes services to restore victims' "independence, physical, mental, social and vocational ability."[118] Accordingly, these measures should relate to the provision of medical and legal services (both emergency and long-term), including psychosocial support.[119] Additionally, these services should be gender sensitive in

115 At [23(a), (b), (f)].

116 See for example General Comment No 3, above n 72, at [5], [9] and [11]; see also R Manjoo *Report of the Special Rapporteur on Violence against Women, Its Causes and Consequences* A/HRC/23/49 (2013) at [75].

117 See for example Committee against Torture *Concluding Observations on the combined fifth and sixth periodic reports of Portugal* CAT/C/PRT/CO/5–6 (2013) at [16]; Committee against Torture *Concluding Observations on the combined third to fifth periodic reports of Latvia* CAT/C/LVA/Co/3–5 (2013) at [22]; Human Rights Committee *Concluding Observations on the fifth periodic report of Peru adopted at its 107th Session* CCPR/C/PER/CO/5 (2013) at [12]; Human Rights Committee *Concluding Observations on the seventh periodic report of Ukraine* CCPR/C/UKR/CO/7 (2013) at [6]; Human Rights Committee *Concluding Observations on the fourth periodic report of Ireland* CCPR/C/IRL/CO/4 (2014) at [10]; and *General Recommendation 19*, above n 104, at [24(k)].

118 General Comment No 3, above n 72, at [11]. See also Committee against Torture *Concluding Observations on the third periodic report of Belgium* CAT/C/BEL/CO/3 (2014) at [23]; and Committee against Torture *Concluding Observations on the third initial report of Burkina Faso* CAT/C/BFA/CO/1 (2014) at [18].

119 See for example Committee against Torture *Concluding Observations on the third initial report of Burkina Faso*, above n 118, at [18]; Committee against Torture *Concluding Observations on the combined fifth and sixth periodic reports of Poland* CAT/C/POL/CO/5–6 (2013) at [22(e)]; Human Rights Committee *Concluding Observations on the initial report of Sierra Leone* CCPR/C/SLE/CO/1 (2014) at [15]; Committee on the Rights of the Child *Concluding Observations on the combined third and fourth periodic reports of Portugal* CRC/C/PRT/CO/3–4 (2014) at [36 (c)-(d)]; Committee on the Rights of the Child *Concluding Observations on the combined second to fourth periodic reports of the Democratic Republic of the Congo* CRC/C/COG/CO/2–4 (2014) at [43(b)]; Committee on the Rights of the Child *Concluding Observations on the combined third and fourth periodic reports of Croatia* CRC/C/HRV/CO/3–4 (2014) at [37(f)]; Committee on the Elimination of Discrimination against Women *Hakan Goekce, Handan Goekce and Guelue Goekce v Austria* CEDAW/C/39/D/5/2005 Communication No 5/2005 (2007) at [12.1.1]; Committee on the Elimination of Discrimination against Women *SVP v Bulgaria* CEDAW/C/53/D/31/2011 Communication No 31/2011 (2012) at [9.11]; Committee on the Elimination of Discrimination against Women *Concluding Observations on the combined initial and second to fifth reports of the Central African Republic* CEDAW/C/CAF/CO/1–5 (2014) at [28(b)]; Committee on the Elimination of Discrimination against Women *Concluding Observations on the combined*

providing for the specific needs of sexual abuse victims.[120] This includes rehabilitative programmes with specialised personnel to deal with the psychological needs of victims of gendered violence.[121] Moreover, states parties are expected to implement protective measures such as safe shelters.[122] The needs of vulnerable or marginalised groups should be prioritised when developing these rehabilitative services.[123]

The Special Rapporteur on Violence against Women has argued that reparations should serve additional societal goals.[124] Moreover, reparations should link to both individual and structural transformation.[125] Essentially, gendered violence exists within a context of negative gender stereotypes and inequalities and structural oppression over women particularly.[126] Peacekeeping operations are inherently gendered, and sexual exploitation and abuse are an example of this gendered hierarchy. Any pre-existing gender inequalities and discrimination against women (or groups that are considered feminine, who do not conform to heteronormative stereotypes, or are otherwise "othered" by the dominant group) are then compounded by post-conflict circumstances, poverty, and the introduction of military forces that are overwhelmingly male. As a result, a significantly disproportionate power imbalance exists between peacekeepers and the local population. Therefore, reparations should not reinforce structural oppression. In fact, the Special Rapporteur argued that reparations should aim to dismantle such negative structures and address the "root causes of violence".[127] Similarly, the CEDAW Committee has urged states parties to develop comprehensive strategies when responding to violence against women to tackle the wider societal context that fosters gendered violence.[128]

fourth and fifth periodic reports of Cameroon CEDAW/C/CMR/CO/4–5 (2014) at [19(e)]; and Committee on the Elimination of Discrimination against Women *Concluding Observations on Cote d'Ivoire* CEDAW/C/CIV/CO/1–3 (2011) at [29(c)-(e)].

120 See for example Committee against Torture *Concluding Observations on the combined fifth and sixth periodic reports of Guatemala* CAT/C/GTM/CO/5–6 (2013) at [12].

121 *General Recommendation 19*, above n 104, at [24(k)].

122 See for example *Hakan Goekce, Handan Goekce and Guelue Goekce v Austria*, above n 119, at [12.1.2]; Committee on the Elimination of Discrimination against Women *VK v Bulgaria* CEDAW/C/49/D/20/2008 Communication No 20/2008 (2011) at [9.13]; Committee on the Elimination of Discrimination against Women *Concluding Observations on the combined fourth and fifth periodic reports of Georgia* CEDAW/C/GEO/CO/4–5 (2014) at [21(c)]; Committee on the Elimination of Discrimination against Women *Concluding Observations on the sixth periodic report of Sierra Leone* CEDAW/C/SLE/CO/6 (2014) at [21(f)]; and *Concluding Observations on Cote d'Ivoire*, above n 118, at [29(f)]; See also Committee on the Elimination of Discrimination against Women *AT v Hungary* A/60/38 (Part 1) Communication No 2/2003 (2005) Annex III.

123 See for example Human Rights Committee *Concluding Observations on the sixth periodic report of Germany* CCPR/CDEU/Co/6 (2012) at [9].

124 Manjoo (2010), above n 72, at [12].

125 At [24]. See also Manjoo (2013), above n 116, at [71].

126 Manjoo (2013), above n 116, at [31].

127 At [31].

128 See for example, Committee on the Elimination of Discrimination against Women *Banu Akbak, Gulen Khan, and Melissa Ozdemir v Austria* CEDAW/C/39/D/6/2005 Commination No 5/2005 (2007) at [12.2] and [12.3(b)-(c)]; Committee on

The above discussion indicates that there are identifiable trends in international human rights law: firstly, that rehabilitation reparations are favoured in response to violations of a sexual nature; and secondly, that transformative reparations are being argued as a response to gendered violence. Transformative reparations are forward looking and go beyond providing a remedy for the individual victim. They target institutional and structural transformation, such as removing barriers to justice mechanisms, establishing gender sensitivity training, and installing measures that "strive to change the realities of people that are impacted by violence".[129]

Both rehabilitation and transformative reparations fit within the principles of this book, especially the principles of centralising the interests of victims and recognising the (gendered) context where abuse takes place. For sexual exploitation and abuse, transformative reparations would require an understanding of the specific cultural and social contexts of each host state. The implementation of such reparations would centralise the interests of victims and their communities more broadly as they necessitate the participation of local actors, particularly of victims themselves, in the development of any reparations scheme.[130]

The UN Strategy and the recent establishment of the Trust Fund in Support of Victims of Sexual Exploitation and Abuse and the Victims' Rights Advocate reflect the trend in international human rights law to some extent. The intention to provide emergency medical and psychosocial support (for both complainants and victims) aligns with full rehabilitation reparations discussed above. Additionally, the Strategy requires close work with local actors and implementation of services through local organisations, which are supported by the jurisprudence of human

the Elimination of Discrimination against Women *Cecilia Kell v Canada* CEDAW/C/51/D/19/2008 Communication No 19/2008 (2012) at [10.2] and [11(b)(i)]; *Hakan Goekce, Handan Goekce and Guelue Goekce v Austria*, above n 118, at [12.2]; Committee on the Elimination of Discrimination against Women *Isatou Jallow v Bulgaria* CEDAW/C/52/D/32/2011 Communication No 32/2011 (2012) at [8.6]; Committee on the Elimination of Discrimination against Women *Maria de Lourdes da Silva Pimentel v Brazil* CEDAW/C/49/D/17/2008 Communication No 17/2008 (2011) at [7.7]; Committee on the Elimination of Discrimination against Women *Concluding Observations on the combined fourth and fifth periodic reports of India* CEDAW/C/IND/CO/4–5 (2014) at [11(b)]; Committee on the Elimination of Discrimination against Women *Concluding Observations on the combined seventh and eighth periodic reports of Peru* CEDAW/C/PER/CO/7–8 (2014) at [18]; and *Observations on the combined sixth and seventh periodic reports of the Democratic Republic of the Congo*, above n 118, at [10ff]. This has similarly been observed by the Human Rights Committee, see *Concluding Observations on the initial report of Sierra Leone*, above n 118, at [15]; Human Rights Committee *Concluding Observations on the initial report of Indonesia* CCPR/C/IDN/CO/1 (2013) at [13]; and Human Rights Committee *Concluding Observations adopted by the Human Rights Committee at its 105th session, 9–27 July 2012 Maldives* CCPR/C/MDV/CO/1 (2012) at [11].

129 R Manjoo "Introduction: Reflections on the Concept and Implementation of Transformative Reparations" (2017) 21 *The International Journal of Human Rights* 1193 at 1199.

130 At 1272.

rights bodies. The proposed meeting with victims and representative organisations to discuss support and assistance is also a positive move supported by human rights jurisprudence (particularly that addresses violence against women).[131]

However, transformative or forward-looking support mechanisms are missing from the current UN Strategy. There is an absence of forward-looking reparations for individual victims (such as vocational training)[132] and no indication of structural reforms. Although the UN has established in-house training and awareness raising among their personnel about sexual exploitation and abuse,[133] nothing suggests that this has been linked to transforming communities or dismantling harmful masculinities that foster gendered violence. Overall, the status quo requires significant improvement to offer *effective* remedies for victims of sexual exploitation and abuse.

A mechanism that has attempted to implement transformative reparations, both individual and structural, is the ICC Trust Fund for Victims. As the Trust Fund is closely linked to an international criminal institution, it is insightful to examine its practice (so far) and glean possible ideas for reparation mechanisms that might attach to or sit alongside a series of hybrid courts for peacekeepers.

Example – ICC Trust Fund for Victims

The ICC has the power to order cost of reparations against a convicted person (in the form of restitution, compensation, or rehabilitation).[134] However, where the convicted person is unlikely to deliver on costs or it is deemed appropriate by the Court, the ICC may order reparations to be made through the Trust Fund for Victims.[135] The Trust Fund may be utilised in various ways: reparations may be awarded directly to the victim, collective reparations may be awarded, or general assistance may be made available to intergovernmental, international, or national organisations previously approved by the Trust Fund.[136] Additionally, the Trust Fund is an independent organ of the Court itself, and so may provide assistance to victims and their communities of its own accord (within an active situation of the Court and not inconsistent with the rights of any accused).[137] In this way, the Trust Fund aims to implement transformative reparations that have an impact beyond the individual victim.

131 *Special Measures for Protection from Sexual Exploitation and Sexual Abuse* (2017), above n 96, at [27]-[35].
132 See for example General Comment No 3, above n 72, at [11]; see also *Concluding Observations on the third periodic report of Belgium*, above n 118, at [23]; *Concluding Observations on the third initial report of Burkina Faso*, above n 118, at [18].
133 See for example, *Special Measures for Protection from Sexual Exploitation and Sexual Abuse* (2015), above n 94, at [76]-[79].
134 Rome Statute, art 75(2); Rules of Procedure and Evidence, above n 42, at Rule 98(3).
135 Rome Statute, art 75(2); Rules of Procedure and Evidence, above n 42, at Rule 98(3).
136 Rules of Procedure and Evidence, above n 42, at Rules 98(2), 98(3) and 98(4).
137 International Criminal Court *Regulations of the Trust Fund for Victims* ICC-ASP/4/Res.3 (2005) at [50(a)(i)]. See also, Evans, above n 36, at 106.

In its first order for reparations (March 2015), the ICC fleshed out a number of general principles.[138] The Appeals Chamber noted that reparations must be ordered and implemented with full consultation with victims and their communities.[139] Reparations (whether restitution, compensatory, rehabilitative, or symbolic) must be prompt, appropriate, and proportional to the harm caused to the victims and their communities.[140] Additionally, reparations aimed at community programmes should "reflect local cultural and customary practices unless these are discriminatory, exclusive or deny victims equal access to their rights".[141] In the particular case of *Lubanga* all modalities of reparations were made against Lubanga (convicted for *inter alia* the recruitment of child soldiers).[142] For example, the Court ordered reparation in the form of rehabilitation measures: to reintegrate former child soldiers into their society, to address their shame and victimisation, and to include education programmes implemented within the victims' community.[143]

Through its regulations, the Trust Fund has a mandate to partner with NGOs and international and national organisations to help provide assistance to victims and their communities in countries where the ICC investigates (situations).[144] The Trust Fund for Victims takes a holistic view when providing assistance measures and projects. When deciding on such projects, the Trust Fund's board of directors[145] will consider the wider context (for example, conflict, post-conflict, post-disaster, human rights crimes) and take into consideration a number of factors when developing responses. Such factors include the following: transitional justice; gender mainstreaming; the physical, mental, and social wellbeing of victims; economic security; material support (food and shelter); and wider peace and reconciliation of victim communities.[146] Examples of current Trust Fund programmes (partnered with the appropriate international and national organisations) include employment skills training, financial

138 *Prosecutor v Lubanga Dyilo (Situation in the Democratic Republic of the Congo) Annex A: Principles of Reparations* ICC Appeals Chamber ICC-01/04–01/06–3129 3 March 2015 [ICC Reparation Principles]; *Prosecutor v Lubanga Dyilo (Situation in the Democratic Republic of the Congo) Submission on reparations issue* ICC Trial Chamber I ICC-01/04–01/06–2879, 10 May 2012 at [4].

139 ICC Reparation Principles, above n 138, at [29]-[32].

140 At [44]-[45].

141 At [47].

142 *Prosecutor v Lubanga Dyilo (Situation in the Democratic Republic of Congo) Annex A: Order for Reparations against Mr Lubanga* ICC Appeals Chamber ICC-01/04–01/06–3129, 3 March 2015 [Order for Reparations].

143 At [67(iii)]-[67(v)].

144 *Regulations of the Trust Fund for Victims*, above n 137, at [50].

145 The Trust Fund's board of directors is made up of five members representing the five major world regions (Asia, Africa, Americas and Caribbean states, Eastern European states, and Western European and "other" states), see J McCleary-Sills and S Mukasa *External Evaluation of the Trust Fund for Victims Programmes in Northern Uganda and the Democratic Republic of the Congo: Towards a Perspective for Upcoming Interventions* (International Center for Research on Women, The Hague, 2013) at 10.

146 See generally The Trust Fund for Victims "A Road to Recovery: Healing Empowerment and Reconciliation" *Programme Progress Report* (Winter, 2014); The Trust Fund for Victims *TFV Strategic Plan 2014–2017* (The Hague, 2014).

literacy education, and dedicated groups assisting survivors of sexual violence with reintegration.[147] Moreover, local outreach programmes to reduce stigmatisation of sexual violence has also been a key aspect of the Trust Fund's work.[148] The focus of such programmes is community leadership and participation, which has been highlighted as one of the key aspects of the perceived success of the Trust Fund.[149]

In terms of response to gendered violence, the Trust Fund's measures have emphasised the empowerment of women and girls. Such measures include financial literacy for financial independence and community leadership.[150] Therefore, the development of programmes and assistance seek to involve the full participation of local women and girls.[151] This can help dismantle gendered stereotypes that foster violence against women and provide a more complete perspective for implementation strategies.[152] The ICC Trust Fund itself places its reparations programmes within the structure of gender justice; therefore, they are remedies that aim to acknowledge the context of unequal power dynamics based on gender and to avoid magnifying such inequalities.[153]

The ICC Trust Fund's approach has both expanded and challenged the traditional concept of reparations for victims with its focus on rehabilitation (reparations have often been limited to restitution and compensation).[154] The Trust Fund's notion of transformative justice has been drawn from several sources, particularly from human rights norms.[155] As discussed above, the approach to victim reparations taken by the Special Rapporteur on Violence against Women has been one with particular emphasis on long-term remedies, and it includes reparations aimed at changing negative social/economic/cultural structures that foster gendered violence. This approach is reflected in the Trust Fund. Again, by focusing on community-driven transformative reparations, the framework is context specific

147 "A Road to Recovery: Healing Empowerment and Reconciliation" above n at 146. See also "The Trust Fund for Victims Launches New Assistance Projects in Northern Uganda" (press release, 3 July 2015) available online: <www.icc-cpi.int>.

148 Assembly of State Parties *Resolution on Victims and Affected Communities, Reparations and Trust Fund for Victims* ICC-ASP/13/Res.4 (2014) at 8; *TFV Strategic Plan 2014–2017,* above n 146, at 20–21.

149 McCleary and Mukasa, above n 145, at 8.

150 At 34.

151 "A Road to Recovery: Healing Empowerment and Reconciliation" above n 146, at 4; *TFV Strategic Plan 2014–2017,* above n 146, at 20–21; *Resolution on Victims and Affected Communities, Reparations and Trust Fund for Victims,* above n 148, at 8; McCleary and Mukasa, above n 145, at 13.

152 McCleary and Mukasa, above n 145, at 34.

153 E Rehn "Speech: Achieving Gender Justice: The Case of Reparations" *57th Session of the Commission on the Status of Women* (2013) at 3.

154 Hoyle and Ullrich, above n 7, at 13.

155 Particularly influenced by the Nairobi Declaration, above n 100. The Declaration arose out of a meeting between women's rights organisations and survivors of wartime sexual violence from Asia, Europe, South and North America, and Africa, and it details implementation of the right to an effective remedy in the context of sexual violence during armed conflict. Development of the Declaration was led by women.

and victim centred. These are positive attributes to build within or alongside a series of hybrid courts for peacekeepers in order to provide *effective* remedies for victims of sexual exploitation and abuse.

However, implementation of reparations by the Trust Fund has not been without its challenges. Although there has been the development of broader reparations for victims, many reparations are attached to convictions.[156] This can cause problems for certain groups of victims who have not been reflected in the particular charges brought by the prosecution. For example, in the *Lubanga* case, while there were victims of sexual violence, the charges exclusively related to the recruitment of child soldiers.[157] This decision was made based on the evidence available and the expeditiousness of proceedings.[158] Upon conviction, those victims of sexual violence were left without reparations. This has been criticised as a perpetrator-centred approach, which leaves reparations as an afterthought once conviction has been sought.[159] Moreover, victims may also lose out on reparations under this system where the accused was not convicted due to insufficient evidence or acquittal.[160] For a truly victim-centred approach, broader transformative reparations should be based on need and detached from actual conviction of the perpetrator.[161] Development of such a mechanism must then be guided by victims and their communities in order to reflect reparations that are appropriate according to genuine need.[162]

Overall, the ICC Trust Fund for Victims focuses on transformative and forward-looking reparations. This goes further than just immediate or emergency care for victims. The Trust Fund takes a holistic view of human rights violations to tackle the wider context that fosters such violations. In relation to sexual violence, this view is similar to that under international human rights law, which supports reparations that have transformative goals. The ICC Trust Fund offers a blueprint for a possible reparations scheme for victims of sexual exploitation and abuse. However, as noted above, there have been challenges in implementation where repatriations are attached to convictions.

Reparations for victims of sexual exploitation and abuse – a separate mechanism

Victims of sexual exploitation and abuse are victims of human rights violations and should receive reparations to address the harm caused. Victims deserve to be

156 L Moffett "Reparations for Victims at the International Criminal Court: A New Way Forward?" (2017) 21 *The International Journal of Human Rights* 1204, at 1204.
157 At 1206; see also L Chappell "The Gender Injustice Cascade: 'Transformative' Reparations for Victims of Sexual and Gender-Based Crimes in the Lubanga Case at the International Criminal Court (2017) 21 *The International Journal of Human Rights* 1223.
158 Moffett, above n 156, at 1206.
159 At 1206.
160 At 1208.
161 A Durbach and L Chappell "Leaving Behind the Age of Impunity" (2014) *16 International Feminist Journal of Politics* 543, at 555.
162 See generally Manjoo "Introduction", above n 129.

treated with dignity and respect. Following the overall trend in international human rights law, in addition to individual reparations that might be awarded upon conviction, rehabilitation and transformative reparations should be developed to sit alongside a series of hybrid courts for peacekeepers. A new Victim Reparations Fund should be established and could be administered under the proposed new UN organ that would oversee the hybrid courts.[163] Such a fund would be utilised by local entities to deliver rehabilitation and transformative reparations. Dialogue between the UN-level Victim Reparations Fund and the local entities could be facilitated through the Victims' Rights Advocate(s). However, in order to reflect appropriate reparations according to the unique context of each host state, a necessary first step is the leadership of victims and their communities in the development of such reparations.

Generally, rehabilitation should include (as it does currently under the UN Strategy) access to emergency medical and psychosocial support. Additionally, safe shelters and legal assistance should be part of this support. In order to be victim-centred, rehabilitation should respond to the needs of the victim and their community and not be attached to the outcome of a trial.

Victims should have access to not only immediate and emergency material care, but also long-term or forward-looking reparations (such as education and vocational skills). Moreover, responses should take into consideration the wider context; reparations should not enforce pre-existing societal or cultural structures that foster gendered violence, but should instead aim to dismantle them. This includes negative stereotypes associated with hypermasculinity in military forces (within peacekeeping) and within the local community in which the UN operates. As with victim participation, transformative reparations must be guided by the needs of the victims.

Furthermore, the UN Strategy's preference for working with local organisations in order to provide assistance to victims represents international best practice and should be carried over into the Victim Reparations Fund. Moreover, working with networks within the host state and involving victims and communities themselves in development support the principle of host state ownership and bolsters legitimacy. Importantly, it must also be recognised that no one remedy will serve all victims, and compensation must also be left open as an option under the proposed reparations scheme.[164]

Conclusion – the second part of a twofold solution

To centre the interests of victims within a new hybrid framework for accountability, a series of hybrid courts for peacekeepers should be built around a mixed retributive-restorative model. Such a model ensures that perpetrators are

163 See chapter six for further discussion.

164 L Chappell, A Durbach and M Marcus "'Nothing about Us, without Us, Is for Us': Victims and the International Criminal Justice System" (2017) 21 *The International Journal of Human Rights* 1337 at 1342.

prosecuted and punished and also includes victims in that process to guarantee that justice is seen to be done.

This chapter proposed the establishment of two mechanisms, which serve two different sides to restorative justice. The first is a Victim Support Unit within the series of hybrid courts for peacekeepers. Victim Support Units should facilitate victim participatory rights. Guided by the needs of victims, these tasks could include helping victims with reporting complaints, referring legal assistance, offering security and protection where appropriate, and keeping victims informed about their cases.

The second mechanism is a Victim Reparations Fund to sit alongside the hybrid courts. The Fund should go further than the current UN Strategy for victim support and assistance by developing full rehabilitation and transformative reparations. These must be both led by victims and their communities and implemented locally, responding to the particular needs of those victims. Placing victims and their communities in such an empowering position challenges the differential power dynamics between peacekeepers and beneficiaries of assistance (which creates the potential for exploitation).

A series of hybrid courts for peacekeepers would only serve one aspect of accountability. The two broad responses explored in this chapter, participation and reparations, aim to deliver the second, yet equally important, aspect of accountability: effective remedies for victims of sexual exploitation and abuse. The UN is required to take leadership in the establishment of the above two additional mechanisms and positively engage with relevant local actors for their implementation.

References

K Annan *Comprehensive Review of the Whole Question of Peacekeeping Operations in All Their Aspects* Letter dated 25 May 2006 from the Secretary-General to the President of the General Assembly GA A/60/877 (2006)

Assembly of State Parties *Resolution on Victims and Affected Communities, Reparations and Trust Fund for Victims* ICC-ASP/13/Res.4 (2014)

Basic Principles and Guidelines on the Right to a Remedy and Reparation for Victims of Gross Violations of International Human Rights Law and Serious Violations of International Humanitarian Law GA Res, A/RES/60/147 (Annex) (2006)

MC Bassiouni "International Recognition of Victims' Rights" (2006) 6 *Human Rights Law Review* 203

R Burke "Shaming the State: Sexual Offences by UN Military Peacekeepers and the Rhetoric of Zero Tolerance" in G Heathcore and D Otto (eds) *Rethinking Peacekeeping, Gender and Equality and Collective Security* (Palgrave Macmillan, Basingstoke, 2014)

AM Cellini "The Proposed Victims' Rights Amendment to the Constitution of the United States: Opening the Door of the Criminal Justice System to the Victim" (1997) 14 *Arizona Journal of International and Comparative Law* 839

L Chappell, A Durbach and M Marcus "'Nothing about Us, without Us, Is for Us': Victims and the International Criminal Justice System" (2017) 21 *The International Journal of Human Rights* 1337

L Chappell "The Gender Injustice Cascade: 'Transformative' Reparations for Victims of Sexual and Gender-Based Crimes in the Lubanga Case at the International Criminal Court" (2017) 21 *The International Journal of Human Rights* 1223

Committee against Torture *Concluding Observations on the combined fifth and sixth periodic reports of Guatemala* CAT/C/GTM/CO/5–6 (2013)

Committee against Torture *Concluding Observations on the combined fifth and sixth periodic reports of Poland* CAT/C/POL/CO/5–6 (2013)

Committee against Torture *Concluding Observations on the combined fifth and sixth periodic reports of Portugal* CAT/C/PRT/CO/5–6 (2013)

Committee against Torture *Concluding Observations on the combined third to fifth periodic reports of Latvia* CAT/C/LVA/Co/3–5 (2013)

Committee against Torture *Concluding Observations on the third initial report of Burkina Faso* CAT/C/BFA/CO/1 (2014)

Committee against Torture *Concluding Observations on the third periodic report of Belgium* CAT/C/BEL/CO/3 (2014)Committee on the Elimination of Discrimination against Women *AT v Hungary* A/60/38 (Part 1) Communication No 2/2003 (2005)

Committee on the Elimination of Discrimination against Women *Banu Akbak, Gulen Khan, and Melissa Ozdemir v Austria* CEDAW/C/39/D/6/2005 Commination No 5/2005 (2007)

Committee on the Elimination of Discrimination against Women *Cecilia Kell v Canada* CEDAW/C/51/D/19/2008 Communication No 19/2008 (2012)

Committee on the Elimination of Discrimination against Women *Concluding Observations on Cote d'Ivoire* CEDAW/C/CIV/CO/1–3 (2011)

Committee on the Elimination of Discrimination against Women *Concluding Observations on the combined fourth and fifth periodic reports of Cameroon* CEDAW/C/CMR/CO/4–5 (2014)

Committee on the Elimination of Discrimination against Women *Concluding Observations on the combined fourth and fifth periodic reports of Georgia* CEDAW/C/GEO/CO/4–5 (2014)

Committee on the Elimination of Discrimination against Women *Concluding Observations on the combined fourth and fifth periodic reports of India* CEDAW/C/IND/CO/4–5 (2014)

Committee on the Elimination of Discrimination against Women *Concluding Observations on the combined initial and second to fifth reports of the Central African Republic* CEDAW/C/CAF/CO/1–5 (2014)

Committee on the Elimination of Discrimination against Women *Concluding Observations on the combined seventh and eighth periodic reports of Peru* CEDAW/C/PER/CO/7–8 (2014)

Committee on the Elimination of Discrimination against Women *Concluding Observations on the combined sixth and seventh periodic reports of the Democratic Republic of the Congo* CEDAW/C/COD/CO/6–7 (2013)

Committee on the Elimination of Discrimination against Women *Concluding Observations on the sixth periodic report of Sierra Leone* CEDAW/C/SLE/CO/6 (2014)

Committee on the Elimination of Discrimination against Women *General Recommendation 19* CEDAW/C/GC/19 (1992)

Committee on the Elimination of Discrimination Against Women *General Recommendation No 28 on the Core Obligations of States Parties under Article 2 of the Convention on the Elimination of All Forms of Discrimination against Women* CEDAW/C/2010/47/GC.2 (2010)

Committee on the Elimination of Discrimination against Women *Hakan Goekce, Handan Goekce and Guelue Goekce v Austria* CEDAW/C/39/D/5/2005 Communication No 5/2005 (2007)

Committee on the Elimination of Discrimination against Women *Isatou Jallow v Bulgaria* CEDAW/C/52/D/32/2011 Communication No 32/2011 (2012)

Committee on the Elimination of Discrimination against Women *Maria de Lourdes da Silva Pimentel v Brazil* CEDAW/C/49/D/17/2008 Communication No 17/2008 (2011)

Committee on the Elimination of Discrimination against Women *SVP v Bulgaria* CEDAW/C/53/D/31/2011 Communication No 31/2011 (2012)

Committee on the Elimination of Discrimination against Women *VK v Bulgaria* CEDAW/C/49/D/20/2008 Communication No 20/2008 (2011)

Committee on the Rights of the Child *Concluding Observations on the combined second to fourth periodic reports of the Democratic Republic of the Congo* CRC/C/COG/CO/2–4 (2014)

Committee on the Rights of the Child *Concluding Observations on the combined third and fifth periodic reports of Hungary* CRC/C/HUN/CO/3–5 (2014)

Committee on the Rights of the Child *Concluding Observations on the combined third and fourth periodic reports of Croatia* CRC/C/HRV/CO/3–4 (2014)

Committee on the Rights of the Child *Concluding Observations on the combined third and fourth periodic reports of Portugal* CRC/C/PRT/CO/3–4 (2014)

Committee on the Rights of the Child *Concluding Observations on the combined third, fourth and fifth periodic reports of Hungary* CRC/C/HUN/CO/3–5 (2014)

Convention against Torture and Other Cruel, Inhuman or Degrading Treatment or Punishment 1465 UNTS 85 (opened for signature 10 December 1984, entered into force 26 June 1987)

Convention on the Rights of the Child 1577 UNTS 3 (opened for signature 20 November 1989, entered into force 2 September 1990)

M Damaska "What Is International Criminal Justice?" (2008) 83 *Chicago-Kent Law Review* 329

JT Davis "The Grassroots Beginnings of the Victims' Rights Movement" (2005) *National Crime Victim Law Institute News*

M Deschamps, HB Jallow and Y Sooka *Taking Action on Sexual Exploitation and Abuse by Peacekeepers: Report of an Independent Review on Sexual Exploitation and Abuse by International Peacekeeping Forces in the Central African Republic* (December, 2015)

A Durbach and L Chappell "Leaving Behind the Age of Impunity" (2014) 16 *International Feminist Journal of Politics* 543

ECHA/ECPS UN and NGO Task Force on Protection from Sexual Exploitation and Abuse *Sexual Exploitation and Abuse Victim Assistance Guide: Establishing Country-Based Mechanisms or Assisting Victims of Sexual Exploitation and Abuse by UN/NGO/IGO Staff and Related Personnel* (April, 2009)

E Evans *The Right to Reparation in International Law for Victims of Armed Conflict* (Cambridge University Press, Cambridge, 2012)

Extraordinary Chambers in the Courts of Cambodia Internal Rules (Rev. 9) ECCC (January 2015)

H Friman "The International Criminal Court and Participation of Victims: A Third Party to the Proceedings?" (2009) 22 *Leiden Journal of International Law* 485

R Henham and M Findlay *Exploring the Boundaries of International Criminal Justice* (Ashgate, Farnham, 2011)

C Hoyle and L Ullrich "New Court, New Justice? The Evolution of 'Justice for Victims' at Domestic Courts and at the International Criminal Court" (2014) *International Criminal Justice* 1

Human Rights Committee *Concluding Observations adopted by the Human Rights Committee at its 105th session, 9–27 July 2012 Maldives* CCPR/C/MDV/CO/1 (2012)

Human Rights Committee *Concluding Observations on the fifth periodic report of Peru adopted at its 107th Session* CCPR/C/PER/CO/5 (2013)

Human Rights Committee *Concluding Observations on the fourth periodic report of Ireland* CCPR/C/IRL/CO/4 (2014)

Human Rights Committee *Concluding Observations on the initial report of Indonesia* CCPR/C/IDN/CO/1 (2013)

Human Rights Committee *Concluding Observations on the initial report of Sierra Leone* CCPR/C/SLE/CO/1 (2014)

Human Rights Committee Concluding Observations on the seventh periodic report of Ukraine CCPR/C/UKR/CO/7 (2013)

Human Rights Committee Concluding Observations on the sixth periodic report of Germany CCPR/CDEU/Co/6 (2012)

Human Rights Committee *General Comment No 31: The Nature of the General Legal Obligation Imposed on States Parties to the Covenant* CCPR/C/21/Rev.1/Add.13 (2004)

International Covenant on Civil and Political Rights 999 UNTS 171 (opened for signature 16 December 1966, entered into force 23 March 1976)

International Criminal Court *Regulations of the Trust Fund for Victims* ICC-ASP/4/Res.3 (2005)

A Kasparian "Justice Beyond Bars: Exploring the Restorative Justice Alternative for Victims of Rape and Sexual Assault" (2014) 37 *Suffolk Transnational Law Review* 1

S Kelly "The Role of Victims in the International Criminal Court: Challenges & Opportunities" (2012) 18 *New England Journal of International & Comparative Law* 243

B Leyh *Procedural Justice? Victim Participation in International Criminal Proceedings* (Intersentia, Cambridge, 2011)

B Leyh "Victim-Orientated Measures at International Criminal Institutions: Participation and Its Pitfalls" (2012) 12 *International Criminal Law Review* 375

R Manjoo "Introduction: Reflections on the Concept and Implementation of Transformative Reparations" (2017) 21 *The International Journal of Human Rights* 1193

R Manjoo *Report of the Special Rapporteur on Violence against Women, Its Causes and Consequences* A/HRC/23/49 (2013)

R Manjoo *Report of the Special Rapporteur on Violence against Women, Its Causes and Consequences* A/HRC/14/22 (2010)

F Marsh and N Wager "Restorative Justice in Cases of Sexual Violence: Exploring the Views of the Public and Survivors" (2015) 62 *Probation Journal* 336

C McCarthy *Reparations and Victim Support in the International Criminal Court* (Cambridge University Press, Cambridge, 2012)

J McCleary-Sills and S Mukasa *External Evaluation of the Trust Fund for Victims Programmes in Northern Uganda and the Democratic Republic of the Congo: Towards a Perspective for Upcoming Interventions* (International Center for Research on Women, The Hague, 2013)

SM Mitchell "Restorative Justice, RPF Rule, and the Success of Gacaca" in HF Carey and SM Mitchell (eds) *Trials and Tribulations of International Prosecution* (Lexington Books, Lanham, 2013)

L Moffett "Reparations for Victims at the International Criminal Court: A New Way Forward?" (2017) 21 *The International Journal of Human Rights* 1204

Nairobi Declaration on Women's and Girls' Rights to a Remedy and Reparation (2007) available online: <www.redress.org>

SN Ngane "Witnesses before the International Criminal Court" (2009) 8 *The Law and Practice of International Courts and Tribunals* 431

M Pena and G Carayon "Is the ICC Making the Most of Victim Participation?" (2013) *The International Journal of Transitional Justice* 1

Prosecutor v Lubanga Dyilo Judgment on the Appeals of the Prosecutor and the Defence against Trial Chamber I's Decision on Victims' Participation of 18 January 2008 ICC Appeals Chamber ICC-01/04–01/06–1432, 11 July 2008

Prosecutor v Lubanga Dyilo (Situation in the Democratic Republic of the Congo) Annex A: Order for Reparations against Mr Lubanga ICC Appeals Chamber ICC-01/04–01/06–3129, 3 March 2015

Prosecutor v Lubanga Dyilo (Situation in the Democratic Republic of the Congo) Annex A: Principles of Reparations ICC Appeals Chamber ICC-01/04–01/06–3129 3 March 2015

Prosecutor v Lubanga Dyilo (Situation in the Democratic Republic of the Congo) Decision on the Arrangements for Participation of Victims a/0001/06, a/0002/06, and a/0003/06 at the Confirmation Hearing ICC Pre-Trial Chamber ICC-01/04–01/06, 22 September 2006

Prosecutor v Lubanga Dyilo (Situation in the Democratic Republic of the Congo) Decision on Victims' Participation ICC Trial Chamber ICC-01/04–01/06–1119, 18 January 2008

Prosecutor v Lubanga Dyilo (Situation in the Democratic Republic of the Congo) Submission on Reparations Issue ICC Trial Chamber I ICC-01/04–01/06–2879, 10 May 2012

REDRESS "Hundreds of Victims Prevented from Participating in Crucial Court Hearings due to Lack of Resources at the International Criminal Court" (press release, 15 July 2011)

REDRESS *Participation in Transitional Justice Processes by Survivors of Sexual and Gender-Based Violence* (Submission to the Office of the High Commissioner of Human Rights, 2014)

REDRESS *The Participation of the Practice and Consideration of Options for the Future* (London, 2012)

Regulation 2000/30 On Transitional Rules of Criminal Procedure UNTAET/REG/2000/30 (2000)

Regulation 2001/25 (amendment) On Transitional Rules of Criminal Procedure UNTAET/REG/2000/25 (2000)

E Rehn "Speech: Achieving Gender Justice: The Case of Reparations" *57th Session of the Commission on the Status of Women* (2013)

Resolution Adopted by the General Assembly, Further Actions and Initiatives to Implement the Beijing Declaration and Platform for Action GA Res, A/RES/S-23/3 (2000)

Report of the Secretary-General *Overview of the Financing of the United Nations Peacekeeping Operations: Budget Performance for the Period from 1 July 2010 to 30 June 2011 and Budget for the Period 1 July 2012 to 30 June 2013* GA, A/66/679 (2010)

Report to the Secretary General of the Commission of Experts to Review the Prosecution of Serious Violations of Human Rights in Timor-Leste (then East Timor) in 1999 S/2005/458 (Annex II) (2005)

Rome Statute of the International Criminal Court 2187 UNTS 3 (opened for signature 17 July 1998, entered into force 1 July 2002)

WA Schabas "Internationalised Courts and Their Relationship with Alternative Accountability Mechanisms: The Case of Sierra Leone" in CR Romano, A Nollkaemper and JK Kleffner (eds) *International Criminal Courts: Sierra Leone, East Timor, Kosovo, and Cambodia* (Oxford University Press, Oxford, 2004)

Secretary-General *A Comprehensive Strategy to Eliminate Future Sexual Exploitation and Abuse in United Nations Peacekeeping Operations* GA, A/59/710 (2005)

Secretary-General *Special Measures for Protection from Sexual Exploitation and Sexual Abuse* GA, A/69/779 (2015)

Secretary-General *Special Measures for Protection from Sexual Exploitation and Sexual Abuse* GA, A/71/818 (2017)

LW Sherman *Trust and Confidence in Criminal Justice* (2001) available online: <www.ncjrs.org>

Situation in Democratic Republic of the Congo Decision on the Applications for Participation on the Proceedings of VPRS 1, VPRS 2, VPRS 3, VPRS 4, VPRS 5 and VPRS 6 ICC Pre-Trial Chamber ICC-01/04–101, 17 January 2006.

H Strange "Exploring the Effects of Restorative Justice on Crime Victims for Victims of Conflict in Transitional Societies" in SG Sholham, P Knepper and M Kett (eds) *International Handbook of Victimology* (Taylor and Francis, Hoboken, 2010)

Terms of Reference Victims' Rights Advocate (2017) available online: <www.un.org>

The Declaration of Basic Principles of Justice for Victims of Crime and Abuse of Power GA Res, A/Res/40/43 (1985)

The Rules of Procedure and Evidence *Official Records of the Assembly of States Parties to the Rome Statute of the International Criminal Court* ICC-ASP/1/3 and Corr. 1 Part II.A (New York, 2002)

The Trust Fund for Victims "A Road to Recovery: Healing Empowerment and Reconciliation" *Programme Progress Report* (Winter, 2014)

"The Trust Fund for Victims Launches New Assistance Projects in Northern Uganda" (press release, 3 July 2015)

The Trust Fund for Victims *TFV Strategic Plan 2014–2017* (The Hague, 2014)

J Thibaut and L Walker *Procedural Justice: A Psychological Analysis* (Lawrence Erlbaim, New Jersey, 1975)

CP Trumbull "The Victims of Victim Participation in International Criminal Proceedings" (2008) 29 *Michigan Journal of International Law* 777

United Nations Comprehensive Strategy on Assistance and Support to Victims of Sexual Exploitation and Abuse by United Nations Staff and Related Personnel GA Res, A/RES/62/214 (2008)

C Van der Wyngaert "Victims before International Criminal Courts: Some Views and Concerns of an ICC Trial Judge" (2011) 44 *Case Western Reserve Journal of International Law* 475

JP Vevan, G Hall, I Froyland, B Steels and D Goulding "Restoration or Renovation? Evaluating Restorative Justice Outcomes" (2005) 12 *Psychiatry, Psychology and Law* 194

Victims' Rights Working Group, "Making Victim Participation Effective and Meaningful" (June 2014)

J Wemmers "The Meaning of Justice for Victims" in SG Sholham, P Knepper and M Kett (eds) *International Handbook of Victimology* (Taylor and Francis, Hoboken, 2010)

S Zappala "The Rights of Victims v the Rights of the Accused" (2010) 8 *Journal of International Criminal Justice* 137

Conclusion

"I want justice by finding the person who did this. I want to hear what he has to say to me… I am walking around the streets feeling destitute because of the UN."
Maria Kalichi, in Port-au-Prince, Haiti[1]

The aim of this book was to explore various ways in which the United Nations (UN) can improve accountability for sexual exploitation and abuse committed by military contingent members. Under the status quo, the troop-contributing country (TCC) has exclusive criminal jurisdiction over its military forces, which is currently preventing the UN from doing more than repatriating individual offenders or entire contingents in certain circumstances. Current international agreements also prevent the host state from taking action against perpetrators. Ultimately, criminal investigation and prosecution is up to the whim of the particular TCC, and successful (or thorough) investigations and prosecutions have been few and far between. Instead, there is a culture of silence and a reluctance to enforce standards. The result is an accountability gap and impunity. The preceding chapters discussed options for greater accountability to victims, their communities, and the host state while also focusing on the UN's role in improving accountability.

Past UN reforms have made some progress, but have not gone far enough to address the accountability gap. Drawing on previous scholarship and official UN reports, there are three broad categories of avenues for improvement that were examined in this book: firstly, that the UN should sanction states that fail to investigate and prosecute their nationals for sexual exploitation and abuse (chapter three); secondly, that alternative mechanisms to investigate and prosecute military contingent members should be pursued (chapters four, five, and six); and thirdly, that victims should receive adequate reparations and significantly better support from the UN (chapter seven).

The analysis was informed by a feminist lens placed within the feminist theories of anti-essentialism and intersectionality. Overall, anti-essentialism and

1 (Maria Kalichi is a pseudonym) A Essa "Is the UN Doing Enough to Stop Peacekeeper Abuse?" *Al Jazeera* (6 August 2017) <www.aljazeera.com> Maria was raped by a peacekeeper close to where she lived when she was 17 years old.

intersectionality focus on the context in which gender discrimination exists. This feminist lens favours bottom-up approaches to accountability, centralising the role of victims of violence and their communities. In addition to the feminist lens, there were three core principles or "guiding lights" that underlined analysis: firstly, the theory of open justice – that justice should be seen to be done; secondly, host state ownership; and thirdly, UN leadership. Ultimately, these principles are about legitimacy in responding to sexual exploitation and abuse, inclusivity of the host state and victims, and transparency to the international and local community.

As a starting reference point, chapters one and two explored the existence of international obligations on TCCs to exercise their criminal jurisdiction in respect of sexual exploitation and abuse. Having discussed the legal status of the Memorandum of Understanding (MOU), chapter one argued that it is a bilateral treaty and that there might be far-reaching implications as a result. For instance, states may be in breach of treaty obligations, rather than merely in breach of UN policy, for failing to exercise their criminal jurisdiction in response to sexual exploitation and abuse. Additionally, the MOU's provisions relating to accountability may carry more normative weight if it is interpreted as a treaty. Chapter two argued that there are further obligations on TCCs to actively respond under international human rights law. However, it was determined that there are notable gaps in the law. Although obligations relating to sexual abuse may be attached to human rights standards dealing with rape, sexual violence, and sexual activity with children, obligations to respond to sexual exploitation as survival sex do not currently exist.

Chapter three investigated whether the UN should sanction TCCs that fail to investigate and prosecute their nationals as per their obligations under individual MOUs and international human rights law. The introduction of Security Council Resolution 2272 is an example of coercive measures that are not supported by the laws of state responsibility or the responsibility of international organisations. Furthermore, although the resolution withdraws troops and so achieves the immediate removal of perpetrators from the host state community, there is no assurance that the offender will be brought to justice. This top-down approach is not sufficient. The three conceptual principles are not reflected in this direction taken by the Security Council; although they involve UN leadership, they do not achieve justice being seen to be done and do not involve host state ownership. The resolution only serves as a partial response.

The first three chapters illustrated that sexual exploitation and abuse are human rights violations and that UN measures against TCC inaction does not go far enough to appropriately respond to those violations. The next three chapters explored alternative ways to investigate and prosecute offenders.

Chapter four demonstrated that the conceptual principles may be better served by host state jurisdiction. Trials performed within the victim's community will assure that justice is seen to be done, and the host state would have at least some ownership over that process. However, host state jurisdiction may not always be possible or appropriate; for example, the host state may be in a post-conflict situation and may be without a fully functioning criminal justice system. Instead, host state jurisdiction may need to be facilitated by an internationally mandated structure.

Chapter five considered the role of the International Criminal Court (ICC). Although the ICC offers an existing formal structure for investigation and prosecution, it has too many limitations in the context of sexual exploitation and abuse by peacekeepers. It is unlikely that this conduct would fulfil the narrowly defined crimes listed under the Rome Statute or be included as a separate crime. The complementarity principle means that the ICC may have secondary jurisdiction; however, the required evidence to prove that a state is unable or unwilling to prosecute their nationals would mean long delays for cases. Finally, the discretion of the ICC Prosecutor favours prosecution of high-ranking officials in cases with a large number of victims.

Overall, chapters four and five illustrated that while alternative mechanisms are desirable, sole host state ownership and the ICC are ultimately unsatisfactory and unlikely to improve accountability. An appropriate solution to the accountability gap would need to incorporate the ownership of several host states, each with its own unique historic, legal, and cultural contexts. Alongside this, a new framework would also need to acknowledge the essential participation of TCCs and the UN in peacekeeping operations generally, while at the same time attempting to centralise the interests of those most affected by sexual exploitation and abuse.

As a result, chapter six argued for a hybrid solution that would encourage cooperation between the three relevant international actors: host states, TCCs, and the UN. This chapter proposed the establishment of an entirely new framework, which would aim to better centralise the role of victims and their communities and decentralise the primary role of TCCs. A series of hybrid courts for peacekeepers was asserted as the best option for improving accountability and providing justice for victims. It was argued that these courts should prosecute sexual exploitation and abuse as international crimes. Having these crimes prosecuted on the international stage would recognise the seriousness of such conduct, which has long been treated as inevitable.[2]

A hybrid model fulfils all three of the guiding principles. Justice is seen to be done, because the tribunal would operate within the territory where the crime took place and would be witnessed by the victim and their community. Where appropriate, mixed personnel in investigation, prosecution, and day-to-day running of the court, including the host state community, would ensure host state ownership. UN leadership should be facilitated by centralised administration and the establishment of a new UN body (a *UN Commission for Hybrid Courts in Peacekeeping Operations*). This new body would also manage a roster of expertise that could be rapidly deployed to fill skills gaps and work in hybrid teams (in investigation and the judiciary, for instance).

A series of hybrid courts must also be courts of first instance. A court with secondary jurisdiction will not materially change the accountability gap, as TCCs would have to be deemed unwilling and unable to exercise jurisdiction. The evidence necessary to prove a state was unwilling or unable to investigate and/or prosecute would cause lengthy delays, and such delays would hinder the chances

2 Refer to the quote included in the Introduction from Jane Hull Lute, Special UN Coordinator on Preventing Sexual Exploitation and Abuse.

of successful investigation or prosecution. Taking into consideration the myriad attempts the UN has made to solve the accountability gap and that it has failed to do so, it is perhaps time for the international community to have uncomfortable conversations about the primary role of TCCs.

However, a new framework for accountability cannot be solely based on retributive justice (the prosecution and punishment of the perpetrator). To centre the interests of victims, a series of hybrid courts must reflect a mixed retributive-restorative model. Chapter seven argued for the participation of victims in the criminal justice process and for the provision of transformative reparations. This may mean the realisation of victim participatory rights, such as the right to be heard, the right to information, and the right to be protected. A separate *Victim Support Unit* should be established to realise these rights.

Under the status quo, victims rarely receive any support. Therefore, chapter seven argued that the UN should implement a separate mechanism to deliver transformative reparations, alongside individual reparations that might be awarded through the court system. Transformative reparations are forward looking and aimed at dismantling structural inequalities that manifest as gendered and sexual violence. In the context of peacekeeping, this may mean sensitising personnel to sexual exploitation and abuse and breaking down harmful masculinities that can exist within military forces. Moreover, the UN partnering with local (host state) networks that provide emergency and long-term support for victims should be prioritised. For legitimacy, the development of the *Victim Support Unit* and transformative reparations must be guided by victims (and host state communities). Political support and adequate funding is required for these changes to occur.

It has been over a decade since the reports of sexual exploitation and abuse committed by UN peacekeepers in the Democratic Republic of the Congo prompted the UN to take action in terms of institutional reforms. Reforms so far have failed to challenge the primary role of TCCs. There remains a culture of sexual exploitation within peacekeeping, and victims continue to suffer in silence. It is not a victim-centred approach. The zero-tolerance policy favours the perpetrator, and the status quo must be changed.

Victims should not have to continue to wait for the UN to take real leadership in responding to these crimes. Victims should not have to wait in limbo, certainly not for another decade, or until the next round of media exposure of sex scandals, before they see justice being done. The time has come for serious consideration of a hybrid solution to improve accountability of offenders and deliver meaningful justice for victims. The UN should be a place where the vulnerable are safe from being sexually exploited or abused by those in positions of power.

References

A Essa "Is the UN Doing Enough to Stop Peacekeeper Abuse?" *Al Jazeera* (6 August 2017) <www.aljazeera.com>

Index

For Product Safety Concerns and Information please contact our EU
representative GPSR@taylorandfrancis.com
Taylor & Francis Verlag GmbH, Kaufingerstraße 24, 80331 München, Germany

www.ingramcontent.com/pod-product-compliance
Ingram Content Group UK Ltd.
Pitfield, Milton Keynes, MK11 3LW, UK
UKHW011016180926
475701UK00004B/778
9780367587284